C000193686

OVER THE AIRWAVES

OVER THE AIRWAVES

My Life in Broadcasting

Trevor Hill

In celebration of 60 years in Broadcasting and of those with whom I was so privileged to work in both Radio and Television

The Book Guild Ltd
Sussex, England

First published in Great Britain in 2005 by
The Book Guild Ltd
25 High Street
Lewes, East Sussex
BN7 2LU

Typesetting in Times by
MRM Graphics Ltd

Printed and bound in Singapore
under the supervision of
MRM Graphics Ltd, Winslow, Bucks

A catalogue record for this book is available from
The British Library.

ISBN 1 85776 832 9

BBC coat of arms

To
the British Broadcasting Corporation,
who made Broadcasting an art,
and in memory of my beloved Margaret

Margaret Potter

CONTENTS

FOREWORD by WALLACE GREVATT

From my own knowledge, Trevor Hill's talents and imaginative skills came at an early age.

The creating of Sound Effects for radio began when he was 17 and he became an effects boy for such wartime programmes as *ITMA* with Tommy Handley.

In the mid 1990s he and the two other former 'effects boys', Harold Rogers and John Ammonds, were to be given an *ITMA* tribute lunch by the Savage Club, London.

Attached to the British Forces Network in Hamburg at the end of 1945 he was soon to be announcing and then to become a notable producer of a varying range of programmes including those aimed at the children and families of Servicemen.

In collaboration with WAAF Margaret Potter he wrote and produced a number of serials and single plays. Their serials were to be successfully repeated by the BBC in later years.

For his Hamburg productions Trevor called on those also serving with BFN and for whom these were to be the introduction to their later distinctions in BBC programmes. Cliff Michelmore, Raymond Baxter, Nigel Davenport, Robin Boyle, Brian Matthew, Geraint Evans, and from Hamburg's Combined Service Entertainment Unit he was to give Bryan Forbes and Roger Moore their first broadcast roles.

Returning to the BBC in 1949 Trevor was to become a General Programme Producer in the BBC's North Region. There he started a weekly film and theatre review, *Showcase*, which he invited a young Geoffrey Wheeler to introduce. Amongst those whom Trevor himself was to interview were Laurence Olivier, Noël Coward, Charlton Heston and Forrest Tucker.

When also producing for Northern *Children's Hour* he chose teenagers Judith Chalmers and Paul Webster, to introduce *Out of School*. Another then teenager, Peter Maxwell Davies, he appointed as the programme's resident composer. He was to team a 16 year old Max with a 14 year old Joyce Palin for recitals on two pianos.

One of his major innovations for radio were the *Cameo Cartoons* he wrote, being a mixture of narrative with highly individual musical scores by Ray Martin and Henry Reed, striking sound effects and character voices. A dozen were to be heard between 1949 and 1955.

For the 1951 Festival of Britain he and Margaret Potter were both commissioned by the then Light Programme to do a musical cartoon combining the two Lewis Carroll *Alice* stories. He cast Joyce Palin in the title role, with other characters to be portrayed by Jeanne de Casalis, Jimmy Edwards and Wilfred Pickles. Their title song was to be sung by Jimmy Young, the then vocalist with the Northern Variety Orchestra, which Trevor announced for the Light Programme. It was conducted by Ray Martin, a former Sergeant in the Pioneer Corps. The *Melody From The Sky* series from Germany, which Ray and he did in 1947, was also relayed by the BBC.

Trevor Hill and Margaret Potter were also commissioned to do an original musical cartoon for NBC, others already having been heard in America, and also to adapt the *Beauty and The Beast* story as a Christmas adult musical for BBC Television starring Sally Bazeley and the Maori bass, Inia Te Wiata.

The BBC in London and North Region continued to commission both Margaret Potter and Trevor Hill for further serials and features after they married in 1952.

Northern *Children's Hour* was to give Trevor the opportunity to do programmes, which became a miniature of a whole broadcast range. The *Afternoon Out* features taking listeners on visits to England's Stately Homes and Castles; *Northern Naturalist*, which he recorded himself on location, with Norman Ellison, or 'Nomad' as he was known, taking them into the countryside.

In collaboration with WH Smith and Son, Trevor was responsible for *A Young Person's Forum on Books*, broadcast from a range of schools throughout the country. This series, with Ivor Brown as his chairman, was to give young people at their own schools the opportunity to put their questions to such personalities as Lady Violet Bonham-Carter, Lord David Cecil, John Betjeman, Elizabeth Packenham, Margaret Rawlings, L.A.G. Strong and W.E. Johns of 'Biggles' fame. For primary schools he chose authors like Noel Streatfeild and George Cansdale.

On one occasion his programme came from the Festival Hall, London for the benefit of young people from 55 schools. It was from here that

Trevor had been invited to do the narration and provided his own character voices for the Grace Williams' composition *The Merry Minstrel* and was accompanied by the London Philharmonic Orchestra. This invitation came about as a direct result of his earlier broadcast performance of that same work with the BBC Northern Orchestra.

When North Region had Television Outside Broadcast facilities, Trevor was to introduce, in front of a camera, a range of programmes from *Speedway* to *Motor Racing*, *Animal Rescue* to *Circus*.

From the mid-1950s he was to become responsible for all Children's Hour and Children's Television originating from the North.

He had two of his own compositions broadcast before coming to Manchester, whilst some of the duets, which he was later to perform on the Home Service with Violet Carson in *Nursery Sing Song*, have since been included in a BBC *Children's Hour* cassette.

For 12 years he was *Sooty's* producer. Yorkshire Television introduced Trevor in a 1990s tribute to Harry Corbett as *the man who did for Sooty what Brian Epstein had done for the Beatles*.

Together with Margaret Potter they were to devise, write and produce the first three of the celebrated *Pinky and Perky* series with Jan and Vlasta Dalibor.

Wishing *Children's Hour* to move with the times in the early 1960s Trevor was to commission a feature on the building of the M1 Motorway and also to cover the Beatles' tour of Germany.

He himself was to write and direct TV features on the International School at Fontainebleau with versions also in French and in German and *Speedbird 933*, BOAC's flight with children from such places as Hong Kong and Bangkok, which brought them back to schools within the UK. *Bread and Cheese* was the story of a young Norwegian boy who is taken mountain fishing for the first time – and leaving the lunch behind! All in this film including *Nils* he cast from the townspeople of Voss.

With Dr James Crabbe of Manchester University and his BBC Audio colleagues, David Fleming-Williams and Chris Webb, Trevor Hill was to be responsible for the very first programme to be broadcast in *Binaural Sound*. Entitled *The Sound of the City*, these were the spoken recollections of artist Harold Riley of what he had heard in his boyhood days in Salford. Actual trams, mill machinery, steam trains, fire engines and factory hooters of the early 1930s were to be recorded and then, in contrast, the now 1970s sounds in 'binaural'. Their programme was broadcast on Radio 3. As a result of reports in the technical press,

Trevor was then invited by both Radio Berlin and by the Danish State radio to go and assist with their own language commentaries to his recordings.

As a result of his technical and programme making experience he was appointed Chairman of Planning for New Broadcasting House, Manchester, producing the opening play, and was later to escort the Hon. James Callaghan round the stereophonic Radio Drama studio complex.

During this period and now as the Assistant Head of Network Radio North, he'd turned his attention to resurrecting both *Round Britain* and *Transatlantic Quiz*, and was responsible for then starting a *Round Europe* series, going himself in search of teams in France, Germany, Poland, Austria, Spain et cetera.

He was granted premature retirement at the end of 1983 owing to a heart condition. Notwithstanding, in the years that followed he edited my own book on *Children's Hour – The Story of Those Magical Years*. He was then invited by the BBC to produce a Celebration for the launch of the book at the Earl's Court Radio and Television Show in 1988.

This was to be followed by yet a further BBC request; to prepare, record and edit the interviews he would himself do with former staff and with current staff for *An Oral History of North Regional Broadcasting*, commencing from the year 1922. It was to take him two and a half years.

As the *Radio Times* archivist, I was to do the research for many of the 67 interviews which, in edited form, have now put some 120 hours into the BBC Sound Archive.

As a result of the above, in 1998 Trevor was to be put in touch with Gregor Prumbs of Krefeld University. Their collaboration has since produced *Songs and Sounds of War* a series of 45 minute Features on wartime radio in Britain and in Germany, and broadcast worldwide by the British Forces Broadcasting Service in September 2000, followed by a CD as issued by *This England* magazine.

In September 2001 Trevor and Gregor worked together on a further series, which they themselves also introduced. *The War of the Airwaves*, dealing mainly with the lighter side of German and English propaganda services, was again broadcast by BFBS.

For the opening of the Allied Museum, Berlin Exhibition, which both attended, a CD entitled *Let's Listen In* was then issued.

I trust the above may give an idea of the extraordinary range of broadcasting in both Radio and Television in which Trevor Hill has been involved.

What remains to this day is what he first created in Manchester when turning *Out of School* into *Children's Television Club*, which included how to make things, News and a dog named 'Conker'. Transferring to London for a regular, rather than a monthly programme, which is all the time and facilities would then allow, the programme was to be re-named and still remains as *Blue Peter*.

Wallace Grevatt
January 2003

AUTHOR'S ACKNOWLEDGEMENTS

It is thanks to my long-serving and last BBC secretary, the splendid Audrey Robins, that I took note of what she had said back in 1981 when I was occasionally giving illustrated talks to such as the Manchester Luncheon Club members at the Free Trade Hall – and with marvellous 'asides' as recorded by two of my special friends in broadcasting, Stuart Hall and Geoffrey Wheeler. At other venues, now in order to raise money for the Church of England Children's Society and with assistance of another very close friend, Violet Carson, it was Audrey who again did all the typing and said, 'You have some good stories to tell. Why not write a book?' That started shortly after retirement – and has only been completed in recent years. I thank Pauline Lyons for a lot of the typing – besides suggesting alterations, whilst a lot of editing has come from my good friend Peter Worsley of *This England* magazine. And for what I trust to be fact rather than fiction on my part, I particularly recognise the contribution which Wallace Grevatt was to make in his role as Archivist to *The Radio Times* in sending me in recent times details of a whole range of programmes with which I'd been associated – yet forgotten all about. Wallace was then to write his own Foreword to this book. Sadly he was to die in 2003.

Undoubtedly a now diminishing number of us were so fortunate to come into broadcasting when we did, at a time within the BBC when for the most part we were a working life-time family – to take the opportunities offered to us but also to give back to 'Auntie' of our time and talents however limited they might have been. I also dwell on what Forces Broadcasting was to do in helping many of us with our careers. In my case and that of Cliff Michelmore and the late Bob Boyle, in also introducing us to our future wives. Back in 1983 I had to retire on health grounds and then continued to write this book – but pausing yet again when 'Auntie' was to give me *An Oral History* to prepare and to record. As a direct result, in 1998 I was so fortunate to meet Dr Gregor Prumbs of Krefeld University. Now, thanks to Rory Higgins of the current British Forces Broadcasting Service and that of my former BBC colleague, the late Antony Askew, Gregor and I were to devise and to produce our two recent four-part series on wartime broadcasting in both Germany and in England. As a further result I now have contact with members of the Vintage Radio Programme Collectors' Circle. It is entirely thanks to their founder, Roger Bickerton, that I now have an Index to *Over The Airwaves*.

For me, Sixty Glorious Years commenced in 1942 and only ended in 2002 when I then settled down to finish this work. As with Wallace Grevatt's 1988 definitive history of *Children's Hour* we both acknowledge the professional help and assistance afforded to us by The Book Guild.

1

Mill Hill, London NW7, and a Famous Pre-War Neighbour

Miss Emerson must have gone to her just reward in the summer of 1938, or if not to Heaven then to her home town of Hove! In any event it was some time during that summer when our new neighbours, the Walkers, moved into No. 21 Holmwood Grove, much taken, no doubt, by the recent interior improvements and by the landscaped garden, something Miss Emerson had seen to since 'coming into money'. Another result of coming-into-money was the renewal of the fencing between the two gardens; far stouter stuff and peep-proof. What is more our Miss Emerson had the whole thing topped off by a sort of diamond lattice trellis – rather a waste really since the only ball games that interested me were rugby and volleyball.

From our side of the fence, I seem to see that summer of 1938 in terms of talk of war and Corona soft drinks. Gone several years since was the Sunday muffin-man with his crisp white-covered tray and gleaming brass bell. And it seemed an age since the blue-and-white chequered Stop-Me-And-Buy-One Walls tricycle had been seen around the Mill Hill area. At least Corona added a bit of sparkle to No. 23. But now that our new neighbours had moved in, the tinkle of Miss Emerson's iced drinks was to be replaced by the sounds of Schumann floating out through the open French windows.

Singing, perhaps, was more in my line. There was that nice young lady at Miss Webb's preparatory school who taught the subject. Father persuaded her to give me private lessons at home and she rose to the challenge. Within a short while, Dr Field-Hyde was tutoring me from time to time and then there I was, father standing a respectful distance back, auditioning for a choral scholarship at St Paul's Cathedral Choir School! When I'd completed the written part of the examination I was invited to take some fresh air. At the end of my vocal performance I was then invited to have my tonsils and adenoids removed!

Fortunately, at Haberdasher Askes' School we had a splendid young music master in Mr Howells. He not only managed to restore vocal confidence, if not tonsils and adenoids, but also to interest most of his classes in music. In my form and House was Alexander Kok who was to become a pupil of Pablo Casals and, later, a cellist of international standing. In the years ahead we were to meet up again when performing together at the Royal Festival Hall in London. In a lower form was Felix Kok, the younger brother who was to become leader of the City of Birmingham Symphony Orchestra, whilst somewhere in between was a young form-mate who didn't sing much because he often seemed to have a cold. But as things turned out, that didn't really matter for Alan Whicker's future career in broadcasting.

Back at No. 21, however, the Walker family soon settled in. I can only describe Mr Walker as distinctly pear-shaped. Susan, his daughter, was a diminutive version, then aged six or seven, but with black, dancing eyes and dancing feet. Ah, but Mrs Walker! A tall elegant lady with long lustrous hair sometimes plaited and worn in Grecian style, at others coiled neatly over each ear. I particularly noticed those 'headphones' as I stood beside her one afternoon when Eileen, my elder sister, and I had been invited in for tea. Mrs Walker was seated at a magnificent grand piano.

'Let's begin with that Handel of yours,' she exclaimed.

Lord, but she must have heard me practice that often enough. 'Laboured' was the word, but not with Mrs Walker as accompanist. She took 'The Harmonious Blacksmith' at a fair old lick, occasionally giving me a sidelong glance as, in jumping one or two of those intervals in the notes, I went horribly flat. Mrs Walker obliged by playing the same wrong notes. Her elegantly cool looks belied a wonderful sense of musical fun.

'Now let's try "The Trout" shall we?'

Her twiddly bits sent us into fits. Susan entertained with a somewhat heavy tap routine on the parquet floor; Eileen with some syncopated hit which Roy Fox and all the other dance bands were playing at that time. And then it was back to Schumann and to several of his songs, which Mrs Walker could sing from memory.

I'm not forgetting Mr Walker. How could I? It's because of him that I'm writing this now. In those pre-war days he seemed to be away from home a lot, although there was always a warm and friendly greeting as we saw him arrive or depart. As it turned out, Mr Walker also sang. In fact *he* had a Signature Tune, as I was shortly to discover!

If the eternal game of cricket loomed large in my father's life then so did the wireless. From Southampton, where he was a young officer in the Customs and Excise, to Highbury, London and then to Mill Hill NW7; in each place we lived there *had* to be a garden big enough for a very long wireless aerial and always the best and latest wireless receiver connected to one end of it.

On the evening of Wednesday, 5th October 1938, when I was aged 13, one younger sister Jennifer, and an even-younger brother Brian, were already upstairs 'in bed-and-no-nonsense', so that the rest of us could catch up with Phil Overdew, Betty Buckshee and, of course, Mrs Bagwash. And we were all dying to know how Lucy and Basil fared at the 'Home for Homesick Homing Pigeons', since that last BBC radio series of *Bandwaggon* had been on the air.

That night, the Fat Stock Prices at the end of the news bulletin seemed to drag on and on as we waited, most of all, to hear from Big-Hearted Arthur Askey and Richard 'Stinker' Murdoch. What had they been up to in that flat of theirs at the top of Broadcasting House? As father's brand new Echo all-mains receiver warmed up, pervading my nostrils with the heady aroma of heating valves and Bakelite, so did my excitement. And I wasn't disappointed by the return of *Bandwaggon*.

How could I be? For on that very night I heard our Mr Walker sing, *and* on the wireless! Nothing quite like Schumann. No, his song went just like this:

Day after day, I'm on my w-a-y,
Any r-a-g-s, bottles or bones ...

In the following weeks I would join in, trying to imitate his deep gruff tones as he said, 'Good evenin', chums. This is your old pal, Syd Walker, a-raisin of 'is 'at an' askin', what would YOU do?'

'Mr Walker Wants to Know' became a very important part of the *Bandwaggon* series, with more than a thousand people responding by post each week to a story concerning the junk man and his barrow, and to the 'poser' he set all those of us who were listening:

'So drop me a postcard with a ha'penny stamp, and write *BAND-WAGGON* in the top left-hand corner!'

Radio Times, November 25, 1938 Vol. 61 No. 791
Registered at the G.P.O. as a Newspaper

Price TWOPENCE

RADIO TIMES

JOURNAL OF THE BRITISH BROADCASTING CORPORATION

PROGRAMMES FOR NOVEMBER 27 – DECEMBER 3

Mr. WALKER WANTS TO KNOW

Here he comes with his old barrow! Syd Walker arrives for his weekly 'Band Waggon' broadcast

Soon, local families were waiting for our Syd to return home in a chauffeur-driven red Daimler in order to ask for his autograph. The next thing, blow me down, there he was almost as large as life and complete with his barrow on the front cover of the *Radio Times*. Such fame!

'Do you have a barrow in the studio, Mr Walker? Are you *really* in a street, Mr Walker? How *do* they make the sound effects, Mr Walker?' Oh, how I longed to see it all for myself.

My modest entry into the world of entertainment was by way of Golders Green Hippodrome and some of the London theatres at Christmas time in order to marvel at the stage effects and those spell-binding 'transformation' scenes. I saved up for a small set of glove puppets, then built what turned out to be a rather ambitious portable theatre complete with lighting on a dimmer. This was a jam jar with Meccano supports and a winding mechanism, which lifted the red wire up through the water and away from the other part of the red wire twisted around a hole in a tin lid at the bottom of the jar. It worked. I even tried putting a finger in whilst operating my 'dimmer' – and lived to tell the tale!

My pal John Doncaster had a father who refurbished cinemas and theatres from his office in Wardour Street, so I had a lovely collection of plain and ornate backcloths. When word of all this got from No. 23 to No. 21, I was formally invited to provide an 'entertainment' at a party for Susan and her young friends. It went quite well, in parts, but with some very long 'intervals' during scene changes; a sort of Punch and Judy show with far too many trimmings but excellent sound effects.

That Christmas, the kind and generous Mr Walker presented me with a lovely set of new glove puppets, together with a few professional hints and tips.

'Keep at it, Trev,' he said. And I did.

By now, the young boy from across the road, Paul Mullins, had been pressed into becoming my assistant. Paul grew up to become quite a distinguished veterinary surgeon; surprising really that he grew up at all in view of the amount of smoking I got him to do with a clay pipe and rubber tube when Mephistopheles appeared in the Hades scene. With young Paul to hand, gone were the long pauses and even the incidental music now came in 'on cue', slowing down at times, admittedly, because there were more pressing things to do besides stopping to wind up the gramophone.

'Keep at it, lads,' we'd been told, and we did.

There followed some children's parties up in the Totteridge and Highwood Hill areas where we were sometimes given seven shillings and sixpence *and* tea.

When war came, the young men at Mill Hill school were evacuated, the noble buildings with the impressive Prince of Wales Gate becoming a services hospital. Besides his parochial duties at St Paul's Church, the Reverend Sheehan seemed to have taken on the task of entertainments officer at the hospital. Could we do a show for them? Well, not Punch and Judy alone. A particular pal of mine in Mill Hill, Tom Scott, did a pretty good ventriloquist act, besides being something of a conjurer, whilst the Ecob brothers from Askes' were good instrumentalists. With only part-time schooling in progress during those early war years there seemed plenty of time for Concert Party rehearsals.

'Keep at it, lads!'

The vicar turned up trumps. Among the wounded soldiery he'd found a man who'd done stage lighting, and another who knew a lot about costume and stage make-up. Very important for the tough, slouch hat, smoking and drinking on-stage characters we boys were to portray in the main sketch!

Can't say I remember much about that Concert Party, except that we had shepherd's pie with the surgeons, doctors and senior nursing staff before the curtain went up. When it came down, Tom had made a decision. Instead of impairing the progress of those convalescing, he would now dedicate himself to becoming a doctor – which he did.

Syd Walker's wartime entertainment record was far more impressive, as one would expect from such a professional. With Britain standing 'on the brink' the great Herbert Morrison himself, as Minister of Supply, had referred to our celebrated next-door neighbour as a 'national figure', and then called upon the comedian to become 'Britain's Dustman Number One to assist with the National Salvage Campaign'. And all because of the wireless.

'I think I'd like to work for the BBC – one day!' I said wistfully.

'Keep at it, Trev.'

It wasn't until after the lovely Syd Walker had gone to his reward that I discovered why he so often used that phrase. In the early 1950s BBC North Region Light Entertainment producers Alick Hayes and Rex Diamond got together and wrote a Radio Feature on Fred Karno, the celebrated showman. Amongst those who learned their skills in his troupe were Charlie Chaplin, Stan Laurel – and Syd Walker.

'Keep at it, lads,' Karno would tell them.

And now, I'd been invited to impersonate Syd! Impersonating him as a young man in his Fred Karno days wasn't difficult, but he used to sing a song entitled, 'Who Put The Bricks in Brixton?' and this was included in the programme. I'd heard Syd Walker sing it himself at one of his parties at home, but even with the aid of good friends in the BBC

Northern Dance Band, I just couldn't reach the bass notes in a 'Syd' voice and so it had to be cut. The best thing for me about that *Fred Karno Boys* feature was that the broadcast put me in touch again with Mrs Walker.

Besides that brand new set of glove puppets – and a great longing to get into the BBC – Syd also had some cards printed for me. In his own wording they read:

'Punch and Judy'
Superior Show for
Schools and Children's Parties

It must have been around this same time that a slightly older lad, then living in Guiseley, Yorkshire, was applying himself to the piano and working hard under one of the best teachers of pianoforte in Bradford. This lad was to take up conjuring as a sideline – and with a most unusual assistant. In later years, *his* card was to read:

Conjuring Pianoforte Film Shows
HARRY CORBETT
Assisted by
SOOTY
The Wonder Teddy Bear

How we worked together will be a chapter in itself.

2

Broadcasting House, Wartime, London W1

Stuart Hibberd turned round in his announcer's chair as *Programme Parade* was going out on the air.

'You say you have put on the wrong record? Well, never mind. How long have you been with the BBC?'

It was only a matter of weeks. I'd arrived at Portland Place on an August morning in 1942 and had waited across the road on the steps of All Souls Church, watching the hands of the imposing clock high up on the front of Broadcasting House slowly creep to the hour of ten. Below, curving away like the bow of some majestic ship, the building itself was swathed in drab wartime dress with sandbags, the windows all pasted up as a protection against further bomb blast. Within only a few minutes I would be a member of the BBC's staff – I would enter that hallowed place which Syd Walker had patiently described in answer to my many questions and see for myself the Concert Hall where the *Bandwaggon* programmes had originated.

A few weeks prior to that, and as a result of my letter of application, I'd been sitting in another building and facing a friendly man with a Scots accent and mild blue eyes. Dr F.W. Alexander, as it turned out, was head of the BBC's Programme Engineering department. From reading *Wireless World* I already knew that it was he who had improved the ribbon microphone. It was a big step forward in sound reproduction but I would need to learn much more about it before passing some BBC engineering exams.

'So you give cinema shows in your father's garage in aid of the Lord Mayor's Distress Fund, eh?'

I explained how I chose records to accompany these 9.5mm silent films, and the sort of sound effects I had for the Punch and Judy show.

'We might consider you for training as a Junior Programme Engineer. Oh, but I see you are not yet seventeen; in that case, a Youth-in-Training!'

The good doctor then sent me to another building for interview by the man in day-to-day charge of such staff, Peter Parish. He growled as he read aloud part of my letter: 'Have you a position for which I may be suited?' He gave me a hard look.

'A bit pedantic but grammatically correct! Now tell me more about *Bandwaggon* from the listeners' end!'

He had to stop me after a few minutes, explaining that he *did* have several other candidates for interview. We shook hands and as I reached the door I asked if I should send the next one in.

'Thank you, Hill. You'll be hearing from us!'

And Hill did. So did that next candidate, Amna Smith, the fair-haired girl who stood only a few feet away from me on the stone steps of All Souls Church that first morning. There were to be some half-dozen of us on the training course conducted from a conglomeration of odd rooms high up in the Langham Hotel opposite Broadcasting House. Our chief instructor was a cheerful man with sleek hair, large glasses and impeccable suits – into which the suave David Godfrey fitted with perfection. In later life as a distinguished producer of radio drama and a colleague of mine, David slipped the initial H into his *Radio Times* and microphone credits. I'd never met anyone before who, by simply pressing the palms of his hands together in order to create a vacuum, could then make the escaping air 'squeak' and form sounds like 'Mary … had … a … lamb'! A pity David never managed to squeak out a sound resembling *little* but he had more important things on his hands – us lot! He trained and trained our course, rarely becoming even slightly dishevelled by the dimmest of his charges, making us 'play-in' gramophone records of music and sound effects in countless 'exercise' scripts, which contained only a few words but a *large* number of recorded inserts, and in double-quick time.

Within those first few weeks, I was scheduled to play-in the records during *Programme Parade*. In wartime, this was a fairly long summary of the day's broadcasting on the Home Programme and, as a rule, there was a rehearsal for it the evening before. I was told that Mr Hibberd would ring when I was to report to him in the studio, but no call came.

As that truly mellifluous voice read the Eight o'clock News to the whole nation the following morning, I stood a respectful distance behind him at the T/D 7. This was a twin turntable desk, with five or six gramophone records up in the racks above me, two more already spinning and waiting to be put on the air. Mr Hibberd wasn't over six feet tall as I had imagined, but I noticed he did sport a splendid pair of canary-coloured spats over his immaculate brown shoes. He led into that record, which was now playing on the turntable, by saying something like, 'Then at a quarter to eight this evening our concert will feature Ravel's *Ma Mère L'Oye*, the Mother Goose suite which includes the "Pavane of the Sleeping Beauty!"'

That is *not* what I had put on. Shaking with nerves, I told Mr Hibberd what I'd done.

'No, now you mention it, it isn't the Pavane. That must be on the other side of the record. Well, never mind. I'm still just a little nervous in the studio myself, and I've been here a good many years. Now, you just fade out the record at the end of this next phrase.'

I did so as he turned back to the microphone again.

'The work also includes the delightful transformation in "Beauty And The Beast", part of which you have just heard,' he announced by way of explanation.

Stuart Hibberd was to assist me again some eight years later. I was to write a *Cameo Cartoon* all about a cat with a difference. This one possessed rather a fine voice. That discovery came about when a certain Italian impresario, Signor Panjoman, inadvertently dropped the heavy sash window of his Milan tenement right on the tip of the sleeping cat's tail, this producing a top C of such exquisite clarity that it shattered glass for miles around. As a result of this, *The Operatic Cat* was eventually to

make his English debut at Covent Garden. Mr Hibberd, in person, announced this unusual event the following day on the BBC News, only this time at *my* special request, sounding very Stuart Hibberdish as he said:

> 'London's world of opera was taken by storm last evening as Timothy demonstrated perfect pitch in his rendition of 'The Anvil Chorus'. Instead of the customary floral tributes, basket after basket of another commodity was handed over the footlights at the final curtain. (pause) Billingsgate market this morning reports a shortage of white fish. (another pause) And that is the end of the News.'

* * *

The BBC in wartime London had converted several buildings into extra offices and studios for broadcasting. From the Maida Vale complex, formerly a large ice-rink, came the first regular radio serial. This was to be heard in the Corporation's expanding Overseas Services as *Front Line Family*. At the end of the hostilities the serial became known as *The Robinson Family*. It was the brainchild of that talented writer, Alan Melville, and a complete change of style from his sparkling material in such West End musical revues as *Sweet and Low*.

Front Line Family began life in the wake of the London Blitz in 1941, with Alan both writing and producing the first hundred or more scripts himself. His six-day-a-week radio serial told, in dramatic form, the story of a British family under fire, to those who were listening in comparative safety overseas. When I joined the production team as the lad who did the 'Spot Fx' – rattle of teacups, door bell, door opened, closed, telephone ringing, rustle of newspaper, et cetera – the serial had been going for over a year. It featured Mr and Mrs Robinson, (Ernest Butcher and Nell Ballantyne) who lived at No. 88 Ashleigh Road. Their son Dick (John Dodsworth) was with the Auxiliary Fire Service and, in one episode, he was awarded the George Medal for his work as a Column Officer. There was also the younger son, Andy, in his early twenties who, in the series, eventually became Squadron Leader Robinson. Alan Melville believed in complete authenticity and, on several occasions, managed to get his Andy into one or two wartime training establishments. Eventually the author himself was to go into the RAF and producers like Peter Watts and Hugh Stewart were to take over.

Andy was my idea of a wartime hero, and actor Tony Halfpenny sounded terrific in this role. I say 'sounded' because in reality I think he'd had polio as a child, which left him somewhat lame. I do know for sure, however, that in between his scenes at the microphone Tony took to pieces and restored a lot of old clock mechanisms. When I had a page or so with no 'Spot Fx' he'd pass me a match-stalk soaked in Brasso and I'd polish a cog or two. Even more enjoyment for me came from being inside the glass-fronted studio Control Cubicle at four or more of those T/D 7 turntable units as I played the recorded effects. On Turntable 1 might be *Background of Spring Bird Song*; Turntable 2, *Distant Aircraft Engines Warming Up*; Turntable 3, *Spitfire on Take-Off*, as Squadron Leader Robinson scrambled with his crews and on Turntable 4, *Closing Music*.

A character named Charlie Williams spent many episodes of the serial worrying that the war would end before he was old enough to fly a bomber and Charlie was always getting into trouble. He was played by teenage actor, Harry Fowler, who had started on radio as the newsboy in a series called, *Papers, Papers!* Another young member of the cast in those early days of *Front Line Family* was a rather shy actress named Dulcie Gray. Nothing shy about another character, though – Mrs Robinson's old school friend, a brisk spinster type who did war work at the local Labour Exchange. She frightened the life out of me, did Gladys Young, long before she was to do radio drama for me.

There was another wartime series I worked on from time to time, and the 'Spot Fx' for this were rather special! You had to be pretty nifty tearing from mic to mic without the sound of footfalls – or panting when you got there. As a result, this particular Spot Fx boy became known as 'Nipper'.

'And what's your real name, Nipper?' enquired the great Tommy Handley after I'd opened and closed the celebrated effects of *ITMA* a time or two. On one occasion he wrote out a cheque, which he thrust into my hand during a brief pause in rehearsal.

'Just tear round for a tenner will you, Nipper?'

I tore as instructed but just as I'd left the bank clutching that large sum of money, so the air raid sirens sounded. It seemed I was away for hours, having been ordered into a shelter. The great Mr Handley laughed.

'Easy to have you "nicked", Nipper. I'd have sent Babs to boot you back!'

Babs was Barbara Price, a girl who lived close to our family at Mill Hill. I thought I knew her well but she never mentioned that she had a famous uncle working for the BBC. I think I have to thank her mother,

Mrs Price, for the fact that I was to be given the initial chance to work on the show. It certainly kept you on your toes, the lines and the Spot Fx coming thick and fast. Sometimes I was down to do *ITMA,* at others, when it was broadcast by the BBC Overseas Service, it was called *Tommy Handley's Half Hour* but either way, I'd be blowing bubbles for, 'Don't forget the diver, sir!' and giving the door a special sort of slam as exit Mrs Mopp with her 'TTFN' and Tommy's tart reply such as:

'DSYG'

'What's that, sir?'

'Don't show your garters!'

Besides Light Entertainment – and it didn't come much lighter than *ITMA* – there were wartime radio features by a line of distinguished writers and producers including Laurence Gilliam, D.G. Bridson, A.L. Lloyd and Louis MacNeice. These often required the use of BBC Gramophone Effects and Spot Fx. Whilst I was doing 'Grams' on one of MacNeice's features, there was a long studio break early on in the afternoon rehearsal. I think someone higher up was re-reading or checking on the script, probably for security reasons. Anyhow during the break several other feature and drama producers wandered down to the studio Control Cubicle to consult together on another matter entirely, including Val Gielgud who, for many years, was the distinguished head of radio drama. I'm pretty sure this unscheduled meeting had something to do with the *remuneration* for those erudite men who were then employed by the British Broadcasting Corporation, and that Louis MacNeice had been deputed to discuss the matter with some of the Senior Management that lunchtime. Now, several of his colleagues had gathered to learn of the outcome. Francis Dillon, a very jovial man whose looks and manner belied his former profession, that of a Collector of Taxes in Manchester, never minced words. In his somewhat high-pitched voice he came directly to the point of this clandestine meeting.

'Well, an' did you tell 'em we all want more money?' was the gist of his enquiry.

Junior staff *never* heard such talk! I buried my nose even deeper into my BBC Engineering Manual by Messrs Amos and Chadder and affected a keen interest in a chapter with a title like 'Simple Studio Signalling Circuits'. At the same time, I couldn't help noticing that Mr Gielgud held open a door and, with a nod of his head, indicated that the conversation should be conducted inside the sound-proof walls of the narrator's studio.

It was at a Gala dinner, given by the Liverpool Soroptomists, many years later, that I sat next to Mr Gielgud and was able to discover more

Val Gielgud, with pipe, Head of Radio Drama

about the wartime 'rebellion'. Louis MacNeice, hadn't *told* the management they wanted more money. On the contrary. Being a good politician, besides poet, he had simply stated that on the money the gentlemen paid him, he felt he could no longer afford to drink champagne for breakfast!

In introducing Val Gielgud at that dinner, I explained how I'd soon come to realise that radio drama was the very stuff of which imaginative broadcasting is made, going on to describe one of his studio productions on which I'd worked as the junior member of his team. It was a very long and involved play entitled *Socrates Asked Why*. The cast and the technical team rehearsed the thing for all of five long days. On the evening of the *live* transmission and with both my eyes firmly closed, I missed the one and only sound effect in fifty-six pages of script. At the end, the cast got the usual 'Thank you, Charles,' or 'Cynthia, darling you were quite magnificent!' All I got was a stony silence, but a look through those thick spectacles said it all. Be that as it may, I did have the pleasure of hearing various members of that cast, working on other programmes in the weeks that followed, wondering to each other what the deuce Socrates was asking about anyway. Having explained all that to the Liverpool gathering and introduced the guest speaker for the evening, I sat down. Val Gielgud rose to his feet saying, 'How strange! At the time, I thought I was the only one who never understood what that play was about!'

* * *

Val Gielgud and I shared a keen understanding and appreciation of the author of the *Hornblower* stories, C.S. Forester. Val, like Horatio's begetter, must have read and re-read over a century's worth of the monthly *Naval Gazette,* written by naval men for naval men and containing a wealth of minute detail. And like Forester, Val possessed a fund of knowledge concerning the Napoleonic Wars.

Strange how things happen. I'd read *Lord Hornblower* shortly after the first book in the series was published in 1946. The author was to be persuaded by readers and publishers to go back in time and to tell about Horatio starting out upon his naval career as a young midshipman. That story came out in 1950. Some years later I was in the Isle of Man for the BBC and staying at a place called Santon in a small hotel named The Arragon. It was indeed a very rare hotel, tastefully furnished down to paintings by Paul Klee and sculptures by Henry Moore – and not reproductions either! The owner of The Arragon, a London builder, had only the best and that included his manager, Peter Pahn, who'd been a German prisoner of war on the island, then married and settled there. Upon my arrival this time, Peter happened to mention that he had a Mr Forester staying in the hotel.

'He is, I think, a good British author? He spends much time sitting under that large tree facing the beach, playing his recorder!'

A good British author indeed! Without wishing to intrude upon a fellow guest, I took a walk. The recorder that C.S. Forester played turned out to be a musical one. He trusted it didn't disturb me! I trusted I wasn't disturbing him, but was soon asking about *Hornblower*. Yes, he had plans for further novels; no he wasn't sure which film companies had the Rights on which stories and I should check with his publishers, Michael Joseph. What particularly pleased me was that he said he always felt these stories of his would make good radio – reading and listening to the radio being so similar. How delightfully perceptive of Cecil Scott Forester. I left *Hornblower's* creator happy in the knowledge that the BBC would almost certainly have the author's approval once our Copyright department had obtained the necessary broadcasting Rights on those novels we'd wish to adapt.

I would not have felt quite so pleased with myself had I known that it would be several years later before that was to happen, by which time the author was dead. When we did go ahead with the project in 1968, it was Val Gielgud who did the adaptations for me for the twenty episodes of *The Hornblower Story*. Johnny Pearson wrote and conducted a magnificent orchestral score of themes and 'background music', whilst two of my colleagues from the BBC's audio department did a trip with the Sail Training Association in order to get actual recordings of sailing ships. The three of us then made up the sounds of nineteenth-century naval guns and all the required battle noises. I had a nice letter from the adaptor when the series was first broadcast. He concluded, '.... and as for all those Sound Effects! There just wasn't time for any of your chaps to fall asleep during transmission!' Eleven years later, we were to do a new production of *The Hornblower Story*, this time in stereophonic sound. I like to think that Val Gielgud and C.S. Forester, both masters of detail, would approve of the fact that our BBC Sound Effects used in the production can now be heard by those who, year by year, visit the Royal Naval Museum at Portsmouth.

I mentioned Johnny Pearson's score for our broadcast series. At one time I fear the way I used music in my own production wasn't exactly 'incidental', but used effectively it certainly adds colour, atmosphere and, above all, emotion. It is part of creating 'scenery' in the mind of the listener, all of which brings me back to the BBC in the early years of the war.

Back in 1940, Val Gielgud as Head of Drama had been discussing the idea of some regular topical feature series with an expert in this field, Laurence Gilliam. How many readers remember the wartime *Junction X*? If such a series was to be done properly and effectively, they concluded that it would require the setting up of a special production unit, and would need the closest co-operation of the BBC's News Division with that of the various wartime ministries and the three services. It would use actors, specially composed music and recorded effects. Such a unit was formed, the series taking its original title from one of those truly rousing speeches by Winston Churchill, who told us that: 'This war must be fought by all of us with all our strength along the road to victory!' By June 1940, it was decided to call the series not *The Road To Victory* but *Marching On*.

Laurence Gilliam was in charge of a unit of producers and writers from the BBC's Manchester offices and studios. Their brief was to go on the air every Friday evening and give listeners a dramatised treatment of stories taken from the week's news, 'the accumulative intention being vigorous statement and the highlighting of encouraging aspects of the Allied war effort.'

The actor Leo Genn was chosen to narrate such stirring stories, and he later became my elder sister Eileen's CO on an 'ack-ack' gunsite! But according to her, the ATS girls missed an awful lot of Captain Gunn's commands as they stared into his film-star eyes.

The music for *Marching On* was composed by Walter Goehr, father of the composer, Alexander Goehr. First, a rousing theme over which the announcer would declare in suitably ringing tones: 'On the Home Front, on the Battle Fronts, behind the frontiers of our enemies, the cause of Freedom is .... Marching On!' Not, I think, Churchill's words; more like Laurence Gilliam's. By the time I joined the series, it was now being produced each week in London by John Glyn-Jones, a happy Welshman *and* a character actor. There was always a bit of a 'performance' as between John and Walter Goehr who, in the mid-thirties, had fled from Nazi Germany, becoming musical director for the Colombia Record Company. Now he too was working for the BBC, quickly and expertly composing incidental and background music to some of the stories featured in *Marching On*.

The Control Cubicle at the Monseigneur Theatre, Marble Arch, wherein sat the producer next to the person 'mixing' on the panel (as a rule the expert 'Laddie' Ladbrook), and the junior on 'Grams', was high up to one side of the stage below. On this were the cast, the musicians and also the lad doing the studio Spot Fx. For one specific programme, Robert Barr dramatised a particularly good story, 'behind the frontiers of our enemies'. It concerned the setting up of the very first 'Underground' newspaper in the heart of occupied Paris, literally under the very noses of the Jerries for it was in a street cellar. But what did a hand-operated simple printing press sound like?

That's where Spot Fx came to the fore. I took a metal music stand and, loosened off the nut, which allowed the inner rod to be raised and lowered producing a sort of metallic swish as the rod slid up and down. On a sheet of aluminium I rolled a steel tube back and forth. 'Swish-clink, swoosh-clonk, swish-clink, swoosh-clonk.' Maestro Goehr hurriedly wrote out the parts for some 'printing press' music and, as the hand-operated machine got into its stride printing out the first message of hope to those who fought for Freedom from Oppression, so listeners also heard the sounds of approaching Nazi jackboots, orchestral interpolations of the German national anthem, a heart-pounding pause as those same boots rang out upon that cellar grill, and then ... the continuation of a hand-printing press and music. Gosh the excitement! I really felt I was worth a little more than two pounds three shillings per week, which the BBC then paid me. I came down to earth as John Glyn-Jones' voice suddenly boomed out over the studio talk-back, the loudspeakers ringing round the large auditorium.

'Wal-ter, ... Wal-t-e-r-r-r-r!'

You could tell from the accentuated Welsh whine that John was about to give 'a performance'. Maestro Goehr stopped his musicians in mid-flight with an impatient shake of his hand, then whipped off the head-phones he wore in order to hear more clearly the dialogue and effects over the sound of the orchestra.

'Vell, Vot NOW?'

'Wal-ter, cannot you keep in time with the Prrrrr-inting ... Prrrr-es-s-s!'

John positively hissed the final syllable. At this, the conductor threw a perfectly good pair of BBC headphones onto the floor.

'Vy...' demanded this former pupil of the great Schoenberg, 'Vy cannot zee bloody leetle boy keep-in-time-viz-ME?'

I don't recall if I was ever scheduled to work on *Marching On* again.

Mind you I did have the perspicacity to note that actor Laidman Browne made a most convincing Nazi and when I later rose to the dizzy heights of being the producer of the W.E. Johns *Biggles* stories in serial form, Laidman Browne was cast as that arch villain, Von Stalhein. My big mistake here (and one really must be honest in writing these things down) is that I was also to put a genuine German actor into the cast as Von Stalhein's henchman. My God, but he sounded so phoney!

* * *

At one Engineering Department staff interview around this time, where you were not invited to sit, I was asked if I would like to go to work on the BBC's Overseas Services and on *Radio Newsreel* in particular. This *might* have had something to do with my personnel file, the contents of which are always kept secret – except in my case. Before retiring as the Assistant Head of BBC Network Radio in the North of England in 1983, I went into Personnel Records where such secrets are kept. The lady in charge, used to seeing me when I had to write staff annual reports, greeted me cheerily as usual, only to then hand me my *own* BBC personnel file. It didn't seem right to take advantage of her slight aberration, but I couldn't help noticing *one* entry! At a wartime Engineering Division interview, the chap who'd seen me was short and to the point as he wrote: 'Not a single original thought in his head, but he does have the gift of the gab!'

At that time, I took my leave of Portland Place, W1, for a while and, in a young life full of such exciting incidents as Engineering Division interviews, I was to be moved down the road nearer to the tube station at Oxford Circus.

3

200 Oxford Street, with the BBC's Overseas Services

J.B. Priestley came into the talks studio and, as usual, handed me his raincoat and old trilby. I bade him good evening as I held back the sound-proof doors between the control cubicle and studio. It was the usual routine. On the studio table were a glass of water and a set of head-phones, for he liked to broadcast with these plugged into 'Local Output' which enabled him to hear his own voice at the microphone. It was a ring main system common to all BBC Studios – Point 1, Home Service; Point 2, Forces Programme et cetera, until you reached Point 8, Local Output, then there was a Point 9 for Talkback to recording.

The great man donned the headphones, took a sip of water and then looked up. On my side of the soundproof observation window I nodded ready to take the level of his voice. He read just the first line of his script then stopped as usual whilst, from my side, I switched to Point 9 for a word with the engineer in the disk recording channel.

'Hello, recording. J.B. Priestley and *Britain Speaks*!'

Before I could say, 'We'll start in ten seconds from now,' a chirpy voice came across my cubicle loudspeaker.

'Good God, is that old gas-bag in again?'

John Boynton Priestley loomed large as, this time, he opened his own studio doors and strode out. My mistake was that I'd left his studio head-phones switched to Point 9!

'I don't come to the British Broadcasting Corporation to be called a gas-bag!' he declared in stern Bradfordian tones – and left.

To get into and out of the BBC's technical areas in what had been this bargain basement of Peter Robinson's department store, and from where the Corporation now conducted most of its Overseas Broadcasting business, it was necessary for everyone, staff included, to show a pass to the men on twenty-four hour security. As I tore along towards that area, I was fortunate enough to meet one of the Presentation Department senior staff.

'Oh sir!' I exclaimed in anguish, and explained what had happened.

'That is rather regrettable,' came the mild reply. 'I will deal with this.'

Fortunately, the injured party in his anger couldn't find the pass he had produced not ten minutes earlier in order to get into the studio area.

'Yes, yes, I *know* who you are, Mr Priestley, Sir, but I *do* have to see your pass, Sir, on leaving as well as entering,' said the distant voice of Security, by which time Presentation had caught up with the celebrated man. He apologised profusely, and we were back in the studio again.

'Hello, recording. *Britain Speaks.*'

When asked for a voice level, Mr Priestley leant forward and said,

'I've been a bit of a bugger! That alright for level?'

Amongst ourselves we junior Programme Engineers often referred to this regular series as 'JB Spouts'. To accord him just and proper dues, Priestley was one of *the* great broadcasters and his was certainly the voice that braced so many listeners in those dark days of 1940. If you can share the same memories you will surely recall his *Postscript* broadcasts and, perhaps, one in particular early on in the series. Priestley told us about the German propaganda machine; how wonderfully effective it was, how we'd all been told what a clever man Dr Goebbels was – and not by friends of his, either, because this little man didn't appear to *have* any friends!

Those ten-minute Sunday evening talks, which followed the BBC's Nine O'Clock News, showed J.B. Priestley's own remarkable skills as a propagandist, and gave the sort of boost which was needed for the British war effort. Having heard *Postscript*, I think a lot of us went to bed feeling happier, though not, perhaps, some of the Tory backbenchers of the day. They considered Priestley's views were too far left.

Viscount Norwich who, as John Julius Norwich, later worked with me regularly in *Round Britain, Round Europe* and in *Transatlantic Quiz*, often recounted to other participants in these series how his father, Duff Cooper, then head of the wartime Ministry of Information, used to go 'positively puce over Priestley'! The voice which caused such apoplexy came to us on the Overseas Services in 1943, the same year in which *Transatlantic Quiz* first took to the airwaves when it was broadcast on the BBC's North American service. The team included such distinguished names as Alistair Cooke who, like my friend Syd Walker, also hailed from Salford, Manchester, the widely knowledgeable Professor Denis Brogan, and a quite dashing young army major who left the good life and safety of Hollywood to do his part for his country. His name was David Niven. I was the BBC engineer when *Transatlantic Quiz* began. Strangely enough, it was to be the last series I was to produce from the BBC's New York studios in 1983.

* * *

Back in 1943, however, Priestley was to be joined at 200 Oxford Street by two other distinguished men at the microphone, Wickham Steed and Howard Marshall, the latter becoming head of the War Report unit. When I think of Mr Steed, I immediately hear the proud note which crept into the voice of BBC overseas announcer, Albert Moor, as he declaimed at a particularly exciting and tense moment in the conduct of war, 'And here is Wickham Steed to give you some un-interesting details about the Allied landings in Sicily!'

When, tactfully, I mentioned what he'd just said, our Albert went 'bananas', in common parlance.

'But that's typed in the effing script. It is in-the-*script*!'

The timing of programme durations and announcements was of the essence on the various Overseas Services, Pacific, Eastern, African, and perhaps most important of all, the North American Service. These countries re-broadcast many of the programmes originated by the BBC in London on their own transmitters, so the Overseas announcers at 200 Oxford Street had to be really on their toes and watching the studio clock when it came to various programme junctions. There was, for example, a twenty or thirty second 'build up' for all radio stations about to relay a BBC programme and during this, our Mr Moor would say something like, 'This is the African Service of the BBC, Broadcasting on the 18 metre band, the 21 metre band, the 49 metre band …'

I cannot recall the precise frequencies now, but this sort of thing had to be announced at regular intervals. At precisely twenty or thirty seconds into this 'build up' the programme from London would begin its transmission. These metre band announcements were quite frightening things to tackle – until the announcers became used to them and then they became very boring indeed. One day when I was working in the Continuity Studio with our Albert, to break the monotony he flicked the microphone key on and off in quick succession in between yet another of those metre band announcements – only he got things slightly out of sync. In other words, his mic was 'live' when he thought it was 'dead'. What our listeners heard their end was: 'This is the African Service of the BBC Broadcasting on (pause) … hat bands, (pause) … brass bands, (pause) … elastic bands!'

I rather imagine that Mr Grenfell Williams, who was in charge of that particular Overseas Service, heard the announcement himself, for when I last met Mr Moor on the London Underground, he had become more successful in quite another profession – insurance.

* * *

My job, when I started work at 200 Oxford Street in the Continuity Studios, was to play music on gramophone records besides complete programmes recorded by the BBC on seventeen-inch 'slow speed' discs. That was in the days before microgrooves had been invented. The BBC slow speed records would have things like *Front Line Family* recorded on them. Then there was the *Epilogue*. On a particular Sunday evening when I was working in the Continuity Studio for the Pacific Service I had a very nice Australian announcer on duty with me, Isabel Ann Shead. The trusting Ann turned to me and asked what was next on that day's Routine Transmission Schedule. I consulted the document.

'Oh, it's the old E-pill-o-gog,' I replied facetiously.

Miss Shead went into action.

'This is the Pacific Service of the BBC.'

We were allowed the slightest reverential pause for such a Sunday transmission.

'The E-pill-o-gog!' declared the good lady for all to hear.

In our Overseas Presentation Department, situated two or three floors above our underground studios, all 'gaffs' were carefully noted and displayed the following day. I went to explain to the young lady who did the typing that it was all my fault. She couldn't stop laughing, but the head of Presentation, Mr Tom Chalmers, wasn't so amused.

In spite of my misdemeanours and undoubtedly those of other young staff, Tom Chalmers was to help a lot of us along in our Corporation careers. When he wanted to join the BBC, his wish was to become an announcer. 'Go away and DO something first, young man,' was John Reith's advice. And Tom did just that. He got a degree in civil engineering, then politely, but more firmly, knocked on the door again. This time he was admitted and after training began his announcing career at the BBC's pre-war Belfast station. Now he was heading the team of announcers for all the Overseas Networks including people like Joan Griffiths, Majorie Anderson, Margaret Hubble, Georgie Henschel, Sanday Wilshin and Mary Malcolm. On the male announcing team were the dashing Franklin 'Jingles' Engelmann, Guy Belmore, Roy Williams and Philip Robinson.

I always enjoyed working with Philip who originated from Bradford. One of the 'standby' records we had in the studio in case of a breakdown was entitled *Dance of the Daisies*, and if the programme *did* go off the air, as sometimes happened, Philip would pass a hand across his suffering brow, murmuring, 'Oh, *not* those darned Daisies *again*!'

Seven years later, we were both now working in Manchester, I as a junior producer, Philip as the senior man in Outside Broadcasts. He was in charge of a broadcast festival of William Wordsworth. Offers of material on the Lakeland poet came flooding in from home and abroad. One lunchtime he said to me in sheer desperation, 'I'm fair swamped. Let's go round to Mrs Mac's and have a stiff drink!'

On leaving the office he turned to his somewhat prim secretary.

'Ruth, love, if anyone else offers us another bloody daffodil whilst I'm out, tell 'em where to plant it!'

Back home in his native Bradford before the war, Philip had done stage design for some of the first productions of plays by J.B. Priestley. He showed me some of his sketches for the Priestley sets during those wartime nightshifts at 200 Oxford Street. In later times, I was with Mr Priestley in the bar of 'Mrs Mac's', just round the corner from Broadcasting House, Manchester, when a young and eager producer, who'd come up from London and met the great man for the first time, elbowed his way to the front of the bar and loudly asked Priestley what he'd have to drink. As soon as his glass had been drained, the chap was on his feet again.

'My round, I think,' murmured J.B. The producer waved this aside.

'No, no. This is all on expenses. You know, "to entertaining Mr Priestley..." .'

That noble head looked the eager fellow right between the eyes.

'But I'm *not* being entertained!'

It was Philip Robinson, that kindest wartime colleague, who in the very dead of night allowed me to speak into a BBC microphone as I read an announcement for him to the North American continent. His boss, Tom Chalmers, paid us a visit just before our shift ended.

'Heard a new voice on the Network. Quite pleasant too. Better when it is a little deeper!'

He departed with never a glance in my direction.

During another night shift, having come up for air to the BBC canteen, which was on the ground floor, Mr Chalmers paused at my table.

'I think,' he said quietly to me and to me alone, 'the next time you put on those Columbia Blue Label recordings of Delius, it would be better to play the movements in the order the composer intended!'

Undoubtedly the most dramatic of confrontations between the Head of Overseas presentation and this engineer occurred at the very door of Red Continuity. We literally collided. In the split second silence Mr Chalmers looked suddenly alarmed.

'What's happened to the programme?'

I too heard nothing. The slow speed recording which should have been going out on transmission at that very moment was tucked under my arm. I'd lifted the pick-up from the turntable, put the record back into its cover and was now on my way with it to the Recorded Programmes Library where such things were kept – but only *before* or *after* they had been broadcast. I have always prided myself on keeping a tidy studio!

* * *

It was the kind and understanding Tom Chalmers who realised that the young girl he'd heard when telephoning her wartime boss had a lovely voice. He therefore had this secretary transferred to his own department, then suggested to producer Noel Iliff that perhaps Miss Jean Metcalfe might be invited to read a poem or two in his *Chapter and Verse* programmes. Within a short space of time, someone else was typing announcements whilst Jean was reading them on the General Overseas Service of the BBC, and when her boss hit on an idea of a series of record request programmes for the troops abroad, who better than Jean Metcalfe to announce *Forces Favourites.* My contribution was to play-in the records requested, besides finding a suitable signature tune for the series. The André Kostelanetz version of *With a Song in my Heart* was to have special connections for Jean when *Forces Favourites* became *Family Favourites* after the war ended.

It was the studio microphone key which gave the very experienced Joan Griffiths a nasty moment one day when she was doing *Forces Favourites*. The announcers had to keep a Presentation log book, noting the starting and finishing times of each and every programme, besides other information. We'd recently had a spate of incorrect labelling on several wartime commercial gramophone records and when Joan announced, 'Irene sends her love to Corporal Jones somewhere in Egypt and wants "Just to be Near You"...' I put the record on.

After a moment Joan declared, 'I'm *sure* that's not the tune. Fade it out … Fade it out!'

With that, Joan moved the heavy log book to one side, inadvertently placing the edge of it down on the microphone key, and in the silence that followed the end of my 'fade', Miss Griffiths was then clearly heard to cry, 'No! I'm a bloody fool. Put it on again, dear. Quickly! Put it on again!'

Back came the long introduction to the melody and then the vocalist began the refrain, 'Just to be Near You…'

The General Overseas postbag some two or three weeks later was bulging with congratulatory letters from the various Services all saying roughly the same thing; how splendid and heart-warming it was to be *that* near to a charming BBC announcer.

My own BBC Programme Engineer boss was the most understanding of men – shortish, not so much hair on top, very expressive and truth-searching eyes behind those glasses and often given to producing a crisp white handkerchief, which he would drape between chin and shoulder before taking his violin out of the case and bowing away with great flourishes.

'Vivaldi?' I once ventured to enquire.

'My arse,' replied E. St. Clair-Hobbins pausing precisely on the beat.

'Hobby' was a born manager of men – and women too – of a whole host of junior and senior programme engineers. He knew precisely what each of us was up to at most times of the night and day; that which we jolly well should have done, that which we ruddy well should *not* have done.

Trevor Hill, Michael Loftus, Peter Francis, Alan Gowdey (who was to become Canon A. Gowdey), Ken Hicks and one or two others came into the latter category. Well, you had to break the monotony of those long wartime nightshifts at 200 Oxford Street. If you were scheduled to work in the studios rather than in Continuity there would often be two or three hours to kill between looking after those who came in to broadcast for the BBC.

Whilst the Germans were using magnetic tape for recording purposes in wartime, the British were still mainly recording on disc with a coated acetate surface cut by a stylus, or occasionally on what looked like a large spool of fuse-wire, or best of all on film.

There was another system. Part of the job was to go into a special technical area and load up an awesome-looking machine known as a Marconi-Stille. This H.G. Wellsian device recorded and played back an enormous spool of *steel* tape far slimmer in width than today's audio cassettes. Once loaded and started up, the tape, being made of very thin steel, acted as a conductor of electricity. When in motion the tape triggered off a mercury-discharge relay. You could see it dipping into a container of mercury and emitting brilliant blue flashes of light as it controlled the speeds of the right- and left-hand spool motors. We seemed to use this wondrous machine for transmitting such things as the News in Marati – an Indian dialect broadcast by the Eastern Service of the BBC.

That machine was almost as colourful as the Indian staff, an unusual mixture even for wartime. Very much in command was Z.A. Bokhari, a man with dark hypnotic eyes who seemed to me to tower above everyone and everything. Occasionally he sported a jewelled ivory walking stick and wore a large Indian ruby ring. I always felt I must behave in his presence, or young lads like me might be made to vanish up a rope – or worse!

Then there was the very elegant lady in beautifully cut English tweeds, and with a beautifully cut Oxford accent to match, Her Highness Princess Indira of Kapurthala, a province south of Lahore. Less exalted in the Eastern service at that time and certainly far less colourful of dress was an Englishman who generally wore a drab brown suit when he was producing programmes. His name was George Orwell.

The person I knew best and enjoyed working with was a diminutive, cheerful young Indian woman from Poona, Venu Chitale. Her beautifully embroidered sari and those of her countrywomen gave a marvellous splash of colour to a drab wartime building and to drab studios. Venu seemed to be laughing for weeks after my little spot of bother with that Marconi-Stille machine. I had loaded up the large spool, not realising that since recording the News in Marati no one in the recording section had wound the steel tape back to the beginning. So, in all innocence, I threaded up the machine and as the red light came on, so I started the News transmission.

Mind you, I thought it sounded a little odd because each bulletin in that language always began and ended with a sort of sung prayer. It went: '*Mazhab nahin sikhata apa mein bair rakhna*', or put quite literally another way, 'Religion not teaches between in animosity to keep'. You may of course already have worked that out for yourself. Frankly I was more familiar with the BBC's variation on the same theme: 'Nation Shall Speak Peace Unto Nation'.

If like me, however, you are not entirely familiar with the Indian language and a Marati prayer, then you are also unlikely to realise if you are playing a tape backwards!

When I had programmes on steel tape to put out during the long night-shifts, I'd turn off the lights above the large machine. Transmitting in the darkness was just as exciting as that film scene in which Frankenstein's monster has 20,000 volts of flashing blue light belted through the iron bolt embedded in his neck. Even better, if that steel tape broke you couldn't glue it, you had to weld it! There was a welding device on each machine, besides a pair of goggles. I became an expert tape-welder – just as broadcaster Teresa MacGonnagle, who was then a girl in the Control Room, became *the* expert with a soldering iron on really intricate technical wiring jobs. The chaps managed to grin and bear it since, occasionally, Teresa brought in her iron or toaster for them to repair. My welding handiwork was displayed over the Christmas of 1943 when both Red and Green Network Continuity suites were decked out with yards and yards of steel 'paperchains'.

* * *

'Hobby' sent for me the moment the festive spirit waned. He had a bevy of quite splendid women Programme and Junior Programme Engineers, with the honours going to Mrs Jo Grimes for sheer elegance of dress, manner and make-up, coupled with expert experience at a Studio Control Panel. Then there was the rousing young Jane Hunt who gave us some wonderful wartime parties in her home in the country, and the demure dark-haired young lady named Rosanne Snelling, who was decoratively perched on the corner of the boss's desk on the one occasion when I was instructed to report.

'But Hobby dah-ling,' she was saying in persuasive tones as she gently licked the tip of a well-manicured finger and dabbed at an imaginary ladder in one of her sheer silk stockings. 'Mother does *so* want me to go with her to the Sales. Can't someone *else* do my day shift?'

Hobby was firm but kind. 'Sorry to disappoint Mummy, but there are already three away with 'flu. Now bugger off there's a dear!'

I wasn't spoken to in any endearing tones that day over the steel paperchain incident and the waste of Corporation time, materials and electricity. Hobby was truly concerned, however, when in the following weeks, after spending several extra night shifts underground and then sleeping in the building because of Air Raids, I eventually surfaced inside a ward of the Middlesex hospital. 'We are sending you off for some fresh air and a rest at Hitchin,' declared Hobby. 'You and Hicks!'

Was there a faint note of relief in his voice? Be that as it may, off went Ken and I to the BBC's own hostel, a large well-furnished house in the countryside. Even in February it was marvellous to be out and about in the crisp air.

'Show your BBC passes to any of the gamekeepers and you can go through the Astor estate,' we were told the morning after our arrival.

The BBC even provided bicycles, which we signed for with a promise that on no account would we leave them unpadlocked in the countryside for fear of German parachutists cycling straight up to Buckingham Palace.

I have always had an absolute passion for water and boats, and to my delight the River Thames wound its majestic way through the Astor estate. In fact, Ken and I hadn't gone far when we came upon a magnificent boathouse built and timbered in Elizabethan style. Propping up the bikes, we ran to take a look through the latticed windows. Bound to be a splendid Thames launch in there! But I couldn't see much so, without a moment's thought or hesitation, I ran round in front of the imposing building. In the next two seconds, and looking far less imposing, I was sailing down Lady Astor's slipway upon steel rollers and straight into the cold river water.

When her Ladyship's gamekeeper came upon us, having noticed the curl of smoke from damp green bracken, I was endeavouring to dry out. From the limp bundle that was my trousers I produced my BBC pass. Two hours later I felt able to move on. At one of the Thames locks we were able to hire a canoe, so leaving the bikes firmly padlocked together in the care of the lock keeper, Hicks and Hill set off with a paddle each, cutting something of a dash upon the deserted river. About a mile further down stream was a weir and, with the river in winter spate, a good head of water was running swiftly over it.

'What do we do?' I enquired. 'Shoot?'

And shoot we did – several times. It really was thrilling, except for the haul back again of some fifty yards before re-boarding and attempting another shoot. As we shot that weir for about the fifth time, so a cushion passed me in the bottom of the canoe, coming to rest at the prow. Funny, I thought! Next moment a few more floatables passed, then down we went under water as the canoe turned on its side.

'You get … the … canoe!' I shouted to Ken, as in the 'boil' of the swirling weir waters I saw a square of wood begin to spin round in the whirlpool – and on that was the padlock key for the bikes! Too late. Down it went. But Ken had pulled the large canoe to the mud shallows whilst I retrieved several cushions downstream. We did our best to wipe off the mud and slime.

'Sorry lads, wife's none so good,' replied the lock keeper when asked if we might dry out.

I didn't really blame him. Thames mud is like any other winter mud.

He did oblige with a hacksaw and so we got going on the bikes back to the BBC hostel. Creeping up the backstairs we were unseen. Then into a bathroom and on with the large hot tap. Wet clothes stick, so both Hicks and Hill were in the same tub stripping off our things in warm water for a change when the bathroom door was thrust open by the hostel manageress.

'Baths not really before 8 p.m.!' she declared sweeping up just the trousers. 'And if you wish to do any washing and drying, there's a place downstairs. Alright?'

Later, I managed to burn a perfect imprint of an electric iron onto the seat of my new trousers, but that evening in the local pub at Hitchin my ten-shilling note, which had been dried and hand-pressed, came under the close scrutiny of the landlord. It passed muster.

* * *

I think Hobby was quite pleased to see us back, for he gave us a nice smile, me in particular.

'You look much better for the rest. Good. Now, Hill, I'm sending you on an Engineering Course!'

As a Technical Assistant, Class 2, upon my return I was promoted from playing records and doing effects to sitting at the Studio Control Panel. *Britain Speaks* was a regular series I worked on, as I've already mentioned. I was often at the Panel when another wartime broadcaster of the calibre of Priestley came into the basement area of 200 Oxford Street. Dr V.K. Wellington Koo may have been His Excellency, the Chinese Ambassador, but he left that side of him at Reception.

As a boy at Highwood Hill prep school, I had tripped up some steps with a fountain pen lodged in my top blazer pocket. The top of the pen had fallen off as the nib stabbed my nose, leaving what looked like a dark birthmark.

'I have been considering your mark,' declared Dr Koo one day as we were waiting to record his Talk. 'If you were Chinese and that mark were a little more central, why, you could be heir to the throne of China!'

At the end of a studio booking he would invariably whisk his engineer into the lift with him.

'Let us now go and see what delights your canteen has to offer.' Greeting the lift attendant he would say; 'And how is Tillie today?' or make some enquiry about her family.

Dr Koo had done some of the Sunday Home Service *Postscripts*, but what I remember best about him was his style of writing and delivery – that and his interest in people.

In more recent times I was to spend a nostalgic day with the BBC Written Archives section at Caversham Park, made all the more interesting for me because Barry Took was also there. He was researching for an article he was about to write for *The Listener*. We spent a lunchtime of 'what-ever-happened-to-so-and-so?' together. There was also a young woman doing research for a programme on George Orwell.

The archive assistant, Neil Somerville, knew exactly where to find everything each of us asked of him, with hardly a glance at the comprehensive Index system. I was particularly pleased when Neil turned up a copy of the very script I wanted. I'm sure Dr Wellington Koo would permit me to quote just the opening paragraph from one of his wartime broadcasts that I remember so well, having been his Programme Engineer the day it went out. He began:

> 'It used to be said that if every Chinese cut his coat only a few inches longer, the fabric needed will keep your textile mills busy all the year round. When the standard of living of the Chinese people is raised – and raised it will be – they will not only want to be better dressed but will multiply their other needs.'

Another man we looked forward to seeing when he came to broadcast was Jan Masaryk, at that time the Czechoslovak Minister of Foreign Affairs and the Deputy Prime Minister of his beleaguered country. He'd arrived one day to find me sitting at the Control Desk in Home Guard uniform. His talk began on this note:

> 'In the same manner in which the Germans undertook a systematic destroying of the Czechoslovak nation, so has the Czech nation responded by large-scale sabotage. At the Zrrojooovka works in Brno, technical designs for an urgent order were inexplicably lost.'

Mr Masarky beamed at me as he came back into the Control Cubicle.

'I sincerely hope they are going to issue your BBC Home Guard with some of our fine Bren guns from Brno!'

I had to explain that I was only the latest and lowliest recruit in the BBC Home Guard. Yet Jan Masaryk's wish for me was to be fulfilled. I didn't know it then but within a year I was to become a Bren-gunner with the Royal Scots regiment.

* * *

Most of those Talk studios at 200 Oxford Street were small affairs; a studio and a Control Cubicle, each about ten feet square. It was to be a Home Guard evening for me the day the General arrived to broadcast, supported by half-a-dozen military men and all with red shoulder tabs. Private Hill took a firm stand.

'I'm sorry, gentlemen. Three or four can stay here in the cubicle but you must leave room for the producer. The rest of you must wait outside.'

The General asked me my name.

'Quite wight, Pwivate Hill, Quite wight!' declared Montgomery.

Duties with the BBC's HQ Home Guard unit began with a parade. For some strange reason we lined up in alphabetical order: Hill, Hobbins, and House, medium, short and very tall. It was good to stand shoulder to shoulder with Hobby. I used to glance in his direction and think how reassuring it would be if he came into the Services with me when it was my time to go; he was a really reliable man who had proved himself a splendid CO to his civilian staff in the Programme Engineering Department.

Hill, Hobbins and House went on to the Army Gas Course together. It was out at Aldershot. After a few lectures and dabs of mustard gas applied on sensitive areas like the wrist and a 'now carry out your First Precaution', we were herded into a long concrete hut, sat down on wooden benches and, with gas masks in place, checked out by one of the regular army instructors. He passed Hill and Hobbins but stopped dead in front of House. Two grubby fingers were thrust against the unfortunate man's cheek and the mask rubber pulled back. The voice bellowed: 'Do you want to be effing well gassed?'

There was a loud 'thwap' as the rubber was released and the offending mask adjusted. This was more than I could take.

'Do you mind,' I said, and then said it again, this time with more clarity, having whipped off my own mask. 'You are talking to one of our Religious Broadcasting assistants!'

'One of your ex h'assistants if he don't put his bloody mask on proper!' came the icy retort. The Reverend Francis House didn't keel over, but I cried more than most when the order came: 'Remove masks'. We were then subjected to a strong whiff of some noxious gas, which stung eyes and throat.

My only other problem with the BBC Home Guard was Major Strode, M.M. A nice chap who'd been something in Publications and before that had had the misfortune to lose an eye, probably in the First World War. The substitute was made of gleaming glass. As Company Runner, being by far the youngest and so they thought the fittest, I had to report almost everything to the major.

'Not on the tarmac, Hill, not on the *tarmac*!' he yelled in a hoarse whisper as we did a night-time exercise in Hyde Park. 'The enemy'll hear your damned boots. On the grass, man. Run on the *grass*!'

But that, I fear, had been criss-crossed with stout wires in order to stop enemy gliders from swooping down and landing under the cover of darkness. It also stopped Home Guard Company Runners in their tracks. Unsound in wind and limb, I never knew which eye to report to half the time!

* * *

One day Hobby told me to nip down and have a word with Mr Chegwidden. He was the senior Presentation assistant, who supported a lot of the announcers and a very large moustache. It seemed he had taken on a new girl. Would I go back and work with her in Continuity for a couple of weeks whilst she got to know the Service and how to tackle all those frightening 'Metre Band' announcements? She was only in her teens and what confidence she had was rapidly vanishing.

At the end of the fortnight, and now beginning to enjoy the work of a BBC Overseas announcer, she said to me, 'You really have been so kind. I've told Daddy all about you! Can you come and have lunch with us sometime next week?'

We arranged to meet at Oxford Street underground station. There was Jill, but in a large chauffeur-driven limousine! As we purred along in the direction of Ealing, Jill said, 'I know you're interested in films. Well, Daddy is going to show you round his studios!'

Then, and only then, did the penny drop. 'Daddy' was Sir Michael

Balcon – and I was now on my way to Ealing film studios for the day. Jill was right. I still had my home Cinema in a garage, and spent most days off working as a projectionist at the Capitol Cinema in Mill Hill Broadway. On other free days I was at the Central Office of Information Film Unit, surreptitiously endeavouring to fit gramophone record music to things like, 'Are YOU Saving Fuel on YOUR tractor?'.

That visit to Ealing with Jill Balcon was a day to remember. I met two of Ealing's most celebrated directors, Charles Frend and Cavalcanti; was taken to the Special Effects department where I saw the model of the ship used in the film *San Demetrio London*, which they were currently working on. I was given enough coloured smoke-powders, greens, blues, yellows and blacks, to keep my puppet show going for the next decade and then, with palpitating heart, I was invited to take lunch in the senior staff section of Ealing's restaurant. There was Sir Michael himself, daughter Jill, Cavalcanti and that flower of English womanhood, the beautiful and demure Patricia Roc.

If you've ever seen pre-war pictures of British Imperial Airways and the sort of large basket chairs in which the favoured few travelled aloft, then those are just the sort upon which sat the favoured few at Ealing Film Studios, but when the enchanting Miss Roc sat down on her chair so the basketwork caught her best silk stockings. On that day, my English Rose uttered something short and Saxon, and thus I was to lose the last of my boyhood illusions.

However, I gained, a 'Pass', signed by Sir Michael Balcon, which enabled me to visit Ealing Studios as often as I wished. I took full advantage of that, making contact with some of the Ealing staff who were to prove very useful in the years ahead when I had the good fortune to produce a programme for the BBC in celebration of Ealing's twenty-first birthday. The sad time was to come later when I arrived, unannounced, in order to do a last-minute interview for one of the BBC Film programmes.

'Can I come in?' I enquired hopefully. Ealing's head of Publicity looked decidedly down in the mouth.

'Why not, you own the place now – or haven't you seen the morning paper?'

Not that morning, when it was announced that the BBC had taken over Ealing Studios.

What a marvellous organisation they'd been; what a gathering of creative people from Call Boy to Carpenter, Projectionist to Producer. If Dr Alexander and the BBC hadn't responded to my letter from school, I think I would have applied to work for this company – always supposing they might have taken me on.

I returned from my wartime visit to Ealing studios by tube train, in time for an evening shift at 200 Oxford Street and to work on what had now become a regular series for me. It was Peter Pooley, as Overseas News Talks Editor, who thought up the idea of a newsreel for radio, an idea that was to prove an outstanding development in broadcast journalism. By the time I came to join the ranks of *Radio Newsreel*, it was an established success. The twice-nightly editions were relayed by an enormous number of American stations for the *Reel* had become one of the major sources of war news for the American continent.

To package these North American editions, in view of their undoubted prestige, we were soon to 'head' the programme's signature tune, *Imperial Echoes*, with another André Kostelanetz recording, this time, the fanfare opening to *Melodies from Victor Herbert*: 'Tara-la, tara-la, tar-a-laar!' Then came the Canadian voice of announcer Byng Whitaker.

'Whilst Britain awaits another dawn, we bring you news from the Battle Fronts of the World in – *Radio Newsreel!*'

Then followed *Imperial Echoes*. That entire opening was copied onto a BBC Watts acetate disc, one of our own recordings, together with Byng's transatlantic voice.

One memorable night, on went the Red transmission light. Recorded Programme assistant Charles Farmer put on the recorded opening sequence. Lovely fanfare:

'Whilst Britain awaits – kerwark–awaits–kerwark–awaits–kerwark ...'

What a moment to have a repeating groove. I quickly fade out the offending disc and give Mr Whitaker a Green light – his cue to do the 'menu' for *Newsreel* tonight.

'In this edition, our gallant Russian Allies ...'

Slowly the quiver in his voice breaks into a chuckle and then into the sort of uncontrollable laughter only contained within a large man. We are taken off the air by the Control Room.

'Yes, yes,' I say over the telephone. 'He is *quite* recovered now! Give us back our transmission!'

Even without that incident, *Radio Newsreel* was an exciting programme on which to work, hearing stories coming in from such War reporters as A.R. (Phil) Phillips, who was with a BBC Mobile Recording Unit even before the collapse of France, also Richard Dimbleby, Chester Wilmot, Frank Gillard, reporters who were right there in the field of battle. Sometimes there was a despatch from American correspondent,

George Hicks, who was on the Allied convoys at sea. The BBC's War Report Unit came with another well-known voice in Broadcasting, that of Howard Marshall whom I've already mentioned.

Those North American editions of *Radio Newsreel* on Red network, which we broadcast at 2345–2400 hours GMT and then from 0300–0315 hours, seemed to highlight the talents of reporters, writers, editors and producers. How poor, it seemed to me, was to be the later coverage of the Falklands Campaign by comparison.

Whilst adrenaline was generated in all of us by the North American editions, it was nice to be able to relax more in the preparation of *Radio Newsreel* for the Pacific Service edition, which was broadcast from 0700 to 0725 GMT. Then there was time for pre-broadcast talking. *Newsreel* producer George Innes, who began his BBC career as a boy messenger, would discuss with Ian Messiter the series he wanted to do once this lot was over. Something about popular ballads mixed with Minstrel songs. It was George's dream, which was to become a very successful Television reality with *The Black and White Minstrel Show*.

And Ian, one of the Recorded Programme assistants? He was always doing conjuring tricks or something exciting to amuse the younger members of staff.

'I'll stand behind you and together we take d-e-e-p breaths. On the count of ten, hold it!'

You did – and passed clean out for a magic moment.

* * *

The nearest most of us on the *Reel* were to come to the physical look, and indeed the actual whiff of war was on September 27th 1944, the day Canadian reporter Stanley Maxted reached Nijmegen and, with the last of the few, got finally out of that hell that was Arnhem. He came straight as he was, in a strained and stained state, to 200 Oxford Street and broadcast 'live' – well almost live after all he had endured.

'They came out because they had nothing left to fight with except their bare hands, maybe,' he said.

Only a few months earlier, I'd been on duty at 200 Oxford Street as Programme Engineering shift-leader when Tom Chalmers' presentation assistant, Sybil Hall, phoned the Programme Engineering office. She told me to get the News studio ready for an important transmission. On the way, I waited at the Recorded Programmes library for an army dispatch rider to arrive from Bushey Heath, which I knew to be the headquarters of the Supreme Allied Commander. I switched everything on, then set up the disc recording marked AFRS (Armed Forces Radio Service) on one of the turntables. I knew what had occurred as I heard the first few seconds.

I was joined by Tom Chalmers. After a very long wait, because of weather conditions, a somewhat nervous-looking John Snagge arrived with two other BBC senior staff in tow. We settled John in the News studio. Then came the go-ahead.

'This is London! London calling in the Home, Overseas and European Services of the BBC!'

I already knew what was coming next from hearing the start of that recording.

'People of Western Europe! A landing was made this morning on the coast of France!'

On that morning of June 6th, 1944, General Dwight Eisenhower told us that this was 'D' Day. There had obviously been a time for propaganda but now it was time for absolute truth. The BBC gave the clearest of instructions to all editors, writers and production staff, even down to my own level of responsibility, on how War Report material should be treated once the Invasion began. If a reporter used a phrase like 'fighting today', it was essential to state *when* the despatch was recorded and *where*, for instance in Normandy, off direct transmission from that area, or an actual recording made on location with the background of an actual battle. It seemed to me a far cry from *Marching On*. And it was.

The first of our correspondents to speak from the soil of France, on June 8th, was Guy Byam. He was something of a hero to us for he'd already survived the torpedoing of the *Jarvis Bay* and later, in the course of the Allied Invasion, he was to swim the River Rhine. The third time, Guy wasn't to be so lucky. He was reported missing in the 'Rose of York', a flying fortress, which took part in a raid over Berlin less than a year later.

Byam's Invasion despatch was followed the same day by Chester Wilmot; 'We came by Glider.' Then it was the turn of Richard Dimbleby doing a recorded commentary from an aircraft over the coast of France.

On June 17th we broadcast Michael Standing's eyewitness account of the visit of His Majesty the King to Normandy. Yes, it certainly *was* an exciting time to be working on *Radio Newsreel*. There were of course lighter moments before and after 'D' Day. From time to time those of us in Programme Engineering were down at the Stage Door Canteen, Broadcasting such celebrities as Fred Astaire, Jack Buchanan, Dinah Shore, Noel Coward, and Beatrice Lillie.

The very day after 'D' Day, and with that veteran of the best of Broadcasting Cecil Madden as our producer-in-charge, the BBC launched the Allied Expeditionary Forces programme. It ran from June 7th 1944 until over a year later, with not only the BBC's resources but also those of NBC and CBS in America and those of the Canadian Broadcasting Company. Gerry Wilmott was already with us at 200 Oxford Street producing programmes for Canadian listeners to the General Overseas Service. From a small studio in nearby Ramilies Place, I'd often balance a sextet accompanying the lyrical voice of Corporal Edmund Hockeridge who, in post-war London, was to star in *The Pyjama Game*. Once the AEF programme was launched, we had things on a really large musical scale with three bands based in and around the London area. The American musicians were directed by Captain Glenn Miller, the Canadians by Robert Farnon of the same military rank, and for the British band, Sergeant George Melachrino.

Cecil Madden's brief was not only to give the Allied Expeditionary Force entertainment and all-important News, but also to link them with their homelands. Working on those Forces programmes proved helpful to me and to Gerry Wilmott, for we were to meet up and to work together again with another Broadcasting Service for the troops, this time on German soil once the war was over. But I'm jumping ahead a bit. Let's go back to that disc recording of General Dwight Eisenhower, which dramatically announced the long-awaited invasion of Europe.

Funny, but in all the excitement of 'D' Day the AFRS recording was left sitting in the record rack above the turntables in the News studio. I discovered it myself a full day later, having returned there after the early morning launch of the AEF service from studios in Portland Place. In my usual efficient and hygienic manner, I decided to tidy up that studio.

It was long after the war ended that someone in the BBC did a bit of careful checking up. Who had been on duty that sixth day of June 1944 when one of the most historic moments in Broadcasting had happened? Now Hobby had a delightful secretary during those war years, Veronica Manoukian, who managed to keep most of us cheerful as she dished out extra shift duties from Management. Veronica went on to the BBC's Transcription Service after the war had ended to do great work in that department. No, Veronica would never have split on me – although had *she* made the discovery she would have said to herself, 'H'm, that heel, Hill!'

By one way or another I got the message. Would Hill kindly return the Eisenhower 'D' Day recording to the BBC's Recorded Archives section? First, I took a copy!

4

British Forces Network, Hamburg (1945–1948)

The handsome Lieutenant Roger Moore looked slightly dishevelled for once as he alighted from the coach outside the Boccaccio Hotel in Hamburg, home of the Combined Services Entertainment Unit.
‘’Strewth, old boy!’ he said, taking breath, ‘Have *you* ever been kissed by an entire section of brass players?’

It was a new experience for the young man destined to have even more exciting encounters on the cinema screen as 007. Roger, I should quickly add, was then followed off that coach by Ivy Benson’s All Girls’ Band. They’d just completed a tour of the British Army of the Rhine with stage appearances at Bonn, at the CSEU Garrison theatre, Minden, and finally at a place called Celle – not far from Luneburg Heath where, some fourteen months earlier on May 5th 1945, Field Marshal ‘Quite Wight’ Montgomery had signed the German Peace Treaty.

The dependable Lieutenant Moore was often sent as the CSEU representative and chaperone to various touring stage companies and top-flight bands who arrived from England to entertain the Services. I took Roger into the Crown Prince Hotel almost next door to his HQ wherein were billeted all those of us serving with the British Forces Network broadcasting station in Hamburg, BAOR 3.

The All Girls’ Band had done a good broadcast concert for us from Celle earlier that evening. Ivy trained the musicians as meticulously as any Brigade of Guards. The lady wielding this particular baton had a private as well as a professional responsibility for the members of her band whilst they were away from home.

A fortnight before the Celle concert, I’d been announcing Geraldo

BFN, Hamburg

from Studio B, our Light Entertainment studio in the Musikhalle. Geraldo and his Concert Orchestra had provided our mid-morning *Canteen Break* broadcasts for two or three days that week whilst his talented brother, Syd Bright, had recorded a series of *Piano Playtime* sessions which would alternate with those by our own Sergeant Bill Crozier, another wizard on the keyboard. Within a month of Ivy's return to the UK, we would be doing broadcasts with Bill Cotton and his Bandshow, but right now, Roger Moore was having a nightcap with me in our mess bar. I'd returned to Hamburg an hour or so earlier that evening after the Celle broadcast was over and we'd de-rigged our microphones and equipment, but Lieutenant Moore had to wait around in Celle whilst Ivy and the girls were given supper. They didn't 'Take the A Train' on empty stomachs.

Roger was pleased that a London theatre management was now sending out professional 'leads' for a touring production of the stage play *The Shop at Sly Corner*, which was to be rehearsed at the Garrison Theatre, Hamburg, and directed by ENSA producer, Mac Picton.

'He asked me if I'd like to audition for the part of the naval Lieutenant! I'll have to clear it with 'Bunny' Warren.'

If Roger was pleased about that – and acting would make a very pleasant change from some of his recent duties – then I was equally pleased at having recently discovered something about Colonel Warren, his genial commanding officer. Now I am not boasting when I say that I remember voices very, very clearly. Back in Mill Hill, NW7, before the war, I was always glued to the radio on Sundays – not to the BBC for that was somewhat 'solemn' on this day as decreed by John Reith. No, my elder sister and I would listen to Radio Hilversum and to such things as *Doctor Fumanchu* on the *Milk of Magnesia Show*, or better still I would get out my Secret Code book and begin to write furiously as a deep,

A first sight of Germany at end of 1945

well-modulated voice of the Chief Ovaltiney would, at diction speed, say things like, 'Six … thirty … twenty four.'

Now as every Ovaltiney worth his badge will tell you, the number Two stood for the letter A according to the Code Book, and so on. You may already be one jump ahead of me, having worked out that 'Six … thirty … twenty four,' spells out 'Col'. I looked Roger Moore's commanding officer firmly between the eyes as, in a hushed tone of sudden recognition mingled with reverence because the room was full of other people, I unmasked him.

'Colonel Warren! *You* were the Chief Ovaltiney!'

'Tell anyone that, Sergeant Hill and I'll kill you,' was his response!

* * *

The morning after the Celle concert I was up early and called round to the Boccaccio in order to collect the other half of the BFN Features and Drama Unit, WAAF Sergeant Margaret Potter. Being an army chap, I never got to know many WAAFs, certainly none as well as No. 473788, who was both attractive *and* talented. The first time I set eyes on that particular number in 1947 she was in the Brahmatorium, a rotunda at one

The Musikhalle, Hamburg, 1946

Named 'The Bramatorium' by BFN staff since Johann's statute is on the right

end of the Musikhalle's first-floor level. This area of Hamburg's equivalent to London's Albert Hall as a place for music-making and concerts gets its name from the enormous marble bust of Johannes Brahms, the city's celebrated son. In this pose he is being firmly adhered to by a number of nubile marble ladies in a state of almost total undress. The mass is pivoted on what must surely be a most substantial base in order that the facial features of the great maestro can be turned to the sun as it moves in the heavens throughout the hours of daylight. On dull days, those of us now in occupation of the building sometimes gave him and *les girls* a whirl!

When this decorative and undamaged building was taken over by the Army of Occupation in June 1945 it quickly had rehearsal rooms adapted as radio studios to become the home of the British Forces Network in Hamburg. Now the Brahmatorium housed our library of gramophone records and sound effects under the auspices of Herr Otto Olle. Margaret Potter may, of course, have felt somewhat dwarfed in the shadow cast by the great Brahms, or by the fact that she, then Paddy Flynn, were at the start the only two women amongst a unit of some sixty or seventy army and airforce personnel. In any event when I first addressed her by saying,

'Good morning, Corporal!' the then owner of that rank turned on a smart pair of heels, the footsteps echoing into the far distance, as she hurried away across the acres of marble floor. Not an auspicious beginning to a relationship that was to last a lifetime.

As I entered the Boccaccio – which incidentally had been Hamburg's most celebrated and expensive pre-war brothel where only the best were to be seen – I discovered Margaret Potter and Ivy Benson seated at breakfast in the small area of the ballroom.

'Have a Guinness, luv?' Ivy was saying. What stamina these leaders of bands and women possess. I wanted to smile as I thought back to the previous evening when Roger Moore and I had thought up that new name for the band, after his journey with them in the coach, 'Ivy Bunsen and Her Burners!'

The All Girls' Band had one more concert to do before leaving BAOR this visit, and that was to be a Variety show, part of which would be relayed by the BBC Light Programme. Sergeant Bob Boyle would announce that for us. Had it been the broadcast of serious orchestral music from inside our own splendid concert hall, then that would call for the talents of Corporal Brian Matthew who, at that time in his broadcasting career, had more of a Third Programme tone to his voice.

At the other, more popular end of the musical scale, our daily record request programme, *The 1600 Club* would be introduced by Corporal Derek Jones, a far cry from *The Living World* and other programmes he was to present so well on Radio 4 in later years. Or the record requests may have been announced by airforce Corporal John Jacobs. At that time his brother, David Jacobs, was serving with the British Forces Network out East. And if not John, then it might be the army's turn again with Corporal Jimmy Kingsbury at the microphone, adopting tones of our American broadcasting brothers down the road apace at AFN, Bremen.

Between this range of musical tastes, I produced a Sunday evening record show called *A Melody, A Memory* in which the Services and their families sent in details of a tune linked with some personal memory. This series began after a quietly spoken army Major who had been O.C. Dover Castle was posted out to us. When he discovered that our BFN commanding officer was of the rank of Captain, Major Barney Colehan personally demoted himself, replacing his one crown with three pips.

A Melody, A Memory was Barney's very first contribution to the world of broadcasting – not, I am glad to report his last, for which the BBC and the European Broadcasting Union must have been truly thankful.

There was another weekly record programme which I did myself,

Philistine that I was. The Tuesday evening *Old Wine in New Bottles* series introduced 'swing' versions of some of the more popular classics. In a class of its own, however, was the series of record programmes devised by Captain Ken Mitchell-Taylor, i/c BFN's Variety Department. We only referred to his particular DJ on air as 'Mr Swing'. That young man's elder brother then possessed possibly the finest private collection of jazz recordings in the whole of Europe and he kindly allowed a large number of these to be brought over in his brother's car. Upon arrival they were immediately put into the care of Lance Corporal Korner. Alexis Korner seemed to know quite a bit about this type of music, for all of his nineteen years. He was later to start Blues Incorporated, the first British rhythm and blues band, besides having a large hand in the forming of the Rolling Stones and other groups. Until his death, Alexis's regular BBC series commanded a large and faithful following. But why, you may wonder, did our DJ adopt such a strange *nom-de-plume* as 'Mr Swing'? Well at that time, Captain the Hon. Gerald Lascelles was closely in line to the throne of England.

'Can't manage next week,' he told us at the end of one programme, 'May 26th is Grandmama's birthday!' His Unit ensured that he was back in the UK in time for him to take tea with his Grandmama, Queen Mary, at Buckingham Palace.

* * *

In this strange yet very happy atmosphere I was humbly serving both King and Country, although it *had* taken rather a time since that wartime day at 200 Oxford Street, when 'Hobby' informed me that I was to report to the War Office for interview. I did as instructed.

Captain John MacMillan surveyed me through half-closed eyes as he glanced at the paper on his War Office desk.

'Technical Assistant! And you have passed the equivalent of the Part 2 Post Office engineering exam, I see.'

A smile seemed to hover beneath the black crinkly hair as the Captain then murmured something about the Army Psychological Warfare Unit and that a posting would soon come through. When the call eventually came it was to report in Home Guard uniform to Darlington. A day or so later I found myself in Northern Ireland doing basic training. Despite the fact that I also murmured something about Psychological Warfare at the Selection board, I was booted into the infantry – Scottish at that.

Jean Metcalfe cheered me up with a record request for 'Private T. Hill of the Royal Scots' and a letter or two. On the firing range I tried out one of Jan Masaryk's guns from Brno and, perhaps out of respect for him, was given a Marksman's badge plus a heavy Bren gun to go with it. The very day my battalion went off to Burma, I went by ambulance into hospital with scarlet fever, then to a large Convalescent Camp at Glencorse. Here they had a run-down Radio room and no one who really knew how to run it. I made a rapid recovery from grade C3 to grade A1, wrote a short note to Captain J. MacMillan c/o the War Office: 'Dear Sir, Am really fit now but the C.O. here says I'm not so that I can stay and run the depot Radio room,' and then settled down once more to a very pleasant way of doing army Service by playing records which were relayed to all areas in which service personnel were convalescing or undergoing medical treatment.

It was the Adjutant, complete with spotted dog, who somewhat viciously kicked open the door of the Radio room.

'HILL!' he exploded, 'You are a sod, a stupid sod. I am sorry but I mean it!'

Even his dog hung its noble head in shame. His master was waving my letter.

'The War Office sent this to Army Records, Perth! You are O.U.T!'

And I was – that very same day.

They had to give me sick leave before packing me off to Burma, so I went up to London and into that War Office again. MacMillan was no longer there, but I did talk to a helpful Major John Humphreys – very helpful as it turned out, for he was to become our C.O. in Hamburg. Within ten days he'd got me a posting to Hamburg.

As soon as the war in Europe was over, that Army Psychological Warfare Unit – put into the field of battle to counteract German propaganda broadcasts – had hitched one of its Mobile Studio vans to the powerful Norden transmitter. Now the British Forces Network, Hamburg was being heard loud and clear by listeners as far afield as Denmark, Holland, Belgium, France and in the north of England and the Midlands. Within a short while, the undamaged and spacious Musikhalle had been commandeered as the home of BFN.

John MacMillan's half-smile and half-closed eyes welcomed me on my posting to his unit. He was now a major.

'Glad to have you with us,' said the smile. Not a dickie about the time it had taken waiting to get there!

I was to train some of the Forces personnel in Balance and Control as Programme Engineers, but Corporal Johnny Ammonds was also an ex-

BBC chap, and he knew the job inside out. He was later to be awarded the OBE for his services to broadcasting. Discovering Harry Worth and producing his TV shows, besides doing *Morecombe and Wise* for BBC and ITV, amongst other things, isn't a bad track record. I was therefore to be given a mic test and then put onto announcing duties. It was nice to be back inside a decent Continuity Studio – even if in Forces Broadcasting you played the records yourself. The equivalent of those BBC Overseas 'Metre Band' announcements was in reading out at regular intervals: 'The levels of the Rhine and the Weser as at 07 hundred hours today.'

Well, perhaps the Royal Engineers had to tighten or to lengthen the ropes on the Bailey Bridges, which still spanned these mighty rivers. I know that as I crossed the swollen Rhine for the first time in the comfort of a troop train, I could only think of Guy Byam swimming across.

We played a lot of Overseas Recorded Broadcast Service programmes on our BFN turntables, mainly popular and light music, but we also had a professional Music Department of our own under Captain Trevor Harvey, the conductor. Sergeant James Gibb an accomplished pianist was in his section, also Edward Nash, who was later to produce many delightful music series for the BBC in London. And there was our own BFN Light Orchestra, which I was to look after, under Dr Milo Karatsch, Leader Kurt Theim. Our listeners were also able to enjoy regular broadcast concerts by the Nordwestdeutscher Rudfunk Symphony Orchestra, conducted by Hans Schmidt-Isserstedt whose sister was our chief BFN receptionist. By arrangement with Hugh Carleton Greene and David Porter, now in charge of NWDR, these former BBC colleagues encouraged me to 'work in conjunction' as far as NWDR and BFN were concerned, as they did with Captain Harvey. As a result our concert hall at the Musikhalle would be full to capacity with German civilians on a weekday afternoon and Allied Services personnel on a Sunday for the broadcasts. Besides the NWDR Orchestra there were many visiting orchestras and conductors.

The Berlin Philharmonic came to us for their very first concert after the great Wilhelm Furtwängler had been 'de-Nazified' and was allowed to perform in public again. The Germans queued outside our building for thirty-six hours in order to be able to see and hear the maestro at work again. Hundreds were to be turned away. We decided to balance the German orchestra not only with the usual Telefunken condenser microphones, but also by adding one of Dr Alexander's BBC 'ribbon' microphones. The results were spectacular. We had the advantage of recording the Berlin Phil on the splendid German AEG Magnetophonband Tape recorders. What an improvement on 'steel'. As soon as War Reparations were ended, AEG gave us three of their spanking new high-frequency Studio Tape machines, which recorded and reproduced sound at an amazing thirty inches per second. I sent tape recordings of that Furtwängler concert to London – but the BBC had yet to wait until they'd *also* got Magnetic Tape machines before they could broadcast it on the Third Programme.

It wasn't until the mid 1970s when Zenderfries, Berlin invited me to visit them whilst they did a German version of a programme I'd produced for Radio 3, the first ever in 'Binaural Sound', that I heard their recordings in Stereophonic Sound – and made in that city as long ago as 1936 on discs! Most of our BFN technicians were German civilians who'd made broadcasting their career. They taught us a lot.

In a lighter musical mood and from the same Concert Hall, Sergeant Ray Martin of the Pioneer Corps conducted the 30 Corps Stage Band comprising highly professional Service musicians, some of whom had played in leading American bands. For a series Ray did for us we augmented musicians with the string section from the Hamburg Philharmonic. In between the various items, all to be skilfully arranged and orchestrated by the talented Ray, there were 'links' played by Germany's leading organist, Gerhard Gregor, himself just out of detention. Over these links came the programme announcements. I'd come down from our Control Cubicle, housed in the former box of Kaiser Wilhelm II, in order to have a word with Ray at the end of a rehearsal. Having done so on one occasion, the leader of the Hamburg Phil caught my eye. As I went over to him, he tapped the music stand with his bow:

'Diss, diss tune, "Night Und Die"? Is very good! I think Sergeant Martin he should haf it published, no?'

No, I thought, Cole Porter might object!

BFN's Variety Department did a range of programmes: *Parking Space* a weekly satire written by Sergeants Roy Bradford and Johnny Brandon, which I also produced, *Nuts and Wine*, light music and verse, and a *Services Quiz* on Sundays, arranged and skilfully conducted by a recently arrived Flight Lieutenant Cliff Michelmore, who also did sport along with Sergeant Alan Clarke.

It was now Squadron Leader Michelmore who walked into my office one day and, whilst talking, noticed the photos on my desk top covered by a sheet of glass. They were of the BBC's Overseas women announcers with whom I'd worked at 200 Oxford Street, and all signed. Cliff looked at and studied them all – one several times,

Above left: BFN's scriptwriting team for Features and Drama

Above: Midnight oil at the Musikhalle as Margaret Potter writes our first serial *The Island of Moressa*

"WHAT'S ON BFN"

THIS week BFN has the pleasure of filling for the BBC its dance band hight-spot of the week. Normally called "Band Parade" and featuring the best in British Dance Music, this week the show is called 'Garrison Concert' and comes from C.S.E.U's Hamburg Garrison Theatre. The double bill is Ivy Benson and her Band, and Leslie Douglas and his Orchestra. Time 8.45—9.30 p. m., Monday 27th October. It will be heard by BFN and BBC listeners. Ivy Benson and her Band can be heard again by BFN listeners on Saturday 1st November in a half hour programme at 2.30 p. m.

LISTENERS to "Quiz Time" will be invited presently to join us at the regular time on Sunday evening by tuning into our new interrogation half-hour, "Do You Know?" The line-up for this programme is as for Quiz Time but the content of the programme is changed. Further details follow, but in the meantime watch out for the new title ... DO YOU KNOW???

THE BFN Theatre Orchestra will be in possession of the Concert Hall on Saturday of this week, with a programme which includes the Strauss "Emperor Waltz" and Mozart's Symphony No. 39 in E flat. We hope to continue our series featuring the regimental bands in B.A.O.R. next week.

"TOP TEN"... the programme designed to find out from YOUR voting the tunes which YOU consider to be the "Top Ten" of the week still goes from strength to strength. It's worth while reminding listeners that the tunes to be selected can be taken from any programme originating from BFN — or anywhere else.

NOW the oldest inhabitant of our Variety Department, by virtue of length of service, is Sgt. Trevor Hill who joined us after three years with the BBC, where he assisted with such shows as "Ack-Ack Beer-Beer", "Itma", and "Radio Newsreel". His first job with BFN was that of Continuity Announcer, but on transferring to Variety Department he produced the "Parking Space" series, our first venture at satirical comedy. From comedy he turned to the writing and producing of serial plays for "Children's Magazine" and is at present working on a new series of "Spine Chillers" which he hopes to present round about Christmas. Shows in which he can be heard are "Round and About", in which he does "Puzzle Corner", the light half of "Round the Records", and "Old Wine in New Bottles", which has started on its second run. Ambition: to become a really good producer—his aim since slamming doors and making effects on "Itma".

"HE'S BEEN LISTENING TO THAT TREVOR HILL AGAIN!"

‘Yes, she *is* nice. Very nice!’

No, she isn’t married, I explained – at least she wasn’t the last time I heard from her. Some time later, Cliff returned.

‘I’m going on UK Leave. Er, would you like me to call in at the BBC and give Jean Metcalfe your kind regards?’ he enquired.

Better than that, I sent him with a sealed letter by way of introduction. If she could cope with Continuity, she’d cope with Cliff.

‘He’s quite a smoothy, is your Squadron Leader Michelmore,’ she wrote in reply.

The wedding invitation came sometime after we’d been demobbed.

* * *

BFN’s Presentation Department had long-suffering Captain Campbell Logan in charge. I say long-suffering because occasionally he did have to deal with one young Canadian announcer who *would* say things over the air like: ‘That recording of “Your Tiny Hand is Frozen” was by Benjimmino Gig-lee!’

There was a certain amount of locally produced Drama broadcast by BFN Hamburg but once the languid Sergeant Vivian Milroy was demobbed fairly early on, this faded out. With the arrival of Service families, Control Commission personnel, WVS et cetera, Drama as part of Family Programmes was needed. So Sergeant Hill left Continuity and came together with Sergeant Margaret Potter who’d been busy writing and producing women’s programmes. We became the BFN Features and Drama Unit. Corporal Alexander McKee and Corporal Leon Griffiths were attached to us on the Feature scripting side. I began *Service Spotlight*, a series which covered all that the title implies. *Operation Woodpecker* dealt with timber felling in German forests for rebuilding and much-needed fuel, whilst *The Red Caps* was a feature on the Military Police and their training. We not only had every help from the Provost Marshal of BAOR, he also gave Alex and myself a full General’s escort along the autobahn, complete with outriders on motorcycles and four Jeeps with sirens sounding as we bade his unit goodbye.

There was little to smile about, however, with the scripting and recordings for *The Case of the Missing Flowerpot*. This was the work of the Royal Airforce Missing Persons Bureau and their endeavours to trace aircrews ‘missing, presumed killed’. In this instance, an aircrew had been shot by the Gestapo, but a man from a forced-labour Corps had scratched details of their executioners on a plant pot and dropped this into the shallow grave. We also featured the German police as they assisted in bringing one of the culprits to trial, whilst the War Graves Commission took over the task of reburial in a British Cemetery.

The programme was heard by Tom Chalmers, who by now had been appointed to run the BBC's new Light Programme. Whilst he was on one of several visits to BAOR, he recommended that it should be broadcast by the BBC, but in view of the number of families in England who still had sons and husbands missing, it was decided it might prove too distressing.

Service Spotlight was entirely factual. Fiction provided us with most of the serial plays and series, which Sergeants Potter and Hill wrote and produced in Hamburg, most of which were subsequently to be heard again in later BBC productions. *The Island of Moressa* was our first attempt at doing a radio serial, with William Eedle, later to become a professional actor, in the role of 'Dick', and Corporal John Jacobs as his cockney batman 'Dave'. The extrovert Jimmy Kingsbury, later to become Presentation Editor for Radios 1 and 2, was the villain of the piece, a chap named 'Meldano'. In the story Dick and Dave team up with a certain Professor Selby, a clever Scottish scientist – and who better to portray him than a genuine Scot, ex BBC Empire Service announcer and professional pre-war actor, James Urquhart. To accord him his service rank, he was then Squadron Leader Urqhuart and i/c the Unit's RAF personnel. One Sunday in Studio E after rehearsing most of Episode 1 all morning, we broke for lunch, we other ranks going to the BFN canteen, Squadron Leader Urquhart to the Four Seasons Officers' Club as befitted his rank. It became rather a long lunch hour as we waited his return, and then we rehearsed the ending to the first instalment. The lines went like this:

Dick (puzzled):	'But how are we going to get to this Island of yours, Professor?'
Dave (cheerfully):	Got a plane or summat, eh?'
Professor Selby:	'Not exactly a plane. If you've finished your drinks, gentlemen. (putting down his glass) Come to my workshop!'
<u>*Grams:*</u>	'<u>*Closing Music*</u>'

Well that's what the *script* said. What Squadron Leader Urquhart said and in somewhat slurred tones, was:

Professor Selby: 'Not 'zactly a plane. Have annuver one, and we'll all go into th'workhouse!'

Stunned amazement showed on the face of Corporal John Jacobs as he looked at his Commanding Officer.

'You're DRUNK – er, sir!'

John was to give up acting and introducing Pop Music on the '1600 Club', and to become a most distinguished director of early Television drama, working mainly for Anglia TV. His name on a production became a hallmark of both quality and excellence.

When *The Island of Moressa* was done for the BBC, I was fortunate to get the dashing actor John Bentley as the lead, whilst Jimmie Urquhart, I'm sorry to say, was very much tied up with a West End stage production. Later when touring in the musical *Oliver* he phoned our home, the voice the other end simply saying by way of introduction, 'May I come out to your Workhouse?'

The BBC bought a third serial which Margaret and I had first done in Hamburg, *The Adventures of Robin Hood*. As the producer, once again I wanted to use some of the original Hamburg cast, for by now we were all demobbed. My Masters were quite firm; only professionals and some well-known names. I now cast Tom Fleming as Robin. That was long before his days as the BBC commentator for Royal events. The large and equally effective Francis de Wolff became Guy de Gisborne in the BBC version. To my mind I hadn't done badly with the Hamburg cast so, just for a moment, whistle to yourself the tune *March of the Bowmen* as you now read out the closing announcement to one of those original Hamburg productions:

In Episode 5 of The Adventures of Robin Hood by Margaret Potter and Trevor Hill you heard:
NIGEL DAVENPORT as 'Robin'
CLIFF MICHELMORE as 'Little John'
RAYMOND BAXTER as 'Guy de Gisborne'
KEITH FORDYCE as 'Will Scarlet'
and
BRIAN MATTHEW as 'King Richard'.
The part of 'Blondel the wandering minstrel' was played by GERAINT EVANS
Other parts were by BRYAN FORBES and ROGER MOORE.

Ray Baxter, an ex-fighter pilot, had come to us as our first civilian member of staff and soon began to learn about broadcasting, taking part in and producing radio plays. He'd do a Chekhov one week and appear in *The Man with the Limp*, our own Potter/Hill mystery-horror series the next. As our original 'Guy De Gisborne', Ray had a lovely vocal *sneer* – far better than Basil Rathbone's screen performance. As for our 'Robin', well Corporal Davenport was my room-mate for a while at BFN and my friend or so I thought. When interviewed by a national newspaper in more recent times, the now celebrated star avowed that when a party of Service personnel and families came to look round the BFN studios in Hamburg, some asked if they could meet the radio Robin Hood, as the serial had become very popular. So far, quite true. But then Mr Davenport goes on to report that I quickly said he was away for the day – and all because I didn't want any listener to become disillusioned when coming face to face with 'a somewhat callow, bespectacled youth'!

'And I *was* a bit spotty in those days,' he says. *That* bit is true – the rest, quite, quite false!

When Nigel left BFN he resumed his studies and went up to Trinity, Oxford where he was soon back acting again becoming secretary of OUDS – but more about that later.

I can clearly hear the quietly modulated voice of a young Sergeant Bryan Forbes that night we did a Variety show from the Garrison Theatre, Hamburg, which I mentioned earlier. Apart from the always-professional Ivy Benson Band and some solo artists, we had booked another British band together with a well-known vocalist of the day. It was entirely through a lack of production experience on my part that the second-half broadcast section of the stage show was badly over-running, so I sent word to cut the reprise of the final song whilst we were on air. The 'lady' would have none of it. Sergeant Bob Boyle was to close the show from the stage as the band finished – but the vocalist insisted on carrying on to the bitter end.

Back in Broadcasting House, London, the announcer on duty in Light Programme Continuity just faded Hamburg out and made a closing announcement himself for the benefit of the BBC listeners, so that was fine. For those tuned to BFN, however, the band and the 'lady' became only slightly less audible as in despair I told the stage manager to ring down the curtain. Even so, Bob Boyle had almost to shout the closing announcement since our broadcast time was over-running.

Wringing my hands in woe over such a messy ending, I went straight back to the billet where Mac Picton gave me a large drink. Then Bryan Forbes came quietly up to me.

'Never mind, Trev. You should have got them to ring down the *Safety* Curtain. That would have cut off the cow!'

There is a similar typically Bryan Forbes line in that splendid British film, which he both wrote and appeared in, *League of Gentlemen.* Nigel Patrick descends the grand staircase in the large house owned by the wealthy and debonair Jack Hawkins. They pause on the stairs at the portrait of a beautiful woman as Nigel exclaims, 'A distant relative?'

To which Mr. Hawkins replies in tones to match his immaculate evening dress: 'I'm sorry to say the bitch is still going strong!'

BFN was a good training ground for a lot of Service people who were to make broadcasting, the stage and cinema their careers, whether as writers, performers, directors or producers. Yes, we had our fair share of flops, and the amateur edges certainly protruded at times. Taken as a whole, what was occasionally lacking in professionalism was compensated for by the enthusiasm of those involved – and certainly by the encouragement of the listeners, particularly those civilians who had suffered occupation during the recent war years. The BFN fan mail from Holland and from Denmark resulted in our joining forces with Dutch and Danish radio and with the American Forces Network in Bremen, for such light music series as *Dancing Round the Baltic.*

From Hamburg I would use soloists of the calibre of Helmut Zacharias, former violinist with a distinguished group, and bass player Coco Schumann. BFN late-night music often relayed by other radio stations took the form of series like *Slumber Time* with the Carl Rading Sextet and *Tango Time* with Juan Lossas and his orchestra. Our German Programme Engineers or *Tonemeisters*, as they were called, were particularly adept at doing good music balances and had Tape Editing down to a very fine art. We all got on extremely well, both German civilians and Service personnel. It cannot have been easy for our own German staff when we were covering the notorious Ravensbruck Trial in Hamburg. This brought to book those responsible for making medical experiments on healthy victims. Some of the survivors stayed at the Boccaccio Hotel whilst the trials were in progress. It was particularly poignant that one of our own BFN staff covering the proceedings, Captain 'Sandy' Carlos-Clarke, who in happier times rode the family range in the Argentine, should begin reporting the trial with bitterness and revulsion in his heart as he saw and heard the case for the prosecution, only to fall in love with one of the accused, a doctor, as the case for her defence was presented. Some of us were to realise for the first time what it must have been like to be forced to take orders under the Nazi regime.

Margaret and I were to make close friendships with several of the German staff at BFN and with von Reibnitz in particular. He was one of the Unit drivers and his wife, Lucy, was the accomplished pianist with the BFN Light Orchestra. After doing a broadcast with the Canadian Maple Leaf Four one evening we were having supper at Hamburg's best hotel. I phoned my Unit for transport to take me back to the billet and then returned to the table. Later, realising the time, I thanked my Canadian hosts and hurried out again to the hotel foyer. There I beheld the German manager and some of his senior staff gathered around our driver, bowing low as they shook the hand of a clearly embarrassed man. As we drove back along the Ulster, so von Reibnitz said, 'I'm sorry, but you see at one time I was very well known in this city!'

He certainly was – as Chief of the Hamburg Police until he was drafted into the Luftwaffe and given the rank of Colonel as late as 1943. Having served as a German officer, he was only allowed a job of very minor responsibility by the British.

On another occasion von Reibnitz had taken me to the German Panzer training range right next to the obscenity that was Belsen. The range was now used to train members of the Royal Armoured Corps who were being featured in Alexander McKee's script for that month's *Service Spotlight*. Whenever one or two of us at BFN got the chance, we would stay at the Church of Scotland canteen at Ultzen. It was run by Padre Johnstone and by a most wonderful woman named Edith Macbeth. An entire Royal Armoured Corps Tank Recovery Unit plus tank crew would manage somehow to break down near that canteen and Edith would soon be on the telephone to the CO. 'But have you *seen* the conditions? The poor lads'll be frozen unless we give them hot food!'

After our first day at the Panzer range, Alex and I arrived at Edith's canteen. Von Reibnitz was to take the car to a Services fuel depot, have it filled up and then report back to me with the vehicle.

'He'll be staying at one of those awful places for German drivers,' declared Edith. 'I've *seen* them. They get watery cabbage soup and straw to sleep on. Well he's *not* staying there, he's staying here!'

There was no arguing with such a determined and Christian body.

'Well you tell him!' replied the coward.

In order not to embarrass von Reibnitz, Edith had a room prepared for him at the top of the rambling house. Before we sat to the table for grace she gave me a tray to take upstairs. When I knocked then entered the small room, von Reibnitz was sitting up in bed, the usual monocle in his eye, but now he was wearing what must have once been an exquisite pair of pure silk pyjamas. Only his family coat of arms heavily embroidered on the pocket had survived intact. His family had once owned vast tracts of land in Silesia. He might have lost all of that, but none of his bearing.

With exquisite manners and his sense of humour, von Reibnitz was my perfect Prussian. Just before Margaret and I left Hamburg we had a farewell supper with him and Lucy in the two rooms which were their home. He raised a glass to Margaret.

'Now,' he added with a note of pride, 'I raise my glass to a big, *big* woman!'

One play series Margaret began to write in Hamburg was *The Adventures of Samuel Poppleton*, and continued to do these for the BBC for several years. Back in the UK she wrote a play around Colonel von Reibnitz. The action was set prior to the First World War but still making von Reibnitz in charge of the Hamburg police. There was a theme-tune woven into the storyline; a German tune called *Melodia*. I'd heard it first on the way to Hanover. On the outskirts of the city, playing to nothing more than mile after mile of devastation and rubble and one miserably thin dog, was a man named Ferdinand Büsso with a pipe organ. Herr Büsso trundled away a happy man from our BFN studio a day or two later when we had recorded his pipe organ and *Melodia*, for we paid him in the best of all the then currency, cigarettes.

Two people at least heard the BBC broadcast; von Reibnitz himself, because he wrote and told us so and how he and Lucy were getting on now that he had been promoted to BFN Storekeeper; and musician Ray Martin. We were on holiday, so he sent telegrams halfway round the British Isles to track us down: 'Must have tune. Ray Martin.' What tune was he on about? We phoned and found out. Ray was now Recording Manager at EMI, and having got hold of *Melodia* and the recording of the pipe organ I'd made, he gave it to Norman Newell to arrange and record. Now, Ferdinand Büsso's performance can be heard on the Columbia label. The plaintive pipe organ is taken up by a full orchestra, coming back again as the tune ends.

Another tune, which certainly comes in Barney Colehan's *A Melody, A Memory* class for us is *Muncher G'Schichten* or the *Tales of Munich* waltz by Theo Mackeben, for this introduced our BFN Children's Magazine broadcast twice weekly, whilst *Moonlight on the Ulster* immediately brings back memories of Milo Karatsch and the BFN Light

They usually closed their eyes when I conducted the BFN Orchestra

The Hamburg State Opera wardrobe department dressed us on special occasions

… and from where I am our 'Tyrolean Sketches' don't sound to be *that* bad!

Erhwald Tyrolean Sketches

Orchestra. Milo sometimes parted with his baton when it came to that closing signature tune.

'They played it jolly well,' I said to him one day.

'Yes, yes. When *you* are wavering my baton they *all* keep their eyes closed!'

Whilst I seem to be dwelling for a while on musical memories, there was the Hamburg State Opera House, a splendid building dating only from Hitler's time. It had been burnt out by bombing – except for the original stage and area behind the stage. Taking a leaf from Bryan Forbes's book, someone had 'rung down' the Safety Curtain the night of the raid. Now the Germans had built seating for a smallish audience on the original stage, leaving just enough space to put on operas again. From time to time and for more lavish productions, they took over the Hamburg Garrison Theatre.

One evening a party of us went from BFN. The place was packed to capacity for *Der Rosenkavalier* so our group, which included Geraint Evans, James Gibb and Arthur Langford, all from BFN's music department, were crowded into a small box at the side of the stage and almost in line with the proscenium arch. Very much a side-on view.

Richard Strauss wrote the part of *Baron Ochs*, the thoroughly seedy but endearing country squire, for a singer named Richard Mayr. He in turn tutored Theo Hermann in the role he was to sing that night. For me *Der Rosenkavalier* was a wonderful introduction to opera with all its comedy and colour, besides some of Strauss's loveliest songs. In Act 1, there is the Marschallin's levée. In this role, the formidable figure and voice of Erna Schluter were to the fore. It was a breathtaking performance, as music critics often say. As the curtain came down at the end of the first Act, so the audience sprang to their feet. The principals took four or five calls and still the applause continued – for the Marschallin. This time the curtain was held open at the centre, to reveal the far side of the wings only to those of us from BFN sitting in that box. In her heavy velvet costume, Fraulein Schluter glided majestically forward. We saw her long train catch on a heavy metal lighting stand and pulling her suddenly off balance. Small arms flayed the air as German stagehands rushed forward to support the toppling Marschallin. It was then that her wig slid down over one eye! Seconds later, a picture of composure, she stepped into sight of her adoring audience – but by that time we were already helpless with loud laughter as all eyes turned in amazement to our box. The Management asked us to leave.

It was later that the kind and discerning Sergeant Arthur Langford who took our Welsh chum in hand. Geraint could certainly sing. He would readily oblige when Margaret was short of an item for her weekly *Woman's Magazine* and he was equally entertaining in the Mess with *his* Welsh version of certain rugby songs. Those we really *couldn't* broadcast! Arthur, however, introduced Geraint to Theo Hermann who was so impressed by both the voice and the personality that he took Geraint on as his pupil. We paid him out of our cigarette rations! It was the start of a remarkable musical career.

* * *

Just before Tom Chalmers left us from one of his visits to BFN, Hamburg he listened not only to a playback of that *Missing Persons* feature but, later, to one or two of our *BFN Playhouse* productions.

'You must come and see me when the Army has finished with you,' he said. And I did!

It would have been sooner rather than later had not the War Office by kind agreement with the BBC declared that I was to be 'DOV'. Such does wonders for the ego. In those times it meant 'Delayed Operationally Vital'. And so both Sgts Hill and Potter were to spend an additional time with BFN before our 'demob'.

When that came at the end of 1948 – and within two months of each other – so I returned to Mill Hill, NW7, and Margaret to Birmingham from where the BBC engaged her to write a feature. She was then to become the assistant to the MD of British Non-Ferrous Metals, a kindly man who allowed her time off when required. Writing a sequel to our *Island of Moressa* serial wasn't so easy when we were no longer sharing the same office, so a lot of postage money was spent as we exchanged pages of our proposed serial *The Mystery of Bendreda*. Fortunately for us this was also to be bought by the BBC.

It was only then that I began to realise that life without Margaret just wasn't the same and therefore the best thing *I* ever wrote in my life was a letter asking her if she might marry me. Her reply was brief and to the point: 'Darling, I thought you'd never ask.' I took that to mean 'I do' – but those words were not to be spoken until August 1952 at the Church of St Christopher, Pott Shrigley in Cheshire. Little did we realise that only some four years later we would be living opposite the very church in which we were married. Thanks to 'Royalty' payments from the BBC – although in my case it was often 'SNF' (Staff No Fee) – we were able to put down a deposit on an old farmhouse in nearby Bollington,

Cheshire. It was the father of the then pianist with the BBC Northern Variety Orchestra, Ken Frith, who did much of the required building work for us.

Apart from Vi Carson's lovely wedding present, which I mention in a later chapter, it was actor Norman Sommers who gave us an extremely well-bred Siamese kitten, as cross-eyed as they come and complete with that bent end to the tail which, in another tale, is as the result of a Siamese Princess knotting it having placed her ring there before taking a swim. Be that as it may, 'Cleopatra', as we named her was to feature regularly in the *Macclesfield Times and Courier* and Margaret's weekly *Children's Page* besides becoming, as far as I know, the *only* cat ever to broadcast on the BBC Home Service, such were her vocal talents. After young Joyce Palin's dog 'Spot' was to die –as reported in the National Press, as I hope to explain to you later – how many still recall 'Cleo', as heard in *The Adventures of Samuel Poppleton*? You only had to ask her, 'Are you hungry/tired/happy/cold/thoroughly bored?' etc. in order to get very different vocal responses, such had been her training. Come to think of it, besides a Siamese cat, both Robert Powell and Brian

Wedding of Mr Trevor Hill, BBC Producer and Miss Margaret Potter, script writer at Pott Shrigley Church on Saturday

Trueman were also to make their acting debuts in Margaret's *Poppleton* series.

Fortunately we were not to lose contact with many of those from our 'Hamburg Experience' whose friendships we were still to treasure in the years ahead. But back at the start of 1949 I was on a BBC Production Course, thanks to Mr Chalmers and to former Captain John McMillan of BFN who was also now with our firm. They invited me to attend a performance at Covent Garden. And who did I see but Geraint Evans, not yet in any 'lead' but somewhere in the chorus. I realise now he was distinctly embarrassed when at the end of the opera I was to usher the then Controller of the BBC Light Programme into the Chorus dressing room of the Royal Opera House in order that they should meet. Shortly after Margaret and I were married, however, Geraint was to be singing a lead opposite Adele Leigh at The Opera House in Manchester.

We were both excited at the prospect of hearing Geraint sing a major role and having him stay with us for one night during the Manchester run. At the last moment, however, I was detained at the BBC, so Margaret went to the performance on her own. I was home around 10.00 p.m.

'Cleo' makes her BBC debut

to find that supper had been prepared and the table laid ready for a celebration. I waited and I waited.

Sometime, just before midnight, I decided to feed Cleo. 'Let's face it, puss. She's gone off with an opera singer!' It transpired that in reminiscing in his car about the times spent at BFN, Hamburg, our guest and my wife had got hopelessly lost.

Another ex-BFN visitor to Cheshire was Alexander McKee who had been such an important part of our Features team. Alex had a great interest in military history besides photography, and had written some very good Radio Features on various regiments, including the Royal Hampshires, who were stationed at Minden at the end of the war. *The Tiger and The Rose* stood for the royal tiger of India, signifying their service on that Continent, whilst wild roses from the hedgerows of Westphalia had been picked by men of the regiment as they marched to the battle of Minden.

When he came to stay with us, Alex had turned his attention to things nautical, having just found some wreck or other off the coast of Anglesey. Much later, in 1966, he was to make a far more important discovery when he located the wreck of the *Mary Rose*, joined forces with that remarkable Museum curator, Margaret Rule, and started a project which then captured the imagination and attention of almost the entire nation.

* * *

I must now mention the fourth member of our BFN Features and Drama Team. Corporal Leon Griffiths dutifully spent a week with me at the Army School of Catering in BAOR for *Service Spotlight,* and we both survived such things as Cornish pasties made by beginners yet lived to enjoy the delights produced by some taking their 'Master Cook' diploma. There was far more need of Leon's scripting talents when the Russians decided to blockade the City of Berlin!

Five days after the start of the Berlin Airlift, and as a direct result of a BBC telephone call from London on 27th June 1948, Leon and myself with John Weekes as disc recording engineer were at the former Luftwaffe fighter station at Fuhlsbuettel. From here the Douglas DC 3s and the far larger York transporters were running a twenty-four hour shuttle service carrying food and supplies to the beleaguered city for 'Operation Plainfare'.

I have never been very good at remembering *full* names; first names OK, a fact that will also receive later mention, and Group Captain Whitely proved the point. The Commanding Officer of the Fighter station was explaining to me the work involved in laying steel mesh on the existing runways of what had been a German light aircraft fighter station, in order to take the weight of heavy transporters and in having to extend those runways for larger aircraft. In the recorded interview I referred to the CO as 'Whiting, Watney and Witney' all in the space of some four minutes, which was the maximum time we could record on a Watts acetate disc. His ADC took me aside for a few well-chosen words. Oh well, we'd just have to edit, as we normally now edited disc recordings – but only in Germany!

During the war the German Corps of Signals had a little black box, which you could take anywhere. You recorded onto magnetic tape, the sort I've already mentioned. – no cutting stylus to jump out of an acetate blank through bouncing about on the sea or in the air. Our BBC mobile Recording Engineers had difficulties enough recording the voice of Richard Dimbleby as they flew into flak over Berlin during the bombing of the city. They'd have given their right arms for the compact machine I was about to use. Later, I was able to copy my disc recording of the Group Captain onto tape, cut out all the wrong names I'd given him, and literally stick the interview together again with special adhesive tape.

Leon and I bade John and his heavy disc recording gear *au revoir* and, in lieu of seven sacks of flour that trip, we were then flown into Berlin. Ray Baxter was there to meet us. He handed me the German Midget tape recorder on which we did the rest of the recordings.

The BBC's own representative in Berlin had a lot of useful contacts. I especially wanted to get the views of some of the Berliners. How did they feel? Was enough food coming in? It didn't matter to me if their English wasn't good enough to use their own voice. We had our German staff back in Hamburg who could easily repeat the words. I cannot remember the precise point at which Leon said he felt he was no longer able or willing to write the script for *Operation Plainfare*. In any event, he asked to be relieved of his duties and to return to Hamburg. I left Berlin two days later in a Sunderland flying boat from Havel Lake, landing in Hamburg docks close to those indestructible U-boat pens.

Working all the rest of that day, through the whole of the night and part of the following day, together with our expert German tape editors and technicians, we got our feature programme finished and off to London. The narration is all I can remember now. It was mostly written and spoken by Ray Baxter. And it was outstanding, punctuated by the sounds of wave after wave of aircraft taking off and landing.

Leon Griffiths at least had the courage of his convictions. It's not easy to exercise those in anyone's Army. After demob I believe he went off to work for the Hungarian Communist Party. Be that as it may I can forgive anyone who left me in the middle of Berlin if, like Leon, they were eventually to delight us all by devising and writing that superb Television series starring George Cole and Denis Waterman: *Minder.* Yes, I was indeed fortunate to work with some talented people in BAOR 3. But you may think, if you flick back to the beginning of this chapter, what about that reference to Roger Moore and *The Shop at Sly Corner*. Did he get the part? Well yes, he certainly did. I then adapted the stage play myself and produced it for *BFN Playhouse* with Lieutenant R. Moore in the role of the naval lieutenant in love with the shop owner's daughter. After the opening night of the play at the Garrison Theatre I went straight round to congratulate actress Phoebe Hodgson, who made a wonderful 'Mrs Cat' and then to see Roger. He was just pulling off a pair of naval trousers and stepping back into army ones.

'Well, and what did you think?'

I tried to be tactful. I told him he *looked* terrific in the part and perhaps he should think about taking up modelling or something like that when he left the Services, which he did. We couldn't *see* that raised eyebrow – well not on radio. In fact no sooner was Roger Moore demobbed than I was to see him sitting in a tank and wearing a beret as a private in the Royal Armoured Corps – it was an Army Recruiting poster. When, later, this international star of the cinema was making the film *Gold,* about mining in South Africa, he sent me a message via a mutual friend, who did the script.

'Tell Trevor, I still can't act – but I'm not doing badly!'

5

Back with the 'BEEB'

'Hello dear, back again doing effects, are we?'

The cheerful greeting in the Drama studio at Broadcasting House, London came from 'Mrs Mopp' of my *ITMA* days. I am not usually modest, but I really didn't know what to say to Dorothy Summers that day in 1948.

'He's not doing effects! You are addressing the co-author of this play, Dorothy dear.'

Martyn C. Webster, one of the great exponents of radio drama, had very kindly invited me to sit in as he produced *Journey into Darkness*. This was a slightly improbable plot about a ballet dancer who is diagnosed as having an incurable disease – only she hadn't, but by that time her husband had taken an overdose! It was the first radio play Margaret Potter and I had submitted to the BBC within a week or so of being demobbed. Now Margaret was doing that feature I mentioned for the BBC in Birmingham, her home town, and I was back again with the BBC in London and attending the play rehearsal. Beryl Calder played the part of the dancer, with Donald Gray as her husband, and Dorothy Summers sounding every bit like the wife of a successful doctor on this occasion, and not a trace of:

'Can I do you now, sir?'

I had *hoped* I wasn't going back to Effects. The Engineering Establishment Officer, Mr P.A. Florence, had been very nice about it, telling me that all the time I had been in the Services the BBC had kept a note of annual increments and now I would receive these, bringing my salary to almost £4.15s a week. I thanked Mr Florence all the same and said I had the chance of returning to Forces Broadcasting as a civilian and at something rather in excess of £4.15s, but I was hopefully waiting to hear if I had been accepted for a Producer's Course at BBC Staff training.

I was later to learn that I had Martyn C Webster, Tom Chalmers and John McMillan to thank for a recommendation. Fortunately, production courses had nothing to do with Engineering Training and those responsible for a previous course I'd been on, which had started sometime in 1943 at Maida Vale. There some of us managed on one memorable day to get served with morning coffee ahead of the Course Instructors, and all because I noticed that the man delivering the lecture had a sneaky habit of pressing a bell-button just before the coffee break. That warned his office to go and queue up before all the students arrived in the canteen. On this particular morning, I'd borrowed a small bottle from my elder sister's dressing table before leaving home. I got to Maida Vale nice and early, unscrewed the bell push, and put a liberal coating of nail varnish on the bell contacts.

We had enjoyed another brief moment of triumph when the course went down to Wood Norton, the BBC's final wartime bastion should London be invaded by the German hordes. Barbed wire and an electrified fence surrounded the whole perimeter of this large country house as well as a regular Army Defence Unit to guard the place. A.V. Roe helped to make aviation history; his grandson, 'Tig', got my medal for BBC bravery in wartime Britain. He agreed to don a pair of dry socks and thick rubber boots, then to touch that 'live' perimeter wire without earthing it. Had he done so, that part of the perimeter fence would have flashed a warning light in the Control post. 'Tig' succeeded in not being detected, but of far more importance to the rest of the students, proved fairly conclusively that we wouldn't all be electrocuted by something carrying a lethal voltage. Those of us that possessed them, synchronised watches and at precisely 2300 hours one dark November night the alarm board inside the Control post at the entrance to Wood Norton lit up like a premature Christmas Tree.

Needless to say, Mr Bruce Purslow, the engineer in charge, ticked us off for our rank stupidity. Well, we'd never had done this had not 'Smithy' the chief instructor told us on several occasions that he'd never met such a dim lot in all his days. If I may refer back to that Engineers Division report on me that I mentioned at the end of Chapter 2, Hill had now demonstrated he had at least two fairly original thoughts left in his head. The 'gift of the gab' came at the end of the course and the final exams. The students had been given permission to use a studio and to record a sketch I'd written in which a load of us were on a tumbrel, being carried inexorably towards our fate. To the rhythm of the rattling cart-wheels could be heard the voices of some of our lecturers instilling words of Engineering Wisdom into our poor heads and with the voice of 'Smithy' heard above our wails and cries of grief. A cheerful chap at the best of times, 'Smithy' kept telling us, 'You'll fall by the wayside!'

Anguished screams and thuds of student bodies could plainly be heard in my student production as they fell from the tumbrel – but they were the fortunate ones. Those that reached journey's end got the chop, for failing their exams. As you will doubtless realise, I survived to relate this tale and will, therefore, continue.

The post-war Producer's Course I was accepted for in early 1949 was one of encouragement and enlightenment all the way. We even had a splendid 'farewell dinner' at Olivelli's Italian restaurant in Store Street. The only snag arose because of our endeavours to give rather a lot of 'farewell' drinks to the lady Course Instructor, who wore wooden beads and lectured us on 'The Analysis of Oral Communication' and things of a similar nature. She also endeavoured to turn both John Dunn and myself into BBC announcers of the required BBC standards, which was uphill work for her but not in John's case! That party, however, went swimmingly on the whole – especially for the head of Staff Training because the wooden beads lady knew all about trainee producers and so she simply passed all our 'farewell' drinks on to her superior sitting at her right hand.

It's strange sort of feeling when you suddenly realise that everyone else has left. There were only two of us in that upper room at Olivelli's when I returned from settling the bill. By now, the head of BBC Staff Training was not at all sure where he lived and when I thought to phone the Duty Officer at the BBC late that night he wasn't exactly forthcoming either.

'We are not permitted to give staff addresses or telephone numbers over the telephone – unless there is an urgent reason!'

A search inside the jacket of the semi-conscious body fortunately produced an envelope with a London address *and* some keys. We went by taxi, the driver being of great assistance. I was thanked for a 'wunner-ful p-arty'! Not long after this celebration, I was to discover it had been arranged for me to be posted well away from Portland Place to the BBC in Bristol as a trainee producer. And so I arrived at Whiteladies Road.

My father's home was Slimbridge by the leisurely river Severn, and the BBC West Region went at an equally steady pace. I was fortunate to be attached, metaphorically speaking, to Desmond Hawkins, a man of great substance and flair, and nice with it, too. He was the Features producer and did things like *County Mixture*, besides excellent Natural History programmes on radio. Desmond was the architect of the BBC's Natural History Unit, which is justly famous throughout the world.

The Drama man in Bristol also taught me more about radio production in the brief time I was there. Owen Reed was a producer of great enthusiasm, which spread to all those around him. As a member of the Casson family he had drama and the theatre in his blood and, on several occasions, he took me down to the Bristol Old Vic to see promising youngsters such as Nigel Stock, whom he shaped for radio drama. Never, in my estimation, have the novels of Thomas Hardy been done with such imaginative flair and care as by Owen. I was to get to know him a lot better in the years ahead.

There was also, in drama terms, West Region's version of *The Robinson Family*, as *Front Line Family* had become since the war ended. Written by Denis Constanduros, son of Mabel, it was called *At the Luscombes*. I took over production of this for a short while whilst the regular producer was on holiday. The two chaps doing the effects for the series were Peter Bale and Duncan Wood. Peter's name was to appear in later years as the Executive Producer of the best of Television's nature programmes from Bristol. He'd also been with Forces Broadcasting. As for Duncan, well he was soon heading for production work too, becoming one of the top names in Bill Cotton's team of Light Entertainment producers and directors on BBC TV. *Hancock's Half Hour* and *Steptoe and Son* were just two of Duncan's screen credits before he left us to become Head of Comedy with Yorkshire Television.

Whilst working on *At The Luscombes* I read a short story by the West of England writer, Ralph Whitlock, called 'The Odstock Curse', which I adapted as a play. The story concerned a gypsy named Joshua Scamp who was hanged for a crime which as it later transpired he did not commit, so his mortal remains were allowed to be interred in the churchyard at Odstock, near Nunton. The curse that followed upon his unjust death and the subsequent train of tragic events made for exciting listening. Not wishing to be unduly cursed myself by the descendants of the Scamp family for getting any of the facts wrong, I managed to track some of them down with the help of the local police. A day or so later, in one of the BBC's large limousines then used for mobile disc recording, I went off to their encampment to record at first hand their manner of talking and to check up on certain facts.

'Good afternoon, I'm from the BBC!'

All I got from that line were dark looks and the slam of a caravan door. Having waited for me in the smart Humber Pullman car for a while, one of our most experienced sound recordists, Harvey Sarney, came to see how I was getting on. Until his arrival, I wasn't. He knocked this time, and greeted the head of the family in an Indian dialect which, as it turned out, is very close to the Romany language. Within minutes, we were all cooped up inside a stifling hot caravan with Harvey chatting away. He then left us to record in the car whilst I held the microphone as they now spoke in English. This was for the benefit of the cast who were to portray their ancestors in our radio play production a week or so later.

'Now DO call and see us,' I gushed as I crossed several stained palms with silver.

The friendly BBC commissionaire at Whiteladies Road was Sergeant Hawkins.

'Reception here, Mr Hill. I have a load of gyppoes to see you. I've put them in the Waiting Room. You will be down?'

They came laden with pegs in baskets, went into every office including that of Frank Gillard the then Head of Programmes in Bristol, and eventually departed after a good tea in the canteen, having sold sprigs of lucky heather to all and sundry who wouldn't take pegs! I did learn a few things about being a producer at Whiteladies Road.

Shortly after that episode – or so it seemed to me – the imposing Controller of West Region, Gerald Beadle, sent for me to suggest that perhaps his region was a little one-foot-in-the-grave for a young man of twenty-three and that I should apply for a Production post which might offer more 'action'.

He brought to my attention a forthcoming vacancy for a General Programme Producer up in Manchester. It was shortly to be boarded. At that point my heart sank in the West!

6

Showcase, Piccadilly, Manchester

'Would anyone like a raspberry?' enquired Lord Simon of Wythenshawe. It is not a line I'd heard before or since from any other Chairman of the BBC Governors, but on this occasion it was a particularly welcome and well-timed remark.

A number of the BBC North's regional staff, the recently appointed General Programme Producer included, had been invited for an evening at Lord and Lady Simon's home. We stood around in small groups in the drawing room making polite conversation. I envied the worldly Philip Dobson, one of the North's announcers, who rose magnificently to the occasion when our hostess summoned her butler across to us and enquired if we would partake of a cheese straw.

'That is most gracious of you, Lady Simon,' declared Dobson. I noticed they were rather long cheese straws upon that silver salver so, politely, I took hold of only the last inch between crooked fingers. In lifting it to my mouth, the other three inches broke off and fell to the carpet. The butler turned away. We chatted as, carefully, I pivoted the heel of my right shoe to cover my indiscretion but then, a sort of nervous 'twitch' seemed to attack me and within a few seconds my foot was pounding the pastry concoction into the Aubusson carpet. It was at that precise moment that Lord Simon chose to lead his guests into the gardens, and to the raspberry canes.

There, I was to meet Miss Denness Roylance for the first time. I say 'Miss' because the spelling of her Christian name sometimes led to letters being addressed to Mr Roylance. For many years, Denness was my guide and mentor, and a friend to me and to many young and not so

Denness Roylance, Assistant to Children's Hour Organiser

No. 33 Piccadilly. Once known as the 'Temple of a Thousand Voices' the premises served the BBC for over forty-five years

young people who came within her particular sphere of broadcasting – that of BBC Northern's *Children's Hour*, of which more later.

For now, let me state without any fear of contradiction that within a short space of meeting and talking with anyone, particularly in listening to them and getting them to answer her questions, Denness could tell you quite a bit about them. No, not 'nosey'; more 'interested'. She took in names and facts like sportsmen take in calories, and stored them away.

Also amongst those raspberry canes was my good friend from wartime days at 200 Oxford Street, Philip Robinson. From Manchester he started *Have A Go.* This had now been taken over by Barney Colehan who was at Lord Simon's party, as was Alan Clarke, another from my BFN days. Alan was now working to Philip as head of North region's Outside Broadcasts and Sport.

My very first Manchester assignment as a producer was, of all things, to attend the New Zealand v Lancashire Test match, as there had to be a BBC representative present during any broadcast and, on this occasion, the match commentary was being done by a new lad named Peter West. Since as a child I had to be 'At Home' every Saturday and 'Away' every Sunday, such was my father's devotion to Mill Hill Cricket Club, you will appreciate my feelings at having to watch, to talk and to eat cricket, for unlike the commentator the BBC representative lunched with the respective teams. Fortunately, I had a helpful and understanding Head of North Regional programmes in Robert Stead who promised that such an assignment would not occur again.

I'd certainly have gone for a series, which Bob himself started, *How Does Your garden Grow?* But since being re-titled *Gardeners' Question Time* some other producer was looking after that. It had been the smooth, well-dressed Robert Stead who first introduced me to North's Controller, a man who looked as if he'd watched a lot of cricket in his day.

'Nar then, cum thee in, lad, an' sit thee dahn!' he said, both thumbs stuck in his outstretched braces.

Oh, my God! I expected it would be all tripe, Rochdale hounds and Gracie Fields up here, but *never* this bad. I thought of Gerald Beadle and how Desmond Hawkins had described West Region's Controller to me as 'one of nature's gentlemen'. And now I was inwardly gulping at the figure of John Coatman. But as Bob Stead's broad smile creased into laughter, so the North's Head of Broadcasting shook me warmly by the hand.

'We don't *really* all talk like that up North,' he said, then added, 'thar knows!'

John Coatman had done distinguished service in India for the Foreign Office and now, like his fellow Regional Controllers, had been building up a team of producers, writers and broadcasters who would reflect this large area of the country to Northern listeners on a regional basis, as well as to the British Isles at large on the Home Service, on the Light Programme, the Third Programme and in the BBC's Overseas and Transcription services.

As a General Programme Producer, I wasn't tied to any particular department but worked to the Head of Programmes and was expected to cover a range of radio production. Philip Robinson himself, something of a gambling man and with a wife who really understood 'form', decided that I should begin by producing a feature on the Doncaster Yearling Sales, so off we went. Philip told me to spend the first day getting the 'atmosphere'. I'd never been on a Racecourse, let alone placed a bet, but the Clerk of the Course, a Mr Perkins, gave me a ticket to the Silver enclosure with the advice, 'Number Two to win, Number Six first place!' All Greek to me but straight from the mouths of the horses, for they came in precisely as predicted!

In my excitement to get to the Tote, I collided somewhat painfully with a stout post. It read 'Exit' – four letters. The next sign I saw had the words 'Race Cards' displayed upon it, so my initial winnings went on No. 4, with No. 9 first place. Again they both came home. I worked on instinct with a horse called 'Cider Apple', such were my Gloucestershire connections. It let me down badly, but I did quite nicely on the rest of the day's racing having reverted to the Signs and Numbers technique.

Philip put a fatherly arm round my shoulder as I crept into the large refreshment marquee.

'Lost it all, eh?' Well never mind, we'll have one on Muriel. She always does well!'

It wasn't until we were on our way back to Manchester, three days later, in the BBC car and with the recordings we'd done, that I told Philip and Muriel dinner was on me. I'd come away from my first and last day at the Races, despite 'Cider Apple' with a few shillings over £28 – or a full week's BBC salary – and all for that initial two bob on each horse on that first race, thanks to Mr Perkins.

Among the *Children's Hour* programmes which Denness Roylance looked after herself, besides doing her main job – the department's Administrative Assistant – was the monthly *Film News* for young listeners, which she did with John Stratton of the *Manchester Evening News*. He was their chief features writer. John was not only very knowledgeable on the subject of films; he had earned himself the title of 'critic' in the eyes of almost everyone in the film business he wished to interview. So, with John's assistance in Manchester and that of Michael Storm in London, I began an adult series entitled *Going to the Pictures*, a guide to the type of film entertainment which listeners could expect to see in the cinemas that particular week. Later, having taken aboard Michael Walsh of the *Daily Express* and John Bolton of the *Yorkshire Post* with *A Theatregoer's Diary*, I altered the title to *Showcase*.

Before the weekly programme's first birthday, Laurence Olivier, Cedrick Hardwicke, Charles Laughton, Agnes Moorhead, Charles Boyer, Danny Kaye, George Formby, Arthur Askey and Ram Gopal and some of his team of Indian Dancers had appeared in person as guests of the programme. We had interviews with many top-line American and British stars, producers, writers and directors and features from time to time, reflecting different aspects of the film industry as a whole. Sir Michael Balcon and our friends at Ealing Studios provided some of the best material, with Walt Disney giving John Stratten carte blanche to record around his Hollywood Empire. He allowed *Showcase* to use

Charlton Heston

excerpts from the sound tracks of all his cartoon features in the early and mid-1950s. When John was away himself on such assignments as talking to Disney and to Donald Duck in America, I did the occasional interview myself. This was reminiscent of Hamburg days and *Calling the Stars* when I'd interviewed Margaret Rutherford and Anna Neagle on a 'phone in' – or rather a 'phone to' by courtesy of Minden telephone exchange. I had accepted Margaret Rutherford's very kind invitation to dinner at her home when I came on my next UK leave. When I arrived, she immediately took me up to her bedroom.

'That is just where I sat when you spoke to me,' she said, 'And Stringer put a vase of flowers by me on the table so that I shouldn't sound too nervous!' Bless the dear soul and her kind husband. All I'd got my end was, 'And don't make a balls of it. This is costing BFN a bomb!'

I found it a little easier with *Showcase*, talking face to face across the studio table. I found that the easiest people to talk to for programme material are Americans. They are so used to it. Charlton Heston was a gift. He and his wife sent me postcards from wherever the filming schedules took them, after we'd met in Manchester and in London and on only those two occasions. Their dissertation on the history of the American Indian, when Charlton Heston was filming *Pony Express* ran to three cards.

When it came to selecting someone to introduce *Showcase*, I remembered a talk I'd heard about catering as a career, by a young man who'd just completed a course. He'd got into that line, I suspect, because his father, John Wheeler, was the very successful manager of the Grand Hotel, Manchester. Anyhow, Geoffrey Wheeler was to give up all thoughts of catering and become the youngest person to announce a BBC weekly series, sharing the introductions with a new member of the North's presentation department, Roger Moffat.

On at least two mornings a week, my secretary, Pat Paull, and I would go to a Press showing of a new release, which was often followed by a publicity lunch. After attending several of these, I couldn't help but notice that Pat appeared to do a 'Bisto kid' act every time the box of cigars was passed round. She would simply close her eyes and quietly inhale. Some of the cinema managers got to know about this, after which there would often be a Havana secreted within the folds of her luncheon napkin.

Cinema visits in the mornings and theatre visits on one or more evenings became the regular routine. As did a phone call from one of the Buxton brothers who owned a chain of cinemas in the centre of Manchester, telling me that he'd got a World Premiere booked, which we

Interviewing Christine Norden on our way to the European Premiere of *Thunder Across the Pacific*

ought to cover in *Showcase*. Further investigation would prove that the film in question had been shown somewhere in the UK before – often several years before. But on one memorable occasion Dave Buxton *did* succeed in getting a European Premiere at one of his theatres, together with all the ballyhoo which, in those days, went with it.

Thunder Across the Pacific, the story of the B29 Super Fortress, was to be premiered in aid of the Royal Airforce Benevolent Fund, at the Theatre Royal, Manchester – and on a Monday evening in order to coincide with the BBC *Showcase* programme. Herbert J. Yates and his Republic Pictures Corporation spared no expense. I travelled Third Class down to London by train on a BBC allowance and was met at Euston by a chauffeur-driven limousine, hired by the Film Company, which whisked me out to an airfield at Abingdon. Here was waiting a transatlantic Skymaster complete with padded conference room, which was to fly the picture's star, six-foot four Forrest Tucker, together with a plane load of celebrities up to Manchester.

En route, I was to record interviews with the admirable Mr Tucker,

Diana Dors, Kathleen Ryan and with Christine Norden. One of the best interviews I got was with James Jaaché, then the chief photographer of *Picturegoer*. I was only part way through all this assignment when our Skymaster was ready to land. An American airforce colonel, who was on board just to tell me from time to time precisely where we were on our journey and at what altitude, shrugged and said,

'So who's worried? Just you carry on an' we'll do th' Circuit!'

That Skymaster, gobbling up high-octane fuel by the tankful, did just that. It circled the city of Manchester time and time again whilst I completed the interview. As a 'surprise' I was to discover we also had cheerful Charlie Chester aboard and so asked him what *he* was doing on the aircraft when the rest of us were on our way North for the European Premiere of Republic Picture's latest release *Thunder Across the Pacific* (that sort of wording is known as 'a plug').

'But I thought I was on my way to France today,' exclaimed Charlie in mock surprise.

Back on terra firma for the film's debut this side of the Atlantic

'France?'

'Yes, I'm making a rival film. It's called *Clap Across the Channel!*'

Charlie did say it. The trouble is that, what with one thing and another, and getting back late to the studio to put the interviews into *Showcase* within an hour of landing, I later *broadcast* Charlie Chester saying it!

That evening there were searchlights sweeping the Mancunian skies above the Theatre Royal, acres of red carpet and flowers, and two lines of 'Snowdrops'. The American military police from nearby Burton Wood base, wearing their distinctive white helmets, were there to form a guard of honour for high ranking USAFF and RAF officers.

The Buxton brothers also arranged, but without telling me until the time came, that I should interview the stars once again as they stepped out of the limousines, now in all their finery, into the spotlights then into the decorated cinema foyer. They were used to it. I struggled for some new line to take since we last talked! Forrest Tucker declared that he'd hit a new 'high' in film star experiences by being interviewed at 20,000 feet earlier that day by the BBC. Come to think of it, the experience had made my adrenaline flow.

When it was all over in the early hours of the next day, Mr Tucker was to hand me an envelope. Inside he'd written the message: 'To Trevor – just to *tie* the bond of friendship a bit closer! Tuck'

The tie itself was added to a collection, which had begun at the Stage Door canteen in wartime London. There, not realising the generosity of Americans, I had murmured to a certain Mr Crosby that I liked his tie. I all but fainted when, there and then, he took it off and gave it to me. Later, I had another necktie from Senor Mario Cabre who, when not killing bulls in Madrid, was making passes at Ava Gardner. But the only two ties I still retain came from the *Daily Express* sports editor, Henry Rose, undoubtedly one of the nicest and most amusing journalists I had the pleasure of knowing. Tragically, along with Frank Swift and others he was killed in the Munich air crash of February 1958.

I saw Henry only once without his usual wide smile and composure. It was one particular night at the Waverley Hotel in Oldham Street, Manchester. Elise Nichols, a close mutual friend was giving Henry and a large circle of his friends a bumper birthday party in honour of Henry's 21st year with the Express Group. The 'phone rang and I happened to be nearest. The transatlantic voice at the other end asked me to look out of the window and to see if a new white Jaguar car was parked below. It was.

'Then put Henry on, will you?' I did as Lord Beaverbrook instructed.

It was his present to Henry Rose, complete with the registration number HR1, delivered some fifteen minutes earlier that night by Henleys of Manchester.

But back to that Film Premiere at the Theatre Royal. I know Forest Tucker enjoyed at least one part of the sort of film circus he must have been through several times before and since that night. He was signing autographs in the cinema's foyer when young Roger Moffat of the BBC arrived. As a boy, Roger had been selected as a suitable dancing partner to the Princesses of York who lived close by. Now, in elegantly tailored evening dress, Roger looked something of a prince himself. In all the razzmatazz of a pseudo Hollywood event, I suddenly took it into my head to say something like,

'Well, well! We are certainly in for surprises tonight, for I think ... yes, yes, it *is* LANCE GRESHAM!'

The name echoed around outside the theatre over the public-address systems, as the crowds pressed forward to get a closer look. It was a name Roger had never heard of either, but he played the part to perfection. We talked about his recent films in typical showbiz jargon of the 1950s which, like a lot of the showbiz jargon on today's Pop scene, tells you very few hard facts but is intended to leave an overall impression of success. It worked far more effectively when Forrest Tucker joined in with lines like, 'Say Lance, remember when we shot *The Day It All Fell Apart?*' We fell apart when the lights finally dimmed and the film began. The Buxton brothers had their moment of glory!

* * *

Whilst Roger was co-presenting the weekly *Showcase* I'd been approached by Bowker Andrews who was then in charge of *Variety Fanfare* and other Light Entertainment series from Manchester, to announce the Northern Variety Orchestra, which was to begin a run of programmes on the 'Light'. That was something I really enjoyed doing, for the musicians were now conducted by my old BFN mate, Ray Martin. Ray was always a perfectionist and was never very happy that the BBC, unlike the Record industry, had the musicians and the vocalist together in the same studio. He wanted 'separation'. In order that our Balance and Control Engineers could put things like echo onto only the vocalist's voice mic, or keep the orchestral mics at a far lower level than that of the singer, it was arranged that the NVO's leading vocalist and the announcer should work at a microphone placed between the inner and the outer doors of

Manchester's Studio 1. The mic was one of Dr Alexander's double-sided ribbons, so that the singer performed from one side whilst I did the announcements from the other. It is strange to be 'sung at' by a fellow only a few inches away from you, and I never *did* get used to him looking straight at me as he sang lyrics like: 'Just to po-ssess you, my heart's des-I-r-e …' I admit I often tried to make him laugh with some 'finger signs' but Sir Jimmy Young was, and is, far too professional for that.

At one of the BBC staff Christmas parties when goodwill should abound, Roger Moffat was clearly heard to say, 'Oh, I do wish Trevor would drop down dead!'

He said it quite nicely but the point was that *he* wanted to announce the NVO Light Programme series himself. The next time I was going on holiday, I suggested to Bowker Andrews that he give him a try. Bowker wasn't at all keen, saying that Roger sounded too much like a BBC news-reader – which he was.

I returned from that holiday to find I'd lost my job of announcing the Northern Variety Orchestra to Roger Moffat, but made a friend. From that start, with the musicians soon to be renamed The Northern Dance Orchestra, both Roger Moffat and Barney Colehan were to make their names well known to BBC Television audiences when Sheila Buxton joined Roger for *Make Way For Music*, a milestone in Dance Band pres-entation.

I wasn't too downhearted. From the time of my arrival in Manchester I'd taken a special interest in Northern *Children's Hour* and in the output, which made up that programme seven days a week. I found a for-midable Organiser to work to in the person of Nan Macdonald. Never an easy person for staff and artists alike, Nan ran a most successful depart-ment and had set programme standards which were hard to attain, let alone better. Hers was a no-nonsense treat-them-as-intelligent-young-people approach. She offered them a wide range of information and entertainment, so I had no difficulty in persuading her and the North region of the BBC that I should go back to Hamburg in order to arrange a Choral exchange. I'd left a good German friend there, in the person of Eberhard Forck, who worked for Nordwestdeutscher Rudfunk in Hamburg which, in the immediate post-war years as I've mentioned, had been very successfully controlled by Hugh Carleton-Greene and by former BBC Manchester producer David Porter. As a member of NWDR's music department, Eberhard had done some BFN programmes with me and with Sergeant Potter, using their excellent Children's Choir.

Strangely enough, I was to travel out to Hamburg on the very day that Jean Metcalfe travelled to meet Cliff Michelmore on his home ground for the first time. I stayed with my old Unit at the Crown Prince Hotel and met up with Eberhard again. Whilst in the Services during the war, he'd lost the sight of both eyes when they were splashed by a phosphorous bomb. In what I gather was one of the first operations of its kind, the retina of a dead German comrade had been skilfully grafted to one of Eberhard's eyes, thus restoring some sight. Fit only for light duties, he had ended the last few months of the war as a member of the German Information Services, in a bunker along with Hitler and those who still served him. As a result of direct orders from the Führer, Eberhard had left that bombed and beleaguered city towards the end of April 1945, and made his own way back North to Hamburg.

In the summer of 1949 he and I did the journey to Berlin together in order to arrange for Grunewald Saengerknaben to take part in our Choral Exchange between children in Manchester, Hamburg and Berlin. It was to become a series which included other European cities, but from the Manchester end we always had the Darwen Girls' Choir with Joyce Palin

The flags are out for Eberhard and the Queen's Coronation, when living in Bollington, Cheshire

of Withington High School announcing both in German and English, and another 14-year-old, Ulla Schmetzer, doing the same thing in Hamburg. These two became pen friends and then spent holidays together. Sometimes Eberhard stayed with the Palin family in Withington before I had a home of my own and could invite him to stay. I suppose you could say he was an ardent Anglophile. In any event he had insisted on coming to England for the Queen's Coronation in 1953, and he couldn't understand why Margaret and I would not be joining him and his friend, Dieter, in the Mall twenty-four hours beforehand. Incidentally, Dieter, as a prisoner of war in the UK, had worked in the BBC's Gramophone Library at Broadcasting House, London whilst confined within this island – such are the strange ways of war.

We explained to them that the very day after the Coronation, when they both came North to stay with us, we would all be having a grandstand seat of the whole pageant. With my *Showcase* connections we would be attending a special midnight champagne-and-smoked-salmon Film Premiere of this historical event – and in glorious Technicolor!

As the Rank organisation sent us back to our home in Bollington, Cheshire, in one of their cars, Margaret asked Eberhard how things were in a Germany we had left some five years ago.

'Oh, my dear, I am afraid that the Nationalism is again rising up in some of the peoples; the younger peoples. They are again singing "Deutschland, Deutschland, über Alles".'

Was that such a bad thing, we enquired? Eberhard was quite firm on this.

'In England it is all so different. There is no Nationalism rising in any of you, I think, when you sing so well "God Shave ze Queen"!'

The next day we were asking Eberhard how various Hamburg acquaintances of ours were getting on, like the somewhat serious German manager of the Hamburg Musikhalle, Herr Dreyer. We explained how difficult it had been for some of us at BFN not to laugh when saying, 'Good morning, Hair Drier!'

As our German guest didn't quite follow this subtlety of speech, I endeavoured to explain.

'Well, you see it *is* rather like saying, "Good Morning, Hair Tonic"!'

Eberhard nodded wisely. 'Yes, yes, I am knowing him too. He is also well!'

At that time I was not to know that I would be meeting and working on broadcasts with another young German – but in 1953 the year 1998 was still f-a-r ahead!

7

Children's Hour

It came as something of a shock one wartime night in the canteen of 200 Oxford Street to hear actor, Ralph Truman, who was standing just ahead of me in the queue, exclaim in markedly Chinese tones: 'Ah! bl-aked bl-eans.' But in order to put this chapter in true perspective, I must first quote the poet Longfellow:

> Between the dark and the daylight
> When the night is beginning to lower
> Comes a pause in the day's occupation
> That is known as the Children's Hour.

The earlier revelation that Roger Moore's CO had been the voice of the Chief Ovaltiney was one thing; to discover that I was standing right next to the infamous and deadly cunning 'Chang Lee' himself made me lose all interest in food. If the name 'Chang Lee' means nothing to you, it is because you are too young or were unfortunate enough to have missed the radio wonder of two great pre-war London *Children's Hour* serials, *The Island in the Mist* and *The Children of the Sun*. Wasn't it in the latter that a deadly Ray brought down Chang Lee's sophisticated airship – *and* over Hyde Park?

These two Franklyn Kelsey serials awoke my boyhood imagination, just as in later years Josephine Plummer's productions of Masefield's *The Box of Delights* were to awake the creative imagination of author-to-be Alan Garner, to rivet Dudley Moore's boyhood bum to a chair and, like so many *Children's Hour* serials and series of that calibre, to bring forth letters by the sackful.

Those radio serials, *Toytown*, David Davis's readings of stories and his playing of the piano, talks by Commander Stephen King-Hall; all were part of a ritual which could be enjoyed every week and on Saturday, homework and family bereavements permitting. And Sunday? Here the Reithian hand came to the fore with, for some of us, 'Auntie BBC' full of Services, Religious talks – and little in the way of entertainment. We thanked our Good Lord for Radio Luxembourg on most pre-war Sundays!

On arrival in Manchester in 1949, I soon discovered that *Children's Hour* had altered quite a bit since those pre-war days. A far wider range of programmes now catered for varying age-groups. Nan Macdonald's Northern *Children's Hour* covered one of the largest areas of the British Isles. Manchester was her base but her programmes also came from the Leeds studios and from those in Newcastle where the North East transmitter was also heard by listeners living in Northern Ireland. She took a few programmes from London, but the majority of her output was Northern bred and broadcast. And now I'd been told I was to take over for a while as Miss Macdonald was going away. I got the slight impression that this was as much to give the other staff a rest as the lady herself, for Nan worked a seven-day week. When she wasn't rehearsing and producing in the studio and also presenting the programme, she was up in her fifth-floor office putting back sentences and full paragraphs, which her book adapters, like Bertha Lonsdale, had omitted in their treatments for radio.

As we travelled back one Saturday in a BBC staff car after a live broadcast from Leasowe Children's Hospital in Liverpool, Nan told me she wanted me to watch a production the following day. There was a pause.

'Well, you will be in tomorrow?' When fixed with those bright penetrating eyes you did not argue. I did mention, however, that I had intended spending the day in Birmingham with Margaret.

'How will you ever know anything about *Children's Hour* if you are not here to learn?'

I therefore watched her rehearse and broadcast a play that Sunday.

In that first full week I spent shadowing Nan on Northern *Children's Hour*, the programmes were roughly as follows. Monday, 5 p.m. began with *Nursery Sing-Song* with Nan and Violet Carson, sometimes on other days of the week, followed by a story, then *Wandering with Nomad*. This nature programme had replaced *Out with Romany* on the death of The Rev. Bramwell Evens. Like Romany it all came from inside the same studio but instead of studio manager Jack Hollinshead barking as 'Rack', Romany's dog, all the natural history sounds for *Nomad* came from BBC recordings.

The following day began with a feature written by Joan Littlewood in which Wilfred Pickles interviewed people in the Yorkshire Dales for this particular edition of *A Walk with Wilfred*, and ended with *Children's Newsreel,* items covered by the Manchester Mobile Recording Unit and the Leeds unit. This ended with a studio sports page from Kenneth Wolstenholme.

Wednesday's choice of listening offered *Film News* from John Stratten, then the first episode of *The Brydons Undertake a Flitting* by Kathleen Fidler. At 5.50 young listeners joined London for *Children's Hour Prayers* conducted by Donald Soper.

A Russian broadcaster, George Mikhailov, opened Thursday's offering with *My Childhood in Kiev*; an occasional series which Nan did about childhoods in various parts of the world. Then into a larger studio trooped Gerald Isles together with some of his *Animals from Belle Vue Zoo* to face an eager audience of children. 'What does it eat?' and 'How long does it live?' were the usual questions they asked. The programme ended with a talk on Current Affairs by educationalist Harry Ree.

On the Friday, I was delighted to meet Charles Groves for the first time. As conductor of the BBC Northern Orchestra he gave a Concert Preview of the works to be played the following week at the Milton Hall, Manchester, before an audience composed entirely of children. His illustrated talk was followed by *How's it Done?* Whether it was about coal mining, making rubber tyres, putting bubbles into ginger beer, the Northern Mobile Recording Unit with Eric Jolly and Peter Anderson found out. There was a play from the Midlands to end Friday's listening and on Saturday an Outside Broadcast done by London. The Sunday programme broadcast by Northern *Children's Hour* came from Scotland. Just before she left, Nan took away the large pile of books that always cluttered her office desk. The cleaners had strict instructions to move nothing – not even the dust. Now she was to tell me, 'If you polish this, I think it will look quite nice. I've never really noticed the wood before!' She had never had the time!

Nan Macdonald was not to return to the North as a member of the BBC Manchester staff, but after a holiday she was attached to Children's Television at Lime Grove before leaving the staff altogether and becoming a freelancer. She was to do many splendid adaptations for us in later years, including some of the early books by Rosemary Sutcliffe. London

Children's Hour did *The Eagle of the Ninth*, Northern *Children's Hour* did *Brother Dusty Feet*, the story of a company of strolling players in the time of Queen Elizabeth I. For this I commissioned a score from Thomas Pitfield, which was conducted by John Hopkins and played by members of the BBC Northern Orchestra. The great 'Chang Lee' became 'Tobias Pennyfeather', the grand actor-manager of the day who swaggered his way around the country, with the splendid John Slater as the gentle 'Jonathan Whiteleafe'. I swear that he and Ralph Truman existed in an earlier life in those very same roles, such was the impact they made together.

At the time Nan Macdonald left North Region, I held the fort until her successor was appointed, already knowing that in certain parts of the BBC, Mrs Gaskell's 'North and South' syndrome still operated – and particularly as between Miss Nan Macdonald in Manchester and Mr Derek McCulloch in London! *Regional Round* was a *Children's Hour* quiz conducted by Mac between all the BBC regions – except the North!

No sooner had Nan departed than I got a phone call from the Head of *Children's Hour* in London informing Hill that the North *would* be taking part again in this quiz as from next month's edition. Hill thought he should clear this with his own Head of Programmes.

'You tell McCulloch,' declared Bob Stead, 'that we will record next month's edition and if we feel it is up to standard, then the North will take part the following month!'

I took that more as a command than a suggestion.

If some had suffered Nan on occasion, then my widely experienced colleagues in London *Children's Hour* had occasionally also had to understand Derek McCulloch. I was to learn a lot about my Radio hero of boyhood times when, some forty years later I was to be invited to write and to present a Radio 4 feature on that truly remarkable man (see Chapter 21). Now, he appeared to have it in for me when the North of England *did* come into *Regional Round* after a gap of two or more years. Mac would go round the Regions for the introductions at the start of the quiz.

'And who is in Manchester?'

I was to reply, 'It's Trevor, Mac.'

There was a brief silence.

'Oh, and who is Trevor-Mac?'

Bob would have told him precisely where to stick a comma.

It was a lot worse for Cliff Michelmore on what was to be his very first broadcast from a BBC studio. Not long after he left BFN, where he had become Deputy Director, I asked Cliff if he would devise and conduct a Sports Quiz, between the North and the South. McCulloch agreed to this.

'And what is my role to be?' he enquired.

Caught unawares that he would wish to involve himself in this sort of programme, I could only suggest that he might keep the team scores. Not very diplomatic of me! On the live Home Service broadcast that Saturday, young Michelmore was to be put through his paces. It was left to Jack Hardy and *The Little Orchestra* to soothe the way for the rest of that day's *Children's Hour* broadcast, with Cliff returning home to Reigate bloodied but certainly unbeaten!

I got on a whole lot better with the Head of *Children's Hour* after he had paid a visit to Manchester.

'Let me give you a fatherly word of advice,' he said with an arm on my shoulder. 'You should stand up to me more often.'

A new recruit to his staff had been Josephine Plummer who, with a suitable University degree, the highest secretarial qualifications and impeccable references, had begun in the BBC's Typing Pool, only, as she was to tell me herself, to be summoned early on in her probationary period by the lady supervisor who sat behind the glass screen. Miss Plummer was told she should learn to smile a little less during working hours, 'For it creates rather the wrong impression!'

Jo also told me she didn't have much to smile about when, later on in her BBC career, she joined the staff of London's *Children's Hour* quite expecting that when she produced a programme, her name would appear in *Radio Times*. It seems, however, that credits often went to someone else.

'You see,' explained the department head, 'It is rather like a pyramid and *I* happen to be the person at the top!'

At that time Jo was very much the junior of a staff of very well-known names in radio: May E. Jenkin, better known on the air as 'Elizabeth', and the very warm and friendly David Davis, who originally answered a BBC advertisement for the post of an accompanist. Then there was the tall and sedate Geoffrey Dearmer. When he wasn't concocting questions for *Regional Round* and gently tapping that gong when a child got an answer wrong, Geoffrey was one of the Lords Chamberlain. I always had visions of this gentle scholarly man sitting up in bed reading those lurid stage plays, roaring with laughter – at least, at some of the things – then firmly stamping them: 'Banned by the Lord Chamberlain'.

That London department was made up of a very good team, and whilst

I sometimes found it difficult to warm to Derek McCulloch – and perhaps the fault was mine – I was always drawn, like almost every other listener I have ever met, to that splendid broadcaster known as 'Mac', widely known and loved as the very accomplished narrator of *Toytown* who, in the very next breath, *was* 'Larry the Lamb' and had been since the very first programme in that truly memorable radio series.

In the mid-1950s, when I was to be working on Television at Lime Grove, Gordon Murray, a very experienced puppeteer, had precise models made from Hulme Beaman's original drawing of his *Toytown* characters. It wasn't a success. *Toytown* like so much that is best of radio, requires the mind *and* the imagination of a listener – not a viewer.

By 1953 and the 25th year of S.G. Hulme Beaman's evergreen stories, only Derek McCulloch and Ralph de Rohan, as 'Mr Growser' were left of the original cast. Gone were Arthur Wynn as the stalwart 'Ernest the Policeman' and Freddy Burtwell as the comic 'Magician'. No 'Mayor of Toytown' ever reached the heights achieved by Felix Felton. There were never any updated productions of this great *Children's Hour* institution. Like the best of musical compositions, they just kept repeating performances from the original scripts.

It came as a surprise to me to learn that pre-war the BBC regions did their own versions of *Toytown*. In Manchester it was Doris Gambell who played 'Larry'. Surely some of the best lines occur between this lamb and His Worship the Mayor – like the time 'Larry' and 'Dennis the Dachshund' turn up as plumbers at Mr Mayor's house and Larry is heard to bleat, 'If you please, Mr M-maayor, sir, where *is* your baaaa-ath?'

To which a somewhat irate Mr Mayor, with water cascading down his stairs replies, 'The bath? It is in the bath *room*!!!'

There were people in BBC Radio management in the 1960s who imagined right to the end that *Children's Hour* was all *Toytown* and Derek McCulloch saying, 'Hello, twins. If you look in the airing cupboard you will find a birthday present from Auntie Hettie!'

May Jenkin was to succeed Derek in 1950, and then in 1953 David Davis and his 'wind of change' was certainly to ventilate *Children's Hour*. With a younger staff, he was to cater for a far wider range of children's interests on a national basis, as Nan Macdonald had done with Northern *Children's Hour*.

It has always been a happy coincidence that both young and old have insatiable curiosity and can take in a lot of information, especially if it is presented in an interesting and entertaining way. And that is precisely what attracted many young, and many in the grandparent age-range, to

Children's Hour. The latter group had more time to listen, to learn and to add to life's experience. I had a BBC Audience Survey Report stuck on the wall of my Manchester Office. It referred to a *Children's Hour* talk we had done from the North. In an edited form, this was re-broadcast at a later date on the Third Programme. The only editing necessary was to omit some of the tightly packed information in order that the adult Third Programme listener might take it all in!

Under David's encouragement and leadership London took many more programmes from the Regions and vice-versa, and there were to be far more series involving us all. David began *Can I Get There by Candlelight*, using orchestras, choruses and soloists from around the British Isles, interwoven with stories and legends from each region in turn. There was a delightful series of *Children's Hour Music in Miniature* to which various BBC orchestras in London and the regions contributed.

Again from London, John Lane, who joined the department to devise and produce many of the live Outside Broadcasts, began a series on our cathedrals, from Durham in the north to Winchester in the south, from Truro in the west to Norwich in the east. *For Thy Great Glory* always began with a live tour by a visiting 'pilgrim' who, with the Dean and members of the staff, endeavoured to give some impression of these magnificent buildings. Then each programme ended with a special service for a full congregation of young people from that diocese. Instead of radiating the chimes of Big Ben, John decided that each programme should begin with the clock from the cathedral. When it came my turn to do Durham, the BBC engineers discovered that this great clock was ten seconds fast by the Greenwich Time Signal. A helpful verger held me firmly by the legs as I leaned across a great void and held on to a large pendulum for ten arm-aching seconds.

I had rehearsed the 'tour' and other details the night before our live broadcast, run through Dean Wild's address with him and also the hymns with the cathedral choristers and the organist, Conrad Eden, since cathedrals have other things to do on Sundays besides rehearse for the BBC. Almost as an afterthought, I decided to give the organist, high up in his loft, a pair of headphones so that he could not only hear the broadcast tour before the service began, but also any instructions I might wish to give him whilst we were on the air. I also handed him a shortened version of the script, which had things like:

Dean's Address: *ends on words*: ... for the sake of Jesus Christ.

Now it so happened that the phrase occurred *twice* in that Dean's address, The first time he uttered the phrase was not long after he had started – so the mighty organ blared forth with *My Soul Now Praise Thy Maker*.

'Not yet, Mr Eden, NOT YET!' I shouted.

The organ music ended with a suitable coda, and Dean Wild continued to address the nation as if nothing at all unusual had happened.

I also recall it was at Lincoln Cathedral that a somewhat officious head verger decided to lock the great West Door from the inside at about five minutes to five on the Sunday of the broadcast. Fortunately our pilgrim, the Rev. R.T. Brooks on this occasion, thought to give the door a try just before we went on air, or he would have been thumping that Lincoln Imp knocker until the weather forecast, or shouting to the Dean through thick planks of English oak. It was the Dean and Chapter of Lincoln who suggested we might like to take their copy of the Magna Carta out of its case for the broadcast. We certainly did! Nothing was of too much trouble to anyone or any organisation if it was for *Children's Hour*, such was the programme's integrity. How fortunate I was to be contributing to such a department.

A Sunday afternoon series I produced on the National Home Service over a number of years was *Lives of Famous Northerners* by Bertha Lonsdale, who did far more original writing than adapting. We chose Delius as the first subject. Eric Fenby, who for many years had been the ailing composer's hands and eyes, gave us invaluable help with the script; remembering for example that Delius always called his wife *lass*, especially if anyone from Bradford came over to visit him in France. Then he would lapse into quite broad 'Bradfordian'. We also had invaluable help and advice from Sir Thomas Beecham, who, through doing most of the composer's works on the Columbia Blue Label recordings, was to make Delius's music more widely known and appreciated. He told me a lot about the man and about the way he spoke.

Under the circumstances I was not happy to see a letter in the *Radio Times* after the broadcast from an Oxford Don, saying how dare the BBC assume 'that an educated man like Frederick Delius would speak with a Northern accent!'

The BBC allowed me to pen a reply to the bombastic bigot, but since this was also to be printed, it was couched in more polite tones. As producer I heartily agreed, of course, with the sentiments of a Mr Dunbar in the *Radio Times* 'Letters' column two weeks later in which he wrote:

> The BBC can be proud of using its best endeavours to inculcate in the children of this country an appreciation of those standards of

beauty, truth and benevolence, without which humanity is doomed to extinction.

Can't say fairer than that.

Listener correspondence, were it not for the law of libel, would make a fascinating Bedside Companion. In my time the majority was straightforward, honest, helpfully constructive in its criticism, demanding on time, yet fully worthy of a reply. But there *is* another side. A dear old soul wrote a nice letter about a play I had produced. The BBC Post Room had paid excess postage since the envelope bore no stamp. Ah well, we become forgetful as we grow older – as I now know – but after writing about the play in a chatty way, there was this postscript: 'The BBC have more money than me, and anyway, I can't find a bloody stamp!'

Children's Hour certainly received its fair share of correspondence. During *Request Week* it came in sackloads, but there was always plenty of unsolicited comment. Even poor harmless little *Nursery Sing-Song* wasn't exempt. That programme for the very young included *Sing-Song Requests* at 5 p.m., and almost every time we sang 'Ding, Dong, Bell' we

Some of our mail for Northern *Children's Hour* Request Week

received a postcard from Lord Bertie of Thane explaining that cats should *not* be put into wells, whilst the Anti-Drink League of Great Britain were on us like a plague of flies every time we mentioned even so much as a 'grape'! In dramatic terms, 'pish' and 'tosh' were accepted expletives – spoken only, of course, under the greatest duress by the likes of Biggles – but a 'damn' was quite unpardonable! And quite right too, Madam.

On the subject of letters, one I still treasure and *can* write about came in the 1970s from an old coal miner who, as a boy, had been down the pit with D.H. Lawrence. He wrote me long letters after I had produced adaptations of *Sons and Lovers* and *Women in Love* as Radio 4 Sunday night serials. There was a long gap in our correspondence before this came: 'Dear Mr Hill, You said to write to you again if I had anything interesting to report. Well, my wife has just died after fifty-six years of marriage ...'

Newspapers, besides listeners, could write some strange things about our programmes. For another *Lives of Famous Northerners* series I wanted actual brothers to play the sons of William Byrd, the 16th century musician. Families tend to adopt similar speech patterns and rhythms and, therefore, sound alike in many cases. Geoffrey Wheeler had gone on from presenting *Showcase* for me to acting whilst at University as a Law student, and I had persuaded his young brother, Peter Wheeler, who was really far more interested in boxing and things, to take part in a serial, *Peril in Lakeland*. Now I was to cast them as Byrd's sons, but according to the *Daily Express*: 'Mistaken identity last night gave two brothers a chance to broadcast – as brothers.'

A series which Margaret Potter wrote for several years was *The Adventures of Samuel Poppleton*, which she originated whilst in Hamburg. This featured that splendid all-round actor from Oldham, Herbert Smith, who also produced many serials, features and other programmes for us in *Children's Hour*.

'Mr Poppleton' was a retired seafarer who now kept an antique shop, the contents of which provided various stories from his boyhood days as cabin-boy aboard the *Saucy Jane*. I cast young Brian Trueman as Poppleton in his youth, then, when Brian's voice dropped an octave, this role was taken over by Philip Jenkinson. The same sort of thing happened with other long-running series, like *Jennings* where my London colleagues had to find new young actors to take over roles.

It wasn't a question of a voice breaking when it came to *Bunkle*. On taking over production of those popular plays from Nan Macdonald, I thought the leading role should be *played* by a boy, and *not* someone who may have sounded extremely good and happened to have a name that would have done for a lad – Billie Whitelaw. I replaced her, and Billie was furious! I quote: 'That ... "man" got rid of the best boy actor since the days of William Shakespeare! Anyhow, I was delighted when Trevor's choice of substitute turned out to be a disaster. But he *did* give me other roles, and nice ones too!'

Well, I *had* noticed she was filling out her school gym tunic and *looked* like a girl!

But I was telling you about the *Poppleton* plays. Each started with two children, Elizabeth and Peter, visiting the antique dealer. We had a number of 'Peters' in the role, the last being a lad who'd done quite well at audition and I thought he should be encouraged. Not nearly so tall as he sounded. His name, Robert Powell.

I'd cast Joyce Palin, our radio 'Alice', as Elizabeth, whilst her own three-year-old mongrel dog, Spot, became very good at barking and growling to order as old Mr Poppleton spun his yarns to his two eager visitors. We'd already recorded an episode entitled *The Egyptian Vase*

Cast of *Poppleton* (left to right) Brian Trueman, Joyce Palin (with 'Spot'), Herbert Smith and Peter McKendrick when across three columns of a national newspaper was proclaimed: 'Radio's Alice loses her pet and now she asks: "Call off Show".'

The photo of a smiling Joyce with an armful of Spot and script were shown at a BBC microphone below this boxed headline, taking just one column width: *'Alice wants Spot's Broadcast Stopped.'*

By that October, 'Cleopatra' was now billed in the *Radio Times* as Mr Poppleton's cat, and she continued to be heard until the series finished, even during the anxious time of her operation. Well, no, that's going it a bit! We simply had her 'adjusted'. Violet Carson was staying with us the day the vet brought Cleopatra back and the cat was soon sitting on someone's lap and purring, only occasionally stopping to lick the area of shaved Siamese fur and to examine those neatly tied stitches where the adjustment had been made.

'Ah, lover's not!' exclaimed Vi.

When Gwen Pain had been appointed to take over Northern *Children's Hour* in 1950, she introduced various new programmes and series of her own. *Barn Dance* with Bill Cain as the host up in the North East became a very successful musical series, which I later transferred to Children's Television. I then did Outside Broadcasts of *Barn Dance* from places like Alnwick Castle, yet strangely enough some of the best were done inside the old Dickenson Road, Manchester Film studios with a few property 'beams', farm implements hired for the occasion, and loads and loads of straw. When the programme became evening viewing, a fair-haired young man with a Geordie accent introduced it for us. He also provided a book series for me on TV as well. His name was Brian Redhead.

In the early 1950s, however, when Radio was still the big draw, more and more Outside Broadcasts were being done. Gwen started a series of visits to one farm, *Welcome to Whitehill*, taking two young people to hear and learn about farming in the different seasons. She left the drama productions to Herbert Smith and myself. He went in for things like *The Plover Patrol* by Dusty McGarry, whilst I took on production of Bertha Lonsdale's adaptations of the *Biggles* stories with Jack Watson in the title role.

For *Biggles Hunts Big Game*, a six-part serial, I cast Nigel Davenport as the effete 'Lord Bertie Lissie', with Bryan Forbes as the more down-to-earth 'Tug Carrington'. Bryan, at that time, was also appearing in the stage play of *The Holly and The Ivy* at the Duchess Theatre, London. The night Margaret and I went to see our ex-Hamburg colleague, we applauded so loudly the moment he set foot on the stage that the 'lead' stopped speaking in mid-sentence!

The old 'Mancunian Film Studios' at Dickenson Road, Manchester gave me an ideal setting for televised editions of our 'Barn Dance' programmes. A young Brian Redhead introduced these for me

By the time I was casting for *Spy Royal,* an adventure serial by Elleston Trevor, who was better known in those days for all the hilarious *Deep Woodlander* serials in *Children's Hour*, I'd promoted Nigel to the 'lead' part of 'Peregrine the Falcon' – such fame! Mind you, he *had* been the secretary of OUDS whilst up at Trinity College, Oxford after leaving BFN. With Tony Richardson, John Schlesinger, Kenneth Tynan and Lindsay Anderson also involved in the same Society during that period, well, it was better than being at RADA.

I spent a week with OUDS the year they did that unforgettable production of *The Tempest* in the grounds of one of the colleges. When Caliban released Ariel at the end of the play, off went the young actor playing the sprite – and running straight across a stretch of lake water, throwing up his arms and then appearing to shoot a hundred feet into the summer night sky in a shower of falling sparks! I never achieved anything like *that* on radio. OUDS had rigged planks just below the surface of the lake and, from a tripod at the end of Ariel's run, a firework was triggered off. It left the audience truly gasping.

When theatre work was quiet for one or the other, Nigel and Bryan would return to work in radio drama for me in Manchester. Not that things remained 'quiet' for long for either actor. I suppose Nigel got his first real break with the film *High Wind in Jamaica*, to be followed by the role of the Duke of York in the screen version of Robert Bolt's *A Man for All Seasons*. After seeing those in later times I didn't imagine that my sort of programme budgets would be able to attract Mr Davenport – particularly after his star roles in *Play Dirty*, the film about the long-range Desert Group, and *Virgin Soldiers*. But he did return to Radio in the 1960s and to the North when I came to produce Olive Shapley's skilful adaptation of *South Riding* as the Sunday night serial. He portrayed the complex character who is 'Robert Carne', playing opposite Anna Cropper as 'Sarah Burton' the new headmistress in Winifred Holtby's novel.

It was not long after the radio version of this serial that Nigel was to appear in the same role in a Television version of the book. As for young Mr Forbes, well, he was busy acting, and came and did a few more serials for me besides *Biggles*, but he was also now engaged in writing and beginning to do things for the British Film Industry – and in a big way. I hope to include a later mention about others who began acting in plays and serials in Northern *Children's Hour* – but that is only one area in which young people were encouraged to take part.

Besides starting *Nursery Sing-Song* from the North when she was Organiser in the mid 1930s, Olive Shapley also began *Your Own Ideas*, which used poems, stories and musical compositions written and mostly performed by children. There was also a regular spot for *Young Artists*, which Olive began under the title of *The Gingham Umbrella*. Pat Kirkwood made her broadcast debut in that whilst still in her Levenshulme school gym tunic. Each Region had its own variant of these. One of my very first *Children's Hour* announcing jobs was to introduce *Some Outstanding Young Artists* including Joyce Palin appearing as a 13-year-old pianist and a slightly older girl who had a really lovely voice. To her quiet embarrassment, her mother not only came into the studio with her but also brought in a somewhat large teddy bear, saying to me, by way of explanation, 'Well, I *do* like Julie to be like *other* children!'

Despite all that Julie Andrews survived! I imagine her fee is now something rather in excess of the ten shillings and sixpence which we paid her for that broadcast on a Monday in October 1949.

Another *Young Artist* was a 14-year-old violinist who later turned professional and did a lot of work for us before eventually becoming Leader of the Hallé Orchestra. He was Martin Milner. But there is one musician I think I might claim as my protégé. Early in 1950 I received a manuscript from a boy who lived in the Manchester suburb of Swinton. It was a musical composition of his own entitled *Blue Ice.* I couldn't play it so I showed it to Violet Carson for her professional opinion.

'He's either quite brilliant or slightly mad!' she said.

Charles Groves nodded approval. 'I'd get him in.'

Max Davies, or Sir Peter Maxwell Davies as he is now internationally known, made his broadcast debut with me in May 1950 in Northern *Children's Hour* playing three of his own works.

By September I was to be producer at Gwen's suggestion of a Saturday programme for and by teenagers. In that first edition of *Out of School* Max played 'Black and Green Imps', musical sketches he'd done of other boys from his school. He became our resident composer. I teamed Max up with Joyce Palin. Shortly after, her parents at Withington were to prop up the floor of their living room in order to take the weight of *two* grand pianos, so that Max and Joyce could rehearse together. As they became proficient at playing items for two keyboards, so I arranged broadcasts for them.

At some point I told Max he should join me for one of the Children's Concerts from the Milton Hall and took him along to our rehearsal with the Northern Symphony Orchestra. During the break before transmission I introduced him to Charles Groves. The first thing Max wanted to know was why the conductor had left out a section of the work they were about to broadcast. Charles roared with laughter.

'That's a *very* good question, my boy, and there's a very simple answer. Because they couldn't *play* it!'

Apart from a composition that Max wrote for me, entitled *Cameo* – at a time when I was regularly writing radio cartoon musicals – I think *Dance Music* is one of the most lyrical of his boyhood compositions, being a very nice 'pastiche' of the 1930s and 40s. He was to do a similar thing quite brilliantly in later years when Ken Russell invited Max to work on, and to extend, Sandy Wilson's score for the film version of the musical *The Boy Friend.*

All too soon Max's time was taken up with the Royal Manchester College of Music, then he was off to Rome to study. A few years later he was teaching in the West Country and sent me a copy of the Cirencester School's Music Magazine for 1960. One article, signed P.M.D. was about composing music for school use. He was working on *O Magnum Mysterium* at that time and observed, after working with the school choir, that Gloucestershire children are not, by and large, natural singers.

'They are reluctant to make a noise at all – and when they do, it is oddly throaty and gurgling!'

Strange, but Herr Eric H. Bender had said much the same of the youngsters in his Hamburg Children's Choir, only in their case the conductor stated that they were 'hoarse noises'.

I liked another article in Max's School Magazine, which referred to the second period of a Tuesday afternoon which was for the school orchestra and that, according to a Miss Sally Harrison in Form 3, began with P.M.D. having to tune all the violins himself:

> During this entertaining ceremony we began to talk. 'Quiet over there!' roars P.M.D. running his fingers through his hair until he looks more like a golliwog than ever. Then tears off his thick jumper, flings his tie to the winds and undoes half his shirt buttons. 'Steady on,' murmurs someone. 'This isn't the Follies Bergères!

I like to think that we in Northern *Children's Hour* brought out only the best in Peter Maxwell Davies.

There were some very good choirs from the North of England that I announced for the evening Light Programme series *Children Singing*, and certainly nothing remotely 'gurgling' or 'hoarse' about the celebrated Vienna Boys Choir. I had broadcast with them from Hamburg in 1947, and then in the early 1950s I had the pleasure of touring with them when they broadcast concerts during their visit to England. A Northern paper liked the programme but thought that: 'The BBC should use a Northern voice to announce them when performing in the North.'

Strange! I myself never noticed those Wigan accents in which the Vienna Boys sang!

8

On a Musical Note

The Features and Drama Office, which Margaret and I worked from in Hamburg, contained one wall of coloured murals done by Ursula Steveberg and Lore Schalt, both of whom had worked with a German film animation company, and now they had illustrated some of our own British Forces Network programmes. Beneath an enormous candle dripping life-like wax, was a Disney-type character pulling back the pages of a large book out of which sprang other characters from *The Island of Moressa*, *Robin Hood*, and from other plays and serials we had done.

Whilst working on our walls, Ursula had made some rough sketches of a rabbit I'd begun writing about in the hope of doing a sort of radio cartoon. That idea got no further until I arrived to work on programmes from Manchester and, with Nan Macdonald's encouragement, I began to develop the idea. According to the *Radio Times* for September 29th, 1949: 'Floppy was a rabbit who lived in the days before bunnies had white blobs on their tails.' Mark you, that very first of my *Cameo Cartoons was* billed as being for young listeners, and 'Floppy', as you may have guessed, got lost in the dark, causing such an upset that every rabbit you see nowadays has a white powder puff behind!

The next *Cameo Cartoon* was not only far more adult stuff but had the advantage of a musical score, written and conducted by Ray Martin himself, which blended perfectly with all the special sound effects concocted for the cartoon. In this story, 'Marmaduke' was a very ambitious mouse who always wanted things, including the moon. I suppose a lot of us want that at sometime or other in life, but in Marmaduke's case there was good reason for it! Mouseland was infested with raiding cats and the

Trevor and Margaret discuss his ideas for 'The Operatic Cat' cameo cartoon

black ones, especially, always pounced in the dead of night. Had I a childhood obsession with darkness?

Anyway, in the case of *The Mouse Who Wanted the Moon*, young Marmaduke's idea was to bring the moon back from the top of the mountain to the town and hang it in the square so that the citizens of Mouseland wouldn't be caught in the dark. Unable to reach the moon, Marmaduke had an even better idea. He suggested to His Mouse Gracious Majesty that buckets of water should be placed around the city. Whether it was the reflection of the moon in each receptacle that kept the cats away, or the fear of water, I couldn't truthfully say, but Marmaduke was knighted for his endeavours. One of the bow-mice was played by folk singer Ewan McColl, whilst their marching tune, complete with clanking, loose-fitting armour, which was enough to scare anyone away, became a 'hit' when Ray Martin issued the melody on a commercial record under the title *The Dog with Two Tails.*

The next full-length cartoon I embarked upon was *The Operatic Cat*, which I've already mentioned. There was one member of the BBC Manchester Music department who took grave exception to the way in which I had used the Beecham Operatic Chorus and treated some of the well-known operatic arias. It was, therefore, with some delight that I was to inform the head of that department that the cartoon was to be repeated in prime time on the Light Programme and so it couldn't have been in such poor taste after all. Maurice Johnston had a delightfully dry sense of humour, heightened by a rather strange, hesitant speech impediment: 'My d-ear, b-oy, if we were to t-ele-v-ise f-forn-ication in g-lorious T-echnicolor, it would get a v-ery l-arge audience, b-but I w-wouldn't say it would be in g-ood t-taste!'

As I passed the door to Maurice's office one lunchtime, he stopped me in my tracks and, taking me into his office, said he'd heard I did quite a good v-vocal impression of him. Next moment, he'd sat me down and told me to let him hear it for himself. He roared with laughter whilst I felt my face was the colour of boiled beetroot, then he proceeded to tell me the perfectly true story of the man who had phoned Sir Thomas Beecham's residence, asking to speak to Maurice Johnston who'd been working as assistant to this celebrated musician. The Beecham butler explained that Mr Johnston was no longer in their employ, but was now working with the BBC.

'Oh, and what as?' enquired the caller.

'We are given to understand, sir,' related Maurice with obvious delight, 'That M-Mr J-Johnston has g-gone to be an a-a-anoun-cer, s-sir!'

We were not only fortunate in having Maurice 'in our employ' but also the two Staff Orchestras, the BBC Northern and the Northern Variety Orchestra. Producers, like myself, who wanted to use them for incidental music sessions were very popular with the musicians because, in the majority of cases, we booked them on an 'All Rights' contract for the recording sessions, which meant that they were paid a fee additional to their BBC salaries.

It was Jack Hardy who used a section of the BBC Northern together with some members of the Halle for his Little Orchestra, and it was Jack who wrote a very amusing and charming score for the adaptation of Richard Strachey's book *Little Reuben at the North Pole.* Besides adapting, which she did to her usual highly professional standard, Muriel Levy played the part of QOF (Queen of the Fairies to you), whilst I cast the larger-than-life actress and theatre producer Joan Littlewood in the role of 'Woodwind', the witch. Joan did a very good line in 'witches and bitches' for me in the early 1950s, positively excelling in a radio version of the Hans Anderson *Tinder Box* story, which Margaret and I used as the basis for a decidedly adult musical.

This time the composer for the required score was Henry Reed. He wrote a *Witch Circling Then Landing* music cue, which began with a vocal and orchestral 'screech of raucous laughter' at some two hundred feet up, finishing with a 'bass profundo' on hitting terra firma. I was told by the man in charge, *never* to offer such a cartoon for repeat on *Children's Hour*, since he considered it to be very, very frightening. To me there was another reason – that 'risqué' scene in which the beautiful young princess's frustrated old nurse, played by Athene Seyler, follows her charge as she is borne out of the palace in her sleep on the back of a large dog – only to be delivered to the common soldier in his seedy hotel bedroom. There is no dialogue once the dear old nurse has knelt down in order to peer through the keyhole; just sleepy sighs of contentment from the princess, sighs of satisfaction from the soldier, the occasional yawn for the obedient dog, but plenty of 'Ohs', Ooohs' and 'Ahs' from Nanny. With a sequence like this, scored for harp and strings, with occasional woodwind interpolations of an interesting and imaginative nature, I would not have thought that our version of *The Tinder Box was* for the kiddies!

Much more to the *Children's Hour* taste was a work for Narrator and Orchestra by Welsh composer Grace Williams. *The Merry Minstrel* was the main item to be performed by the BBC Northern Orchestra at one of the Milton Hall concerts for young people. In July 1950, Charles Groves was now conducting in Australia, having done an exchange with Joseph Post, then the associate conductor of the Sydney Symphony orchestra. The actor George Baker had been booked to narrate *The Merry Minstrel* but was prevented from coming to Manchester within hours of what was to be a 'live' broadcast performance. Mr Post was the sort of conductor who made executive decisions.

'Here is the score with the Narrator's part,' he said, thrusting it at me. '*You'll* just have to ny-rate this yourself!'

We had time for one rehearsal. I kept one eye fixed on the conductor who 'brought me in' every time I had to narrate and to do the various 'voices'. Thanks to Mr Post's help, I was later invited to perform the same work before a full house of children at the Royal Festival Hall, London, this time with the Philharmonic Orchestra. I felt a little better when, just before the start of the rehearsal, I met up again with my old school friend, Alexander Kok. He was now principal cellist with the Philharmonic. His nods and smiles of encouragement helped me no end.

The Festival Hall was very much in the news, for the year was 1951. When the BBC heard that Walt Disney was bringing out a full-length cinema cartoon of *Alice*, Margaret and I were commissioned to work on

Three wicked tailors read about an Emperor wanting new clothes

'Robert Rocket Esq'

The White Rabbit narrates our musical version of the 'Alice' stories

'Spring Fever'

Joyce Palin, actress, pianist and our 'Alice' in our Festival of Britain radio cartoon

a radio musical version for broadcast Overseas by the BBC's Transcription Service and in the UK by the Light Programme. It was to take the form of another of the *Cameo Cartoons* and would be 'freely adapated'. This enabled us to have a mixture of the two books, *Alice's Adventures in Wonderland* and *Through the Looking-Glass*. We used the character of the White Rabbit, portrayed by Herbert Smith who'd taken part in all the radio cartoons to date, to link selected scenes from the two separate Lewis Carroll stories. The rabbit rode around Wonderland inside an old-fashioned hansom cab, complete with its own theme tune. *Alice's Adventures in Wonderland* starred Wilfred Pickles as the Gryphon. He recited the famous 'Jabberwocky' poem to a score composed by Ray Martin and with the weird and wonderful sound effects of that most unusual of creatures. Jeanne de Casalis as the White Queen used her celebrated 'Mrs Feather' voice when examining Alice and asking her, 'What is one-and-one-and-one-and-one?', whilst Jimmy Edwards clanked and rattled and fell noisily off his horse as the White Knight. We gave him lines which were altered only slightly from those in the book, such as, 'Ah, a gl-orious victory, was it *not*?'

Ray Martin never did things by half. He had leaders of all the London Orchestras sitting in the first desk, besides the services of George Mitchell and the Mitchell Maids and chorus. Although I was not to know it at the time, one of those Mitchell Maids was to become my leading lady in a BBC series some twenty-five years later. With the aid of lyricist Ronnie Taylor, Ray wrote the score for our opening song: *In the Land of Make-Believe* and another entitled: *Wonderland*. They were sung by that chap named Jimmy Young (sorry, Sir Jimmy as he now is!). I have a commercial recording to prove it!

Our radio Alice was Joyce Palin, and when the film *Alice* came to Britain for its European premiere of the Walt Disney version, the two 'voices' were to meet for a day. The Press was out in force as the American voice of the cartoon 'Alice', Miss Kathleen Beaumont, greeted Joyce. Both were then 14 years old but there any similarity ended. As Michael Walsh of the *Daily Express* reported: 'Whilst Miss Beaumont flies back to the U.S.A. to follow her hobby of grafting camellias, so Joyce Palin returns to Withington High School to study for her exams.'

After *Alice's Adventures in Wonderland* had been heard in the States, Margaret and I got a commission from the National Broadcasting Company of America: 'To write an original musical. Something like *A Christmas Carol*, you know!' Yes, we did know and we also knew we couldn't improve upon Dickens any more than we could improve upon the works of Lewis Carroll. Rather than adapt a story, we attempted to create a sort of Dickensian Christmas atmosphere with *The Little Logsellers*, with a score this time by Henry Reed for the BBC Northern Orchestra. It was the story of the old woodcutter's two grandchildren who, for the first time in their lives, go to the Big City in order to sell the logs for him. There they discover what others have and don't have. The programme was produced especially for NBC and, in a slightly different version, was then to be broadcast several times by the BBC.

Our friend, Eberhard Forck from NWDR Hamburg, painstakingly translated our script and lyrics of *The Little Logsellers* into his own language and, under some quite unpronounceable title to us, it was broadcast in Germany the following year.

One thing certainly *does* appear to lead to another. Margaret and I felt that perhaps we really had 'arrived' when BBC producer Francis Essex telephoned to say that the BBC Television service wanted to commission us to write a full-length version of *Beauty and the Beast* for transmission at Christmas time. I hurried down to meet the producer who took me straight over to the Riverside Studios which the BBC had just acquired. In the vast area of the main Sound stage, Francis explained how *he* saw it. A prologue would be filmed at Ealing Studios with the singer, David Hughes as Beauty's swain. He would be seen and heard returning home on her merchant-father's ship – but, at a Grand Ball, held in the merchant's house, news was to reach him that his ship had not come home. It had foundered upon rocks with the loss of cargo and all hands. I listened most carefully as I was told the way the storyline was to go and then returned excitedly back to Manchester and to home.

'We are to write the part of the merchant for Peter Sellers, and that of his steward, in love with Beauty, for George Cole!'

Beauty was played by Sally Bazeley, whom we'd seen in the London stage version of *Bless the Bride,* whilst the part of the Beast was to be written for the Maori bass, Inia Te Wiata. The very next day, we got on to Ronnie Taylor to start work on some of the lyrics, having given him a rough idea of the outline, whilst Margaret and I started somewhat frantically writing *Beauty and the Beast* scene by scene and despatching the script pages to London, for it came as something of a surprise to us to discover that Mr Essex wanted the thing for Christmas *that* year and *not* for the following one!

We completed the Prologue, for which Norman Newell wrote the song, also the final scene, in which Beast meets his end in a house containing flowers of wax and whose beauty would never fade. He was to perish in the flames of a fire. These two scenes in the TV musical were scheduled to be filmed within two weeks of my meeting with the producer. Shortly before that Christmas – and with a slightly uneasy silence from the London end – Margaret and I attended the first day of a three-day camera rehearsal. I sensed all was not well in the Riverside gents, where a now rather forgetful Bobbie Howes was standing at the stalls attempting to get things undone or done up. I greeted him, for we had worked together before and had been out to celebrate the Manchester debut of the musical *Paint your Wagon*, in which his daughter Sally Howes also appeared. I asked Bobbie what he was doing at Riverside.

'Doing, old boy? I'm in a sort of musical thing, playing Sally's dad. Er, not *my* Sally. Sally Bazeley!'

Perhaps Peter Sellers or his agent didn't like the part we'd written for him, I thought. But at least Sally Bazeley was still in the cast. On the way from the gents I bumped into Alma Cogan who'd worked with me on some programmes with the Northern Variety Orchestra. I breathed more easily when she told me she was just seeing about her new TV series for early the following year. On the large Riverside stage were assembled the majority of the cast, now in costume. We peered around, but there was no sign of George Cole for whom we had taken such pains in writing the character of 'Crispin'. However, Leslie Phillips was certainly to be seen. *He* was 'Crispin'! What other surprises were in store? Well, the producer had decided to pep up the action a bit by getting in a couple of gag writers, and now, Inia Te Wiata had a companion in the person of Charlie Drake, cast as 'Wee Beastie'.

My co-author and I felt more assured when we saw the Ball scene in rehearsal. It *was* still our Ball scene as we had conceived it. A fellow named on the credits as Terry Stanford had written a very good theme for the minuet we had indicated, performed by the guests at the merchant's Ball. Then Crispin was to come forward bearing a silver salver – and news of the fate of the merchant's ship. I say 'come forward'. Leslie Phillips had to walk all of fifty feet in precise time to the minuet. The choreography for the dancers was such that, as he approached each couple, so they turned directly to camera and froze as the lights went out on each and every pair of startled faces. Eventually, Crispin reaches the merchant, offers up the salver and, at the same time, lays a discreet hand on Beauty's arm.

Long after most of that BBC Boxing Day version of *The Beauty and the Beast* has been forgotten, we still remember the performances and the voices of Inia Te Wiata and Sally Bazeley. Those, and the required melody for our minuet – for Terry Stanford, better known in musical circles as pianist Russ Conway, was to alter the tempo and re-title it *Side Saddle*.

Looking back, if I'd been asked about Beast having a side-kick, I think I would most certainly have suggested some role for Joan Littlewood. To hear her in some of the cartoon musicals she did for me was one thing. To see her playing the role in a radio studio was quite another thing. Joan did wonders for the theatre as a producer, but I remember her performances of a musical nature. Those and the time she was being most earnestly interviewed by Huw Wheldon on the Arts programme,

Monitor. There she was, a black beret perched on her head, a cigarette thrust to one side of her mouth bringing a down-to-earth whiff of her beloved London Stratford East Theatre to this high-toned Television occasion. Huw was busily consulting the palm of his right hand, as he was wont to do when asking a somewhat long and involved question of his subject, when Joan leaned back on the studio settee. In doing so, her beret fell off and disappeared from sight. When Huw eventually finished asking the question, he looked up. His aquiline nose was no more than three inches away from a large expanse of black knickers, as Joan retrieved the missing beret from behind the *Monitor* settee.

'Sorry, luv, what was that?' enquired Miss Littlewood.

I endeavoured to obtain the services of this very inventive and clever lady when we embarked on a highly original series for *Children's Hour*. However, by that time Joan had more important calls on her time with the London Stratford East Theatre Company and her original productions of *Things Ain't Wot They Used to Be* and *Oh, What a Lovely War*. Instead, the part I intended for Joan went to the author, Muriel Levy.

She and Doris Gambell were definitely two of the radio 'Aunts' in the pre-war days of *Children's Hour* from the BBC Liverpool studios. Muriel could adapt *The Forsyte Saga* for adults on the one hand and write *The Adventures of Lollypop* for children on the other. It was one of the 'stick-iest' productions to originate from the North, what with three Jelly-Babies and Lord and Lady Crème-de-Menthe who could be particularly toffee-nosed at times especially when travelling in their toffee Rolls. Lollypop herself was always torn between looking after the Jelly-Babies and her feelings for Private Praline of the Soft-Centres Regiment. Joyce Palin and Geoffrey Wheeler excelled in these musicals, which were enhanced with scores by Henry Reed and memorable lyrics by Muriel Levy. She, Doris and Violet Carson – the original Three Semis of the 1930s – became the Jelly-Babies. Of all the musicals we did, *The Adventures of Lollypop* was essentially radio – and at its best.

9

Violet Carson

Let me begin by putting the record straight. There certainly *was* an 'Auntie Vi' who broadcast in *Children's Hour* from Manchester, but she wasn't Violet Carson.

'I was never anyone's aunt,' she told me emphatically when in 1981 I was preparing and writing a Radio Feature on this remarkable lady. And the Vi I knew and worked with over many years certainly *could* be emphatic.

'What is more, I don't *intend* to be anyone's aunt.'

Yet the phrase persisted even to the Radio, Television and Press announcements of Violet Carson's death on Boxing Day 1984. Nearly all referred to 'Auntie Vi of *Children's Hour*'. That title rightly belonged to a Miss Violet Fraser, who broadcast from Manchester from 1925 until 1928 when she married another member of the BBC staff and, as was then the custom, had to resign. It is her photo on the *Radio Celebrity* cigarette cards of the late 1920s.

The artist I'd like to tell you more about is Violet Helen Carson, born at No. 1, Corporation Terrace, Ancoats, Manchester, some sixty-three years before the now legendary 'Ena Sharples' came into being as the Grande Dame of *Coronation Street*. That was on Friday, December 9th, 1960, the start of Television's longest running and most successful drama series.

Whilst Vi was travelling back by train to Blackpool from the Granada studios one day, a rather diffident man tapped on the door of her non-smoking First Class compartment, paused a moment, then taking a breath slid the door open.

'You will excuse me for intruding but it *is* Miss Violet Carson, isn't it?'

Vi, then at the very height of her success in *Coronation Street* was delighted to be recognised for once as herself.

'I'd just like to tell you,' continued the man, 'what pleasure you gave to my wife and to myself over all those years on the Radio with your singing and your piano performances. Many won't remember, but we do!' Vi was delighted as the admirer turned to close the door again. Then he paused to add, as something of an afterthought, 'But it's a pity success has come so late in life, isn't it?'

For 'Ena' perhaps. Certainly not for Vi, who said of herself, 'I've not only been very lucky. I've been blessed with gifts that a lot of people would love to have had. I take no credit for any of the things I've been able to do because I haven't been able to help myself. I just happen, so often, to have been at the right place at the right time, and to have done things in front of the right people!'

I would say that 'luck' in life for Vi and for her younger sister, Nellie, began with their choice of parents. Father, William Carson, was a flour miller; Scots, full of music and imagination.

'And you should have seen him on the dance floor,' adds Nellie. 'He wore a waistcoat of velvet, gold cufflinks and looked so dashing in his evening dress!'

Mother was younger, temperamental, self-willed and, according to Vi, her middle name was 'NO', but she was a beautiful singer besides being a firm mama. And Vi? As she said of herself, 'I was just another child at Elementary School in Ancoats who had to ask for time off on Wednesdays in order to have her music lessons; a request often grudgingly given. But from the word go there was a piano in the house, a stool to sit on, a keyboard there, which was no stranger to me at three years old!'

Mr Carson evidently held the view that young ladies stayed and helped in the home until such time as they married, but the First World War stopped all that, so Vi went out and did some office work. Her sister, Nellie, at the tender age of 15, was gaining valuable musical experience at the Market Street Cinema in Manchester, where her fiddle master happened to be the leader of the orchestra. She was also destined to become a musician of renown as lutanist to the English Singers, and accompanied them on various world tours.

When the position of pianist became vacant, Nell suggested they might audition her 17-year-old sister. Playing a programme of orchestral music two or three times a day in the era of the Silent Cinema suited the Carson girls. Vi was to remain as a cinema pianist in the Manchester area until 1926, when she fell in love and married. Her husband, George, died only three short years later. By 1929, the 'Talkies' had started, and so Vi began singing songs to her own accompaniment, spending the occasional evening in the Blackpool and Fylde area entertaining at Masonic Ladies evenings.

'And everywhere I went people said, "You ought to be on the wireless!"'

The man who auditioned her, at the Manchester Piccadilly studios of the BBC, was David Porter, whom I was first to meet in 1946 in Hamburg. David had the rare distinction of getting both Violet Carson and Jimmy Edwards 'airborne'. One he himself announced within a month of her audition, the other he taught to fly in the RAF in the early 1940s!

In that 1936 broadcast, Vi sang one of the folk-songs for which she was to become known: the *Riddle Song*. Not long after her debut, the BBC in Manchester invited the composer and arranger, Henry Reed, who'd been with Henry Hall's Orchestra and was now pianist at the Midland Hotel, to form a Northern Variety Orchestra.

In one BBC programme they featured an arrangement by Henry of *Phil the Fluter's Ball*, which Vi was to sing in her first *Variety Show* engagement. The star of the show was Jimmy O'Dea, with two other established stars of radio: Muriel Levy and Doris Gambell, doing their 'Magg and Alice' Liverpudlian act together. It was whilst waiting for the show to go on air that Henry got them round the piano and scribbled out a three-part song for Muriel, Doris and Vi to sing together in close harmony.

'They fitted in beautifully,' recalls Henry, 'and that was the beginning of what were called, "The Three Semis", and they went on broadcasting under that name well into the 1950s.'

Just three years after the start of a professional career in broadcasting, Vi's note-paper proclaimed: 'Radio's North Star, London and Provincial Concerts.' Such concerts now covered a wide range of items for solo pianist, and folk-songs from as far away as the Appalachian mountains of America, and from much nearer home, from Lancashire. As from the January of 1938, Vi was to add a lot of songs especially for children to her growing repertoire, for it was in that month that the organiser of Northern *Children's Hour* was to say: 'Hello children. We're beginning today with a programme for our smallest listeners, which we've called, *Nursery Sing-Song*!'

Tuesdays, 5.0 p.m. From the north, *Children's Hour* and 'Nursery Sing-Song' with Vi

Then came the tune of *Boys and Girls Come out to Play*, a theme which was to herald that particular programme for over twenty-one years.

There were acting parts too for Vi. First in *Children's Hour* in a range of roles, then in adult radio drama when producer Ted Wilkinson was looking for people to play in Priestley's *Good Companions*. Her first leading role was as Mrs Dorbel in *Love on the Dole*. There were leading roles of an entirely different kind as pianist with the BBC Northern Orchestra under their conductor, Charles Groves, beginning with a performance of the 'Caprice Waltz' from *The Wedding Cake* by Saint-Saens. Unfortunately, as I later discovered when preparing my feature on Violet Carson, no recordings of Vi's performance with the Northern Orchestra exist. I therefore arranged to have the piano part of this same work sent to her home at Bispham, together with a covering letter explaining I would telephone when she and Nell had returned from a brief holiday. Although it was now 1981, I knew from my own visits that there was still a piano and a piano stool in the Carson household. What's more I even offered to have the piano tuned before we came to record.

'Just you tell him when he *does* ring,' declared an emphatic Miss Carson to her bemused sister, 'just you tell him that I haven't touched the blasted thing in over twenty years and what's more, when *he's* over eighty, he'll also have rheumatic joints I shouldn't wonder!'

Then, according to Nellie's own account of the conversation, Vi added with even more force, 'Not that *he* could ever play!'

In the event, when they returned from that holiday, Nellie was out shopping when *he* telephoned. It was a very different tone of voice which said to me, 'Well, dear, I *will* do my best. I've rehearsed and rehearsed it. You *do* only want the opening bars?'

On the day we went to record, Nellie took me aside. 'It's been a tonic to see her playing again. Since Vi's not been well enough to do *The Street*, she's needed something on which to concentrate. This has really made her work, *and* she's enjoyed it despite all the grousing!'

Apart from being fine musicians, Mrs Carson taught her daughters to be highly domesticated and good cooks. It was Nell who'd done a perfectly splendid coq-au-vin, with plenty of the vin, the day we did the recordings. The orders came from her: 'Now, Vi, dear, you go and make the coffee – and don't drop the tray!'

But back in 1949 when I first met Vi, she was at her zenith as a musician. She and Nell gave broadcast recitals together. In contrast, the tune *Have A Go, Joe* was known to millions of listeners to the Light Programme. Week by week, for six seasons, Vi was that most accomplished of accompanists on *Have A Go,* playing anything and everything often on some old instruments, which hardly deserved the name piano and often in keys almost unknown to anyone but the happy contestant, who was encouraged to sing on the wireless by the genial host, Wilfred Pickles.

The first time Vi and I worked together was on that original *Cameo Cartoon*, when she played the part of the baby rabbit, Floppy. A few months later I'd cast her as Marmaduke Mouse's firm and kind mother, who sang her yearning offspring to sleep with the words of my lullaby, which went:

> Be content with what you have,
> Like your other broth-ers.
> They are happy just because,
> They don't envy oth-ers …

Later still, I took the *Pied Piper* story as the basis for another of the musical cartoons. It always seemed a pity that the children of Hamelin were left locked away inside that mountain, so in my version of the story, Hans the cripple boy discovers a way of releasing them. The Pied Piper relents, but not before Hans and one of the grieving townswomen have searched the cold mountaintop for all the missing youngsters. As the boy's cries were echoed back again, so Vi sang, in a beautiful contralto voice:

> No child to care for;
> That child is away.
> No sounds of laughter
> From children at their play.
>
> Doors need no locking
> At the end of day,
> Cradles need no rocking,
> For he's taken them a-way …

In stark contrast was the later re-appearance of 'Floppy', which came about as a result of a phone call from David Davis, who asked if we'd be doing anything special that March 21st.

'Why the twenty-first?' I enquired.

'Because it will be the first day of spring, so how about another *Cameo Cartoon*?'

And so Floppy was to awaken once again, this time from a very deep sleep down a very deep burrow in order to greet the spring. Ray Martin gave a lovely sort of blues treatment to the song, which Vi sang entitled, 'I Feel Terrible' in the cartoon, *Spring Fever*.

In between times she was Mrs Parkinson in the Muriel Levy comedy series of *Tinker and Tapp* the radio handymen; Lollypop's mum; and the person who regularly went over the Piano Examination pieces for those young listeners who were taking their Primary Grade, List A and Grade 7, pointing out during the broadcast the various pitfalls to be avoided. And regularly on Tuesdays at 5.00 p.m. on the National Home Service, she would join us for *Nursery Sing-Song*, often proposing to me over the air as she sang:

> 'Soldier, soldier, won't you marry me …?'
> To which I always had to reply:
> 'Ah no, sweet maid, I cannot marry thee,
> For I've got a wife of my own!'

That was certainly true from 1952 when Vi attended our wedding at Pott Shrigley church in Cheshire, giving Margaret and me a set of beautifully hand-made tablemats as a wedding present. In later times she came, always most willingly, to open local Fetes or to take part in Fund-Raising concerts in the Macclesfield area, something she was to do increasingly in the years ahead. When I asked her on behalf of some local organisation, she always said, 'Of course, dear, but *no* percussion bands!'

As a new broom with *Nursery Sing-Song*, I'd brought in the percussion band of Bramhall County Primary School to make a change and to liven up proceedings. Vi and I finished singing, *They're Changing Guard at Buckingham Palace*, but not the band. Did they heck! They went on banging and clanging away on their drums and cymbals as my 'thank yous' became louder and more anguished as the seconds ticked away, for at 5.15 precisely, we were to join *Children's Hour* from London for the rest of that day's programme. At five seconds to go, our BBC man on the studio control panel did a nice, 'Fade Out on Percussion'.

At other times we had four and five year olds with us in the studio – but never parents. Our *Children's Hour* secretaries, headed by Pat Paull, looked after them, having pinned name cards onto our visitors. During one live programme, a little lad murmured, 'I know a poem!' I looked at his card. 'Do you, Richard? Are you going to let us hear it?'

Richard came closer to the microphone as I beckoned to him. 'It's about Fairies,' he said, then took a very deep breath, and declared to the Nation: 'There are bottoms on the fairies in OUR garden …'

(Cue in Percussion Band – quickly.)

We had older audiences in for two music series that I started after I'd become Organiser of Children's Programmes in the north of England. One was a *Broadcast Rehearsal* with the Northern Variety Orchestra, now under the auspices of the young up-and-coming Alyn Ainsworth, who would rehearse the orchestra and artists whilst 'on the air'. The other, which always featured Doris Gambell and Violet Carson, was simply called *At Home with Doris and Vi*.

One week they were to be followed by another visit from the popular Gerald Isles and his *Animals from Belle Vue Zoo*. Gerald and the Head Keeper, Mr Kelly, arrived whilst Doris and Vi were on the air. In bringing the first two or three animals out of their cages, I noticed that Gerald was holding one end of a lead whilst a very small mischievous monkey was clutching the harness it *should* have been wearing at the other end of the lead. Dropping this, the monkey sprang forward onto the long arm of a microphone boom, running all the way up to the top whilst Doris was right in the middle of a fairly serious aria. The audience greeted the monkey's antics with hardly suppressed laughter. That laughter grew even louder when Vi clenched her fists, firmly closed her eyes and said in a loud voice, 'If it comes near me, I shall scream. I shall scream!'

That's just what the audience did. Long before the coda of Doris's song had finished, I announced to the listeners that Miss Gambell wasn't pulling funny faces or anything like that. We didn't entice the culprit back into his box until long after Gerald's programme had ended. At least on this occasion he stayed to take all his animals home, not like the time we'd been at Leasowe Children's Hospital in Liverpool. The matron phoned me when I'd got back to Manchester to say she'd be obliged if I could contact Belle Vue Zoo and arrange for the collection of a couple of snakes, which had come to light in one of the wards. (Not only books, chocolates and torches are hidden under children's bedclothes!)

But it wasn't all *Children's Hour* for Violet Carson. There were more and more adult plays to do for London and for Regional producers, *Woman's Hour* to introduce from the North, Feature programmes, and, from early in 1951, a series we did together for the Light Programme on alternate Sunday evenings. One week it was Semprini, the next Violet Carson with songs at the piano, which I announced – but not in the same way they'd printed it in the *Radio Times*, which proudly proclaimed: '*Singing and Playing For You* – Songs at the Piano by Violent Carson.'

I suppose I must admit that Vi did get a little 'violent' towards the end of rehearsals for the first episode of a serial I was doing called *The Secret of Hollow Hill.* Philip Jenkinson and Billie Whitelaw were nicely behaved youngsters as usual, but I'd brought over to the Leeds studio a boy from Swinton, named Tony Simpson. A year before we'd tried him out after audition in *Take Your Cue* and, later that same week, given him a small part in one of the popular Molly Griffin serials about the Locke family. Either Vi or Rosalie Williams always seemed to land the 'mother' parts. It was Rosalie who was to give a final performance for me as mother to Ian McKellen in a serialisation of Howard Spring's novel, *Fame is the Spur.*

For *The Secret of Hollow Hill*, however, Vi wasn't anyone's mother or indeed 'Aunt' for a change. No, this time she was plain Bridie, an Irish nurse who had Tony Simpson, in the role of Jonathan, in her charge. But like many youngsters, Tony was keen to learn all he could about Radio and how things were done, and so he kept asking questions and chatting away to all and sundry. After an hour or so of this, Bridie bristled, and said in a voice that carried more of a promise than a threat:

'If that young ... lad doesn't belt up, I'll smack his bottom!'

In bringing Violet Carson and Tony Simpson together that October day in 1951, I think I may possibly have started something, for as Tony was to explain in later years, 'We were to rehearse one episode of that *Hollow Hill* serial and then to record it on what was called 'down the line' to London. And so we got all keyed up ready to do it. The Leeds Control Room talked to London but then lost contact with them. As we waited and waited, Vi decided to entertain us. I remember she sat down at the piano, slid off a knuckle-full of rings, and then she sang, *Bowton's Yard.*'

> At No. 1 in Bowton's Yard,
> Me grannie keeps a school ...
> At No. 3, right facin' pub ...

'I was absolutely transfixed and for years and years, that song stayed in my head!'

It certainly was for all of nine years, because in 1961, having changed his name to Tony Warren he was to create a character named 'Ena

Vi Carson, four years *before* 'Ena Sharples' came on to our TV screens

Sharples' and to devise *Coronation Street*, writing all the early, formative episodes himself. Tony went on to say, 'After *Coronation Street* was a success, Vi, in her own right as a singer, issued an album, and *Bowton's Yard* was on it. And I stopped and thought that song has been in my head all those years! And I wonder? I wonder if that *was* the inspiration for *Coronation Street* – and it was Vi's singing that had given it to me!'

There are many many more of Vi's songs that remain with people of my age: *The Lancashire Lullaby*, *Toad's Courtship* and *The Three Dragons*. This song featured in the very first television appearance Vi was to make for me in a BBC Variety programme I called *Out of the Bran Tub*. It came from the Hulme Hippodrome as an Outside Broadcast because Manchester had no television studio at that time. I was the dithering Director, but Vi was to take to Television as she'd taken to Radio with lead parts in such Manchester-produced BBC TV productions as *Job for the Boy*, *When we are Married,* (a play she did so many times on radio), and *June Evening*.

But then came an invitation from BBC producer, Peter Dews, who offered Vi a small part, as the Duchess of York in his televised Shakespearean series, *An Age of Kings*. To Vi this was one of the true highlights of her whole career.

'Now *that* I revelled in. I was never nervous; I adored the sweep of it, I loved the words – it was more like music. I was playing a *part*; I was not me. I wasn't anyone in a street that I knew; I was the Duchess of York!'

And when viewers saw the Duchess working on a tapestry, it was all done by Vi herself, a tapestry she began at the start of the rehearsals.

In the early 1960s when Margaret was writing the *Pinky and Perky* BBC TV series, we happened to be in Blackpool to see Jan and Vlasta Dalibor, their creators.

'Let's call and see the Carsons,' Margaret declared.

Mrs Carson was in, now almost entirely blind but as bright as a button especially after putting a new battery into her hearing aid. She took us on a tour of the house, which had now been added to and improved, with an even larger and beautifully tended garden. We kept thinking that her daughters might return any moment from Vi's Saturday engagement to open some large Supermarket that demanded a Superstar, for now it was only on such occasions that Nellie managed to get away for a few hours. On a table in the lounge was a lovely photo of Mrs Carson's elder daughter on the day she received her OBE from the Queen.

'You must be very proud of Vi,' I observed.

Turning on the Blackpool Illuminations

'Yes, my dear, I am,' affirmed her aged mama. 'She was wonderful as the Duchess of York!'

I gently explained that I was referring to Vi and to her success in *Coronation Street*.

'Oh *that*! I only watched it once,' came the reply, 'That's not our Vi!'

We phoned Vi and Nellie later that evening, hoping our visit hadn't tired out their mother. Vi sniffed. 'Of course for you she *would* put in a new battery! Nell and I have to shout our heads off as we have to watch the old ones warming up besides the fire!'

I enquired after 'Ena' – only to be told that she is left firmly behind, locked inside the vestry until another episode of *The Street*. But Vi's personal appearances were pretty spectacular – without the hairnet. There was the occasion when Violet Carson switched on the Blackpool lights, only to disappear for a moment in order to don the hairnet and Ena took over. The stars certainly shone all along the Golden Mile that night! Then there was the tour of Australia with sister Nellie and, perhaps the finest accolade of all in Vi's own estimation, the naming of a rose after her by Sam McReady.

Programme Number : RNT 351 V 315

" A PITY SUCCESS HAS COME SO LATE! "

perhaps to Ena Sharples

but not to

VIOLET

CARSON

who recalls her childhood in Manchester
and professional life as a pianist,
singer and actress on radio and tv

Programme introduced
by
GEOFFREY WHEELER

Written and Produced

by

TREVOR HILL

Rehearsal and
Pre-Recording : Monday 12th January, 1981 STUDIO 3, Manchester
1000 - 1800

Tape No : TMR02/351V315N

TRANSMISSION : (WEEK 9) Friday 6th March, 1981 : RADIO 4 1105-1150

Cover for programme about Violet

A love of gardens and of gardening often crept into her radio broadcasts. *Gardening Hints and Tips* was a regular feature of *Children's Hour* with Fred Loads, Doris and Vi. For my feature which I mentioned earlier taking the title from that man on the train: 'A Pity Success Has Come So Late In Life', I went straight from Vi and Nellie's home to record Fred Loads, who was also now laid low. He talked about her roses at some length.

'And you'll be pleased to know I've put "Violet Carson" in a large bed with "Fred Loads" and with "Franklin Engelmann" and we're all doing very well,' he said.

The day after that broadcast, Vi was on the telephone:

'I'm *so* glad to have heard *and* to have taken part in my own obituary,' she said, with more than a note of laughter in her voice.

Sadly, the programme was to be repeated by the BBC as an obituary to Violet Carson within a few days of her death. At her Memorial Service in Manchester Cathedral, where she'd been both baptised and married, Sir Charles Groves and William Roach touched on her many talents. Of herself – and I always knew our Vi to be forthright and completely honest – she said in that final broadcast: 'I'm a very lucky woman, ...

Vi tries her hand at Radio's latest Control Panel

who's been offered all the riches that any woman could be offered, and I *hope* I've made the most of them.'

And then she sang that final verse of *Bowton's Yard*, by her fellow Lancastrian, Samuel Laycock.

And now I've done I'll say goodbye
And leave you for a while.
I know I haven't towd me tale,
In such a fust-rate style;
But if your pleased, I'm satisfied,
An' ask for no reward
For tellin' who mi neighbours are
As live in Bowton's Yard!

10

Wilfred Pickles

The Earl of Derby's butler, Davis, found us in the Stewards' Room at Knowsley.

'Would Mr Pickles oblige by autographing this?' he enquired politely. Resting upon a napkin in the centre of a gleaming silver salver he held was, of all things, a builder's brick. The Comptroller of Lord Derby's household, Captain McKinney, roared with laughter.

'I bet it's the first time you've been invited to sign anything like that!'

It was March 1954. Wilfred had just taken over as interviewer and narrator for *Afternoon Out,* visits to some of the stately homes of England. This radio series was broadcast nationally and had been devised by Margaret a year earlier. Each programme dealt with the history of the family, the house and some of its contents. Scenes from the past were re-enacted by a studio cast of professionals. At that time, Wilfred and his wife, Mabel, had their main home in Disley, Cheshire and we'd been to collect them earlier that day.

Margaret had begun the programme with Wilfred arriving not at the public entrance to Knowsley Hall but at Liverpool Lodge, the impressive main entrance with its round tower on the right and square tower on the left, both joined by an arch. A small sign on a side door proclaimed, 'Bring Good News, and knock boldly.' And he did. Mrs Ellis, whose husband was a forester on the Knowsley estate, welcomed Wilfred and the listeners. After a short recording with her, the BBC staff car and mobile recording car sped up the long drive to the hall itself. It was there that we saw a large gang of bricklayers building a new wall. On her initial visit to Knowsley in order to discuss the programme content with

Lord Derby and his Comptroller, Margaret had noticed that there must be a window in that house for every day of the year. Now, Wilfred was to interview the man who had the job of cleaning them. As our dependable recording engineer for that day, Jimmy Brett, began to set up the equipment, those brickies were quick to recognise the celebrity in their midst.

''Ow do!' called out a voice widely known in those days, by a weekly audience of some seventeen million listeners! Soon, some of the brickies had gathered round Wilfred.

'Think *you* could do this, Wilfred?' quipped one of the younger men, eyeing the neat handmade shoes and an immaculately tailored coat from Saville Row.

''appen I'll try,' came the reply. 'Here Mabel, grab hold of this, will you?' as his coat was folded and draped across her arm. So Wilfred moved up to where the men were laying a recent course. 'Nah than, what exactly do I do?'

An older, more experienced man stepped forward. 'I'll show you, Mr Pickles.'

Then all worked stopped as others were beckoned forward. Wilfred watched intently.

'Just er, ... just do that bit again, eh?'

A hod of bricks was placed by him, also a bucket of mortar, then he was handed a trowel. Standing with legs slightly apart, Wilfred whisked into action, the left hand throwing up a brick, catching it right-side up and correctly balanced, whilst the right hand had already put down and laid out just the right amount of mortar. A tap with the handle of the trowel, a flash of the blade as it cleaned off the surplus mortar and neatly pointed the joint within a matter of seconds, and so another brick seemed to take flight. The nudging and winking ceased more quickly than the smiles on a sea of faces.

'Alright, alright,' said the foreman. 'Come clean!'

And Wilfred did, as he carried on helping to build that wall, but now at a more leisurely pace. Yes, he'd been an apprentice bricklayer himself as a youth; his father, a stonemason, employed Wilfred for a time in his own building firm. Then he went on to tell his new-found friends how he'd been born at No. 24, Conway Street, Halifax in 1904.

'I tell people that I'm proud to say there's a plate outside that door! (pause) It says, Gas Main 15 feet!'

Wilfred Pickles certainly had a knack with people. He was at the pinnacle of his career in those early days of the 1950s, bringing ordinary working folk, as he chose to call them, into the homes of nearly twenty million listeners, topping the bill in variety shows and stage plays. Later he was also to be seen throughout the land on Television as star actor, interviewer and performer.

His springboard was the phenomenal success *Have A Go* which, believe it or not, started life in the USA under the title *Quiz Bang*. It was brought back to Manchester by John Salt, who'd been the BBC representative in New York during some of the war years and, with his wife Olive Shapley, had now returned as Director of Programmes for the North Region of the BBC. Wilfred changed the title himself. The programme changed Wilfred; it almost swamped him.

'Afternoon out' at the Castle Museum York, with Pat Patterson, Curator

As my wife Margaret went ahead in arranging and scripting for *Afternoon Out*, she could sense how some reacted to his name.

'He'll not ask me if I'm courting, or if I've had any embarrassing moments, will he?'

The day we were to commence recordings at the Castle Museum in York the chairman of the committee seemed very concerned.

'I hope he won't call me by my Christian name! Of course I shall refer to him as Mr Pickles ...'

Margaret explained that Mr Pickles would be just as formal as befitted the chairman's office. Things took a different tone from the moment they met and we began recording.

'Hello, Wilfred! Welcome to th' Castle Museum, Wilfred. And where's Mabel?'

We were making the Knowsley Hall recordings during the week of the Grand National at Aintree. The Earl and Countess had a house party and they were all away at the races until the early evening of our first day. Walking through the private apartments to get to the next venue, we noticed two circular tables in one room. The first was laid for dinner with gold plate, the other in solid silver. In an adjoining drawing room, a tea table was set for just the family to partake of tea. Mabel thought it a nice homely touch when she noticed the jar of Marmite reposing on a filigree-edged silver saucer.

'Her Ladyship will not permit it to be decanted,' observed Davis.

Later that day, Captain McKinney came to say that the Earl and Countess would like the four of us to join their house party for drinks before dinner. What I remember most about that evening is seeing Wilfred in animated conversation with a distinguished figure in smart evening dress, but wearing a pair of snakeskin slippers. Lord Rosebery and Wilfred were sitting on a long fireside stool.

'You know I'm mentioned in the song *Burlington Bertie*?' exclaimed his Lordship.

'Of course, so you are,' replied Wilfred. To prove it they broke into song together then and there.

It was the Countess of Derby who'd noticed the scene in the script depicting the opening of the State Dining Room at Knowsley, and what caught her eye were my Technical instructions at the bottom of the previous page. 'String music in background, and the sounds of people chattering and glasses clinking.' I assured the Countess that I had no objection whatsoever to the request she now made. I made a quick phone call to Jimmy Brett, a former member of Lord Louis Mountbatten's staff and used to jumping into action. Leaving his quiet glass of ale in the Steward's Room he was already setting up a microphone as the entire house party adjourned to the State Dining Room in order to provide 'background chatter'. As we took a recording level, I could distinctly hear two distinguished voices saying 'rhubarb-rhubarb-rhubarb' but I soon sorted that out.

'Remember it *is* supposed to be the year 1821!'

But that most gracious of gentlemen, Lord Rosebery, was looking quite sad. He'd taken part in the background chatter which the script called for and then noticed the dialogue to be spoken by the studio cast. In the short speech at the 1821 inaugural dinner a certain General Grosvenor had commented upon the two sixteen-foot high doors. Lord Rosebery now wanted us to record *him* saying, 'Pray, are these great doors to be opened for every pat of butter that comes into th' room, um, um?'

It was Wilfred who had to disappoint him, and explained about Equity, the Actors' Union.

Acting seems to have been in Wilfred's blood since childhood. At the age of 13, and with his father in the army during the First World War, he became a 'half-timer' determined to help out at home, perhaps to start as a 'doffer' as they called the young lads who began in the Weaving Sheds. But his mother would have none of that. She'd been a weaver herself in the mills. Instead, Wilfred presented himself for interview as a likely lad to Mitchell's Gentlemen's Outfitters. He was taken on as errand boy in the mornings, attended half-day school in the afternoons and then in the evenings he was out and about, getting to know the town he was born in. He delivered a trouser press here, with a 6d tip, a box of ladies' blouses there and sometimes only a 3d tip. He was always visiting the local library and going to see plays as often as he could afford to. He certainly found the cash to sit in the gods and watch the great Fred Terry in *The Scarlet Pimpernel*. It was almost too much when Terry walked into Mitchell's and they met face to face – not to discuss theatre with his ardent admirer, you understand, but to purchase a suitable pair of underpants. As they were discreetly proffered for examination, so Wilfred noticed the manufacturer's label. In a flash he now saw the great Fred Terry in another role, as Cardinal 'Wolseley'.

As in all the best showbiz stories, Wilfred was still only of tender years when he trod the boards with actor-manager Henry Baynton, when that worthy brought his renowned Shakespearean Company to Halifax. In the role of Brutus, Baynton, with all eyes upon him, patted young

Pickles upon the head as he strolled among the local amateurs he'd brought into the theatre that week to play the crowd scenes.

Some years later, when an active member of the Halifax Thespians, Wilfred was visiting his family who had recently moved to Ainsdale near Southport. There, he caught up with Arthur Belt, a former producer with the Manchester Repertory Company. Would Wilfred care to attend a read-through of *The Jeffersons,* a play Arthur was hoping to put on with the local Amateur Dramatic Society? Although eager at first, Wilfred then discovered that the producer was really looking and hoping for a replacement to play opposite the attractive red-headed member of the society, who had the role of Jefferson's daughter. Wilfred wasn't going to snatch the lead from the lad who'd been studying it for days on end, and Mabel Mysercough wasn't keen on the idea either. But at least she and Wilfred smiled at each other when they met – if only because both had flaming red hair. Wilfred sat down with the rest of the amateur cast, read the part in for them, then enquired if he might enrol as a member. He was introduced to the red-head's father, a former Theatrical Manager, who had formed this Southport society, and to her two brothers. It was Arthur Belt who provided Wilfred with their home address before he thanked one and all and left.

That Sunday, Miss Mysercough's brother, John, noticed the smart Mr Pickles outside their house. Was it something to do with the play? Being an informal and hospitable family they invited him in. Er, yes, there *was* something. He knew about stage make-up and wondered, could he perhaps help out with that? When asked to take a little refreshment, Wilfred noticed the large and ornate sideboard from which Mrs Mysercough, even now, was taking slim elegant glasses.

'By, but that 'ud look right champion in a pub!' he beamed. The Mysercough family would have referred to 'an hotel'.

That slip apart, it was the start of almost fifty years together for Wilfred and Mabel Pickles. At the beginnings of the depression in Lancashire and Yorkshire in 1930, they were married, with his workmates from his father's building firm making an archway of picks and shovels, and later using them to build the house the newlyweds were to live in. But house buying slumped, the firm went bankrupt and they lost their home. Eventually, having to settle for rented accommodation near Liverpool, Wilfred had various jobs but months of no work at all, and now there was their son, David, to care for. The one luxury they did manage to afford, and even that had to go back on one occasion, was the rented wireless set.

Listening in to an evening play and in particular the actor taking the

Wilfred and Mabel Pickles

lead, Mabel got quite annoyed. She was positive Wilfred could do better than that. The BBC in Piccadilly Gardens in Manchester must have thought he was good at accents, dialects and also at doing straight voices, because not long after his audition came the offer to take the part of Sir Frederick in Jan Bussel's production of *The Mystery of the Cutting*. But no one was to hear it. King George V died that day and Walford Davis's *Solemn Melody* was broadcast instead.

Wilfred did, however, do a lot of broadcasting for Olive Shapley, who before the war was running *Children's Hour* from the North of England. She remembers him popping in and out of engagements and soon twigged that he must have other, more regular work. It was knocking on door after door as the 'Kleeneze' man!

'It's on The Table Mabel!', so Have a Go!

When the Pickles stayed with us, as they sometimes did once they'd left Disley and moved permanently to their London flat, Wilfred would talk to us about those early days, often breaking into dialect for the sort of Lancashire and Yorkshire stories he'd collected since childhood. He'd also set to memory a quite astonishing range of English poetry and prose. The few shillings he'd saved as a boy for the complete works of Shakespeare was money well spent. When the Halifax Thespians did *Julius Caesar* they suddenly found themselves without a Brutus. Wilfred memorised the part for them at short notice, in two days. This gift lasted him all his life.

Wilfred and Mabel were to join Margaret and myself for a short holiday in the Lake District. We waited expectantly for them on the platform of Windermere station. As the local diesel pulled in so a fellow all dolled up in anorak, oilskin trousers tucked into stout climbing boots and with haversack swathed in ropes, was helping an elegantly dressed lady out of the compartment. We instantly recognised Mabel, and then we heard the man's voice just before he turned to face us.

'Nah then, ... Got us togs together, lass?' Her husband had borrowed items from six or seven slightly bewildered but amused young students who were going climbing in the Lakes. We took Wilfred and Mabel to the boat we kept on Windermere, cast off and had lunch as we sailed down to the hotel at Lakeside. The next day I drove us around in the car. We had strict instructions to stop at Varty's bookshop in Keswick. Wilfred had dealt with old man Varty for years, considering it a major victory when he could prise the particular First Edition he wanted away from a dealer who rarely seemed to want to part with such treasure. Now, it was the son who discussed books and old times with this avid collector and reader. Then we were off towards Cockermouth along the Borrowdale valley.

'Er, slow down a moment, will you? Nah then ...' I was given precise instructions. Right at next junction, along for about a mile. Left into the farmyard.

'I wonder if Noble Bland will be at home?' I heard him say to Mabel.

As I turned into the yard, so a young woman was lifting a baby from its pram. Wilfred greeted her by her Christian name. And yes, the Blands were at home. Wilfred remembered interviewing him on *Have A Go*, and shortly afterwards he'd been once to this farm – which had been eighteen years ago!

That holiday was full of such surprises for Margaret and myself and many places we had visited were to be remembered and amusingly recounted by Wilfred in a hand-written letter he sent us, which bore the address, Dove Cottage, Town End, Grasmere, home of the Wordsworths!

My dear friends,

I talk of you perpetually, for then I see you everywhere; here are three days from my journals as I promised.

Feb. 15. A beautiful frosty morning. I am busy making William's woollen waistcoat. Wm unwell and did not walk. Mrs Rushton from the village asked if Wm had tried whiskey. I said 'Yes, that is why he cannot walk.'

I remain your sincere friend,
Dorothy W.

PS I spent the summer of '95 at Halifax. I have no recollection of the family you mention, Builders, I think you said they were? I can only imagine that their name was derived from the Pig-Hills of Sowerby. I am certain that my Aunt Rawson would not associate with anybody with such an obnoxious name.

D

The one thing Wilfred and Mabel rarely talked about was something that had made a great difference to their lives: the death of their seven-year-

An 'evening out' at one of England's stately homes featured in the Margaret Potter series

old son, David, through contracting infantile paralysis. Two things were to grow from that grief. Later, when they were in a position to do so, they insisted that the BBC let them do Radio and Television programmes on Christmas Day from various Children's Hospitals. Those went on for years, but at the time Wilfred made another decision, which was to bring them happiness. David's death completely broke Mabel, who had already lost one child in pregnancy, so Wilfred determined that in future, and where possible, they would go everywhere together.

When Margaret, as scriptwriter, and myself as producer began to work regularly with the Pickles in the mid-1950s, I thought it strange at first that Mabel often accompanied Wilfred when we were away recording on location for *Afternoon Out.* It was our good fortune that she did come, for now we had someone who would chat happily to the under-footman or the Duke, smoothing away nerves as they awaited their turn to be interviewed.

We spent quite a lot of time travelling, working and staying in hotels. And when staying in their home in Devonshire Street in London, Mabel would provide excellent home cooking, and Wilfred the entertainment after the meal, often reading poetry and dialect prose to us late into the night. Not all his stories, however, were suitable for broadcasting.

Wilfred was one of the best read of men I had ever met. He delighted in presenting *The Pleasure's Mine*, his verse series for the Light Programme, or reading sets of the delightful *Matilda Mouse* stories for us in *Children's Hour*. I tried time and time again to persuade J.B. Priestley's agent to let Wilfred read *The Good Companions*, but to no avail.

'He's written better books since then,' was the agent's constant reply.

More in frustration than in anything else, I asked Wilfred to have a word with J.B. Only a matter of days later, the voice I knew so well from those *Postscript* days was speaking to me – and over my own phone at home.

'Yes, yes, Mr Priestley, of *course*, Mr Priestley. I'll let A.D. Peters see the adaptation first. No trouble at all, Mr Priestley!'

But then the tone of voice the other end altered: 'Nah then, ... another of those BBC crawlers?' It was Wilfred. Yes, he had spoken to Jack and added, 'I was just about to tell him what he could do with *The Good Companions*, binding an' all, when the great man said to me, "read on, dear boy, read on"!' and Wilfred did – *The Good Companions* followed by *Angel Pavement*! The voices he gave to Priestley's finely drawn characters were superb, even those for women.

Shortly after Wilfred died, on Easter Monday, 1978, the BBC phoned me at home to ask if I would write his obituary programme. We'd been too close during the years we worked together as colleagues on Radio and on Television and as friends, for me to be completely objective perhaps. But then I felt that Wilfred's *Have A Go* image might be given undue prominence – and that was less than half the man I knew.

I called the programme *Man of Radio* for that was surely his first love. J.B. Priestley, bless him, did a lovely piece. Amongst the things he said about Wilfred was this: 'I've always been told that he did a very fine reading of *The Good Companions*, but I must be truthful and tell you that I didn't listen to it because... (pause) no, no, don't pull a face at me ... (laughs) because I don't want a long work of mine read back to me, however good the reader is. But I'm ready to hear a little of it now.'

I got the BBC Sound Archives to look out a recording of *Aaron's Field*, a 1939 verse play written by one of the founders of the Radio Feature, D.G. Bridson. The Archive assistant rang back. Yes, they had a recording. Which part did Wilfred Pickles play and would I like it copied? I explained that Wilfred played *all* the parts in that feature, except for that of Aaron, the owner of the field. There were Archive recordings of Wilfred doing *A New English Journey* with Priestley in 1940, which gave a picture of just how radically full employment on War Production had altered things for the people Priestley had met five or six years earlier for his book, *English Journey*. There were recordings of Wilfred as a BBC wartime Newsreader in 1941 and 42; of him in a very different role, again created by D.G. Bridson. It was that of 'Billy Welcome' putting across wartime propaganda at Aircraft factories, down Coal mines, in Munitions works. Archives found it difficult, if not impossible, to discern the many voices of Wilfred Pickles when none of the *Have A Go* intonations were present. They were completely baffled when I asked for a copy of his performance as Trimalchio in Louis MacNeice's Third Programme production of *Trimalchio's Feast*. Yes, they had the play, but was that *really* Wilfred Pickles?

Olive Shapley always liked the comment made to her when she was talking about the BBC to a large audience in a school hall. 'Marvellous is that Wilfred Pickles,' an old man explained after Olive had been talking about him as a Radio actor. 'Horatio one moment, a bloody dormouse th' next!'

That distinguished producer of radio features, R.D. Smith once did an update on Bunyon with *Wilfred Pilgrim's Progress*, in which the man of many voices played every part, with the exception of the female, including that of a Viennese. As he was appearing in the stage play *The Gay Dog* at the time the broadcast was going out and wouldn't be able to hear it. He handed me a spanking new tape recorder.

'Would you record the programme for me? Oh and just let me have the tape back, not the contraption. I can't work it anyway!'

We had the machine for years before handing it on to our Village School. Which brings me to the subject of giving. For reasons that I shall never understand, and you'll have this from many who *really* knew him, Wilfred was not a mean man. Quite the reverse. I've listened to people saying, 'Ah, but he told so-and-so that he wanted a fee of £250 and it's for Charity, it's all for Charity!'

Not once have I come face to face with the person Wilfred was supposed to have said that to. All I *do* know beyond any shadow of doubt is that Wilfred and Mabel actively supported many Charities and not one in the name of 'Pickles'. Denness Roylance was not only my Administrative Assistant for many years; she had worked with Wilfred long before we met in Manchester, and whilst working with me, Denness also acted as a part-time secretary to Wilfred. When cheques came in, they came into my office and they were made out to such things as 'The Wilfred Pickles School for Spastics, Dudington'. Various solicitors also contacted us over the years when their clients had intimated they wished to leave a legacy to a charity nominated by Wilfred. Those charities were all, in some form or other, to do with children.

It was in September 1955 that the BBC on Radio and Television celebrated Wilfred and Mabel's Silver Wedding anniversary, with a toast to their continued health and happiness proposed by John Snagge. The following evening the Pickles gave a lavish party for family and friends at the Savoy. That same night they travelled on the sleeper from London to York in order to join us for another programme from the Castle Museum. As Margaret and I sat having an early breakfast, I saw the headline in one of the daily papers: 'Who pays for it? The BBC!' It was Fleet Street at its worst in reporting their party at the Savoy. I wanted to phone Wilfred's agent, Julius Darewski, the moment they arrived. Wilfred glanced at the item then said of me to Margaret, 'A right little worrier, isn't he?' and went on to explain that any comment from him would only be misquoted and, anyway, he'd learned to live with the legend that he was a tight-fisted Yorkshireman. 'It's when they *don't* talk about me, I'll worry!'

When he and Mabel were appearing together in the successful BBC series *Ask Pickles*, the forerunner of *Jim'll Fix It*, only certain requests could be carried out; those of a more unusual appeal or nature. There was nothing unusual about a child writing in to say she'd love a party dress. Without knowing anything about such a request, I was staying with the Pickles whilst editing a film at Shepherd's Bush. One evening they asked if I'd mind driving them to Stepney as, by now, Wilfred had given up driving. Mabel brought out a large box from the one bedroom they used as an office and I took it down in the lift to put into the car. As we drove so they told me what they were up to.

'Are we meeting the Press there?' I enquired.

'We want no damn photographers or reporters, thanks all the same,' was Wilfred's curt reply. I found the street and the house. The three of us went inside and Mabel quietly did the honours. The child was overjoyed but her mother fled the room in tears. It was a lovely dress chosen with thought and care for a young person who wouldn't feel embarrassed by wearing it in her own surroundings, together with a pair of shoes *and* a handbag. The shoe size was only a guess and so Wilfred had them posted back later.

It was at York the morning after the Savoy party that a large crowd of well-wishers gathered on the steps of the Castle Museum to see the arrival of the Pickles. Margaret and I went from the hotel on foot and joined our old friend, Robert Patterson, the Museum Curator, who was waiting to greet them. They arrived a few minutes later in a large limousine. As the 'Hellos', the 'Good Lucks' and the 'God bless yous' rang out, a woman standing next to Margaret said, 'I wonder if they got my card?'

A lot of folk wished them well and drank their health that week, and Wilfred also liked a drink. In point of fact he liked several drinks in his later years. Then, he exercised self-discipline and expected it from those working with him, particularly when he and a cast were in a long-running stage production with hardly an empty seat in all those huge Touring Theatres from Bournemouth to Blackpool. It wasn't a case of 'the hair of the dog' that bit him just before the opening night of *The Gay Dog* in Brighton, but a large Alsatian, which gave the magazine *Punch* a field day. The Pickles named their own Alsatian 'Willie Mossop' after Wilfred's stage role in *Hobson's Choice*. It was *Cure for Love* which proved to be his biggest stage success – yet he had doubts about himself and his ability when he knew he was to take over the part of Jack Hardacre from the one and only Robert Donat.

I always felt Wilfred was at his happiest when reading for his own pleasure and when reading for the listener. When he and I worked together on readings for *A Book at Bedtime*, it was always from Broadcasting House in London. Wilfred would arrive, immaculately dressed as usual, but now he would carry with him a smart black briefcase. I sometimes wondered why the scripts had to travel such a short distance, since his Devonshire Street flat was literally just round the corner, but one day he handed the briefcase to me saying, 'You'd best take charge of this.' He opened it and inside were copies of the scripts and a bottle of Gordons. 'W-e-l-l, pour me out just a little 'un when you feel I'm flagging. And water! Don't forget the water.'

The BBC always provided glasses on the table of every Radio studio and a jug of fresh water that was changed at regular intervals. I used to love the arrival of an elderly Studio Attendant. If the Red Transmission light wasn't on, he'd thrust open the control cubicle door with a cheery, 'How's your water?' Just the sort of thing Army medics used to ask. Some days when Wilfred recorded three or even four episodes of a serial reading, the water seemed to go down at an alarming rate, but the storytelling got better and better!

His experience and understanding of Radio Technique made it a bonus

Wilfred Pickles in *South Riding*

to have him in a cast. He was especially encouraging and helpful to many youngsters like Billie Whitelaw and Judith Chalmers, who came into Broadcasting in their early teens. Whilst his name was often above the title of the play in the *Radio Times* billing, he was always on his feet and doing the right sort of 'rhubarb' in the crowd scenes. When he first broadcast for me in *Children's Hour*, I couldn't get over his fee and neither could Wilfred's agent! It was always around ten guineas when I booked him in 1950.

He gave me the same fee when I rang to say that Margaret and I had been commissioned to write the musical *Alice* for the Festival of Britain, and would he be in it. His agent, Julius Darewski, was delighted when I explained this wasn't for *Children's Hour* and that he should negotiate a 'lead' fee with BBC Variety Bookings. Anything other than *Children's Hour* was considerably in excess of ten guineas!

In later years, I was to direct Wilfred in several of the Sunday serials. There was *Mary Barton* and then *South Riding* opposite Anna Cropper and Nigel Davenport. Wilfred always wanted to play the role of Councillor Huggins in Winifred Holtby's splendid novel. This rascally haulage contractor of Pidsey Buttock was also a lay preacher. As his unctuous tones boom around the small chapel, so his very earthy thoughts about one of the choir girls sear his mind and soul as she begins to sing 'What a Friend we have in Jesus'.

Wilfred was a keen and shrewd observer of people with a finely tuned ear for how they spoke. He certainly met and interviewed those from every walk of life. When it came to portraying characters, I'd say things like, 'Do you see him as that twit in London Programme Contracts?'

'No, no, ... much more like that cheerful undertaker chappie we met in Folkstone.'

When Alfred Bradley first worked with Wilfred on a radio adaptation of *Hobson's Choice,* having got Wilfred to accept that he was casting him not as 'Willie' but as the far older 'Mr Hobson', they finished the read-through.

'Is that how you see him?' enquired Wilfred.

'Make him sound a couple of stone heavier,' was his producer's reply.

I share a wish with others I know, that Wilfred should have become a member of the National Theatre, but as he said in one interview I was to use, 'You know, having a twenty-one year old run like *Have A Go* can be a mixed blessing. It keeps you out of other things!'

Well yes, to a point. Yet he managed during that same period to fit in an enormous amount of radio acting, a little Variety work on both stage and radio, and long runs in stage plays, then once *Have A Go* had finished, in such television series as *Caxton's Tales* in which he was a jobbing printer, in *Yorkie* as the village schoolmaster and, later well into the Top Twenty ITV ratings with *For the Love of Ada.* Come to think of it, the only non-success of his career was *Stars On Sunday.* His acting roles on Television began with *Hobson's Choice* and ended in 1976 with a series for Granada, *The Nearly Man*, in which he played the part of a Labour Party agent opposite the highly professional and polished Tony Britton as the member of Parliament. And there were films too – *The Family Way* with Hayley Mills, who was to pay such a nice tribute to Wilfred in the obituary programme I was soon to write and produce.

The very first production to come from the six million pound Studio Complex, known as New Broadcasting House in Manchester – and, Lord, we waited long enough for that – was appropriately enough to be Wilfred's last appearance. Appropriate because it was at the BBC in Manchester that his career began. Now it was a Saturday Night Theatre play by Northern writer William Keenan entitled, *The Dark Windows of a Room*. There were only two lead parts, that of a young police officer and his inspector. Brian Trueman and Geoffrey Banks filled those roles. But the script called for a host of other parts and so in casting them I took the opportunity of inviting those who, like Wilfred, had begun their professional careers in the North and in *Children's Hour*.

So guest parts were taken by Violet Carson, Judith Chalmers and Sandra Chalmers, then editor of *Woman's Hour*, with Nigel Davenport, Bryan Forbes, Philip Jenkinson, BBC Newsreader Bryan Martin, Wilfred, Geoffrey and Peter Wheeler and Billie Whitelaw. Robert Powell would have been in the play, but the day I had to record his scene was his wedding day. I also tried to get hold of Peter Maxwell Davies as the pianist in a low dive, but he was up on Hoy, beavering away.

In Wilfred's case, I vividly recalled that character in the *Pilgrim's Progress*, the Viennese psychiatrist. In Bill Keenan's play, the whole thing centred on the drug baron who operated from a nightclub. His scene took up precisely half a page, but Wilfred played that minute role to perfection. Although I didn't realise it at the time, Mabel was furious with me for not giving Wilfred a top billing. I simply billed all the guest players in alphabetical order with only Brian Trueman and Geoffrey Banks as leads. Things seemed decidedly cool in our relationship, but then I heard Wilfred hadn't been too well so I travelled down to their Brighton home. He gave me a warm hug as I stepped out of the lift, which is just as well because all I got from Mabel was a very lukewarm cup of tea before she got the whole thing off her chest. We began to laugh about it when I explained that, had he been billed as a lead, people would have surely wondered why they waited one hour and twenty minutes before he came on. Was he so bad that I'd had to cut him out almost completely? It was the only time I'd been in the doghouse with Mabel, at least, I think it was.

I never heard them have a 'tiff' but Margaret and I loved the story

W I L F R E D   P I C K L E S   Programme No: HLF132L339

"M a n O f R a d i o"

an appreciation

introduced
by
TONY BRITTON

with

J.B. PRIESTLEY
BILLIE WHITELAW
JOHN BENNETT
HAYLEY MILLS
D.G. BRIDSON
OLIVE SHAPLEY
BARNEY COLEHAN
MABEL PICKLES

and others who worked with him
during his years of broadcasting

Written and Produced

by

Trevor Hill

Narration Recordings : London - STUDIO 2, Egton 1500 - 1700 hours
Wednesday 12th APRIL
Recording No: TLN14/024W353

Programme Assembly : Manchester - STUDIO 3 1000 - 1800
Thursday 13th APRIL
Recording No: TMR15/132L339N

Editing : Manchester, N6 Friday, 14th APRIL 1000 - 1800 hours

---

TRANSMISSION : (WEEK 16) SUNDAY 16th APRIL 1978
1915 - 2000 RADIO 4

Cover for obituary programme on Wilfred

Wilfred had told us about the time they decided they weren't speaking; neither could remember the reason for this, and each was determined not to be the first to break the silence. That must have been difficult, since they travelled on a long rail journey together and took up their hotel booking together. They were shown up to their suite, silence between them still reigning. When Wilfred followed the porter into the large bedroom there was a single bed in one corner and another some twenty feet away.

'D'you think they've heard then, Mabel?' he exclaimed.

I left Wilfred and Mabel in their Brighton flat and returned home with a promise I'd made to Wilfred, who had asked me to write the final chapter to a book he was working on for the publishers David and Charles, since he was far from well. When I'd finished it I sent it off to Emma Wood, their very conscientious and helpful book editor. To my horror, Emma pointed out that all the way through I had referred to Wilfred in the past tense: ... 'He was ... He did ...' But good book editors sort things like that out for you. The irony of it was that just four days after Wilfred died the book was published.

As we stood with Mabel round the graveside in Southern Cemetery in Manchester, I noticed the small headstone to Wilfred and Mabel's son, David.

> Jesus Christ, Thou Child so wise,
> Bless mine hands and fill mine eyes,
> And bring my soul to Paradise.

Apart from family and close friends, many had turned up that day although it was a private funeral. The woman with a beehive blonde hair-style tied down by a bright lurex-thread scarf, touched Mabel on the arm.

'Excuse me, love, you won't know me from Adam.' She went on to explain that she had been a conductress on the 64 bus route during the war when Wilfred and Mabel lived at Northenden, and how she'd cry, 'Full up, full up' and Wilfred would reply, 'Ooh, come on. It's perishin' standing in this weather,' so she'd give in with a, 'Room for just one more then,' and ring the bell. Then she told how Wilfred would shout, 'Hey up, Mabel, we're on!' The woman beamed at Mabel, then took her leave of us by saying, 'Ah, but he were a right little bugger afore he was famous!'

The last time Margaret and I visited the grave with Mabel was when the masons had just put the new headstone, which I'd been asked to arrange, in place. Mabel had also asked Margaret to choose something appropriate, something perhaps from one of Wilfred's published anthologies of poetry. Margaret chose wisely. Now, beneath the lines of Hilaire Belloc for David, are these by John Donne:

> Death be not proud, though some have called thee
> Mighty and dreadful, for thou art not so;

It was a choice between that or a line from Shakespeare's *Cymbeline*.

Mabel was pleased with the headstone and inscription, but it *was* quite expensive! As she explained, having had a mother who liked nothing more than splashing out on parties, she had learned to be the careful one. Wilfred would have adored her remark as she turned to us and said, 'Yes, yes, I'm glad it's the John Donne. Besides, it's three words less than the Shakespeare!'

11

Natural History and Antics in the Arctic

Whenever I knew I was going to be stuck in the studios for any length of time – and this would be in the winter months if I'd got the Planning Schedule right – I'd endeavour to be out and about a bit at other times in order to get to know the very extensive area covered by the BBC's North Region and to meet some of the people who lived between Lincoln and the Scottish border. So before the winter of 1953 set in, I decided to visit Cicely Matthews, who ran *Children's Hour* in Northern Ireland.

Cicely suggested we get together in Studio 13. Gosh, I thought, Belfast must have a large studio complex. Our venue turned out to be the BBC's local pub in that city, The Elbow Room, which was run by two identical Irish brothers. I thought Pimms No. 1 would be a pretty safe bet for me on a hot August day, especially with all that mint, orange and the number of cherries which came with the first glass. My meeting with Cicely went swimmingly as we discussed drama output and the intricacies of sharing the Newcastle 261 metre transmitter, which meant closer planning of those Children's Programmes to be heard jointly by listeners in the North East and in Northern Ireland. I was introduced to the one brother dispensing drinks in The Elbow Room, at about the fourth Pimms that morning. Lunch wasn't exactly a solid affair, either. After that was over, a now familiar Irish face leaned across the bar.

'So what'll it be, laddie?'

'Same as before,' I replied, 'Cherries!'

He served me about half a dozen on a saucer. This can be explained by the fact that twin number two had come on duty during lunch. I flew back to Ringway airport in Manchester in something of a blur and, arriving home, swore that I'd never meet Miss Matthews in Studio 13 again.

That October I was over at our Leeds studios to produce a serial that Margaret had been working on during the summer and which had now been accepted by the BBC in London who had commissioned it. This was an Elizabethan adventure serial set at the time of the Spanish Armada and entitled *The Seafarers*. The lead was played with suitable dash and 'stap-me-vitals' by the debonair Desmond Carrington, destined to break many a female heart when he became Dr Chris in ITV's *Emergency Ward 10.* My cast list for Episode 2 of the serial had two newcomers to radio acting, Eric Hills and a young man named Philip Waddilove. The serial itself didn't get further away from these shores than the English Channel, but Philip, another romantic at heart, was yet to make a far longer journey with me, of which more later.

There was a further chronicle of Elizabethan times in serial form that autumn with Rosemary Sutcliffe's *Brother Dusty Feet*, the story of a company of strolling players, which I've mentioned in an earlier chapter. Mind you, I'd now made it a firm rule *not* to go with any of the cast over territory we'd covered in the comparative comfort of a studio. I'd learnt that painful lesson back in 1952. All right, so I like to be out and about. But when I allowed a very young Bryan Martin, who was to become a national voice as a BBC newsreader, to talk me into walking over most of the Fell country we'd covered in the serial *Peril in Lakeland*, I didn't realise that a healthy mere teenager would expect me to cover nearly twenty-five miles on day one! Luckily, when I fell exhausted into the first Youth Hostel on the map, the Warden there turned out to be a chap I'd already met a few years before in Hamburg. So, whilst young Martin was given a yard broom in order to undertake the sort of chores expected of those who stayed in Lakeland hostels, his poor producer was given something stiff without bristles! The following day, and a further twenty miles on, a BBC staff car miraculously arrived in order to take me back to Manchester to attend to 'urgent business'.

As soon as we'd gently strolled with *Brother Dusty Feet*, I was planning for 1954 and for many more programmes away from the BBC studios. By March we'd be starting to do the *Afternoon Out* series again but now, for this new series, with Wilfred Pickles as the narrator and interviewer. In previous programmes, this key role had been undertaken by my old friend and BBC colleague, Philip Robinson, but he was becoming more and more engaged in running the Outside Broadcast department in the North, so he'd asked to be dropped. Well, Philip didn't exactly use *that* word. When we'd taken him to meet the Dowager Viscountess Galway for an *Afternoon Out* at her home, Serlby Hall, the first thing Philip had done was to pick up one of those frightfully expensive Chelsea hens from the console table just inside the front door and then to let the base of it fall from the lid. As he carefully retrieved the various pieces now strewn over the carpet, he declared, with admirable aplomb, 'Ah! I see it has already been repaired!'

There would be the annual Outside Broadcast from the Isle of Man, whilst BBC engineers and equipment were over to cover the TT Races. It was always pleasant to spend a week or so in this part of our region. This time *Island Visit* would be the title of a feature programme, introduced by Sir Joseph Qualtrough, the then Speaker of the House of Keyes, or Manx Parliament.

What else? Well, I'd always been a fan of Norman Ellison, better known to listeners as 'Nomad', and of his studio-based programmes, although I think the short time I'd spent under the influence of Desmond Hawkins in Bristol and the way *he* tackled Natural History for radio, made me begin to think that we ought to be 'out and about' during the spring, summer and autumn months. So I asked Nomad to record a new series for *Children's Hour*, which would consist entirely of Field Recordings.

I remember the delightful occasion on which Dr Ludwig Koch from West Region had got up well before dawn in order to record the sounds of the Severn bore for the umpteenth time. In those days, we often used an 'apple-and-biscuit' microphone for OBs. It had the advantage that it acted as a small loudspeaker as well as a microphone. My recordist guide and mentor in Bristol, Harvey Sarney, was sitting in the BBC Recording car that particular dawn. From the far off distance came the dull roar as the river waters performed their wonder of nature, the dull boom reaching a much higher pitch as the bore swept and swirled past the microphone. As the eddies fell to silence, so Ludwig *had* to get a verdict.

'Is it OK Harvey?' A voice with a forced note of excited anticipation answered him. 'Yes, yes. Ready to record when you tell me to start, Dr Koch!'

Was it my young imagination, or did the 'mittel-European' accent of this splendid broadcaster, besides that broad Dorset 'burr' of farmer Ralph Wightman, turn on and off along with studio cue lights? I rather fancy it did, certainly on the many occasions when Farmer Wightman broadcast for us and I was at the Controls at 200 Oxford Street! No such broadcasting histrionics with Nomad. The only time I had to watch

Northern Naturalist

Norman Ellison was when we did things like *Nomad's Christmas party*. He wrote his own scripts and I sometimes had to gently restrain him from such remarks as, 'Ah, Davey, I DO appreciate a really good cigar!' Or, 'By Jove, but a spot of good port goes down well on these festive occasions!' It's not that he'd be hinting to his large and appreciative audience, of course!

Anyhow, we now had the use, for the first time, of the EMI portable tape recorder. I'd planned to begin *Northern Naturalist* in June and to record the first edition on the Farne Islands. That same month we would record another *Afternoon Out*, which the BBC in London had scheduled, with the Duke and Duchess of Devonshire at their family home, Chatsworth.

Margaret hoped that their eleven-year-old daughter, Lady Emma, would tell listeners what it was like to live and to grow up in the Palace of the Peak. The Devonshires' housekeeper, Ilona Solomossy was, amongst other things, a born organiser *and* she had an eye for display! It was she who had a lot of the marble statuary moved into the long

Orangery. Margaret, on her initial visit to the house, was standing in this gallery when a party of WI ladies came through on a tour of Chatsworth. One grey-haired lady surveyed some of the scantily clad, large-busted marbles with a slight look of disapproval, then came straight up to our scriptwriter.

'Excuse me, Miss, could you please tell me which of these is the present Duchess?'

The present Duchess, fully clothed, was standing right next to Margaret!

It undoubtedly helps if a producer's wife is also in the same business – especially so when the husband decides to do what I did the very day we completed those recordings at Chatsworth. A BBC van took a load of Mobile Tape Recording gear and myself to the port of Grimsby, leaving Margaret to return to builders who were even then knocking down part of the old farm cottage we'd bought in Cheshire back in 1951.

Only a fortnight before recording *Afternoon Out,* I'd been to Grimsby to finalise arrangements with the directors of Northern Trawlers Ltd. They'd agreed to let me sign on as a spare hand and sail with their newest vessel to the Arctic. I knew I'd need more than one spare hand if I was to write a Feature about deep-sea trawlermen and to record them during the long journey. To be honest, I spent quite some time deciding *who* the 'other hand' might be.

There was that chap who'd been born with quite a silver spoon in his mouth – his grandfather, Sir Joshua Waddilove, having founded the National Provident Clothing Company and been featured by Arnold Bennett in his novel, *The Card.* Some of the family, thinly disguised, had been material for John Braine when he came to write *Room at the Top*. But Philip Waddilove was the rebel. Not for him a non-job and a big salary in the family firm. He'd chucked that in together with a major part of Pater's allowance to him, and had taken an Assistant Stage Manager's job at £5 a week with David Scase at the Manchester Library Theatre. That's where I'd first seen Philip and told him to come and take an audition with us. After he'd made his debut in *Seafarers*, I'd then cast him in the role which Nigel Davenport had done so well in the previous *Biggles* series, that of Lord Bertie Lissie.

Philip knew his way round the real world of aeronautics and did well with *Biggles in the Blue*. He'd been in one of the very best of British regiments and I even trusted him to take me up from Baildon airport in Yorkshire, since he was an Air Observation Pilot. What I *didn't* know at the time, was that the Auster aircraft we were in would literally 'do' the

Let's have some 'Music whilst you Gut!'

'One that *didn't* get away!'

Berties' view from Up the Pole!

jumps round Aintree Racecourse. Waddilove's CO didn't know this either, until he received an irate phone call from the Racecourse manager, informing him that a light aircraft was 'hedge-hopping' and only just clearing the jumps.

Yes, if I had to be sharing a small two-bunk forrard forecastle with anyone whilst facing the hazards of the sea, then Philip or 'Bertie' as he had now been christened, might be a good choice. He proved an excellent choice. Not only did he arrive with some of his *own* recording gear, but also with a host of up-to-date tapes with which he was to do a regular nightly programme once we were together with other fishing fleets in Arctic Waters. *Music While You Gut* became an immediate hit.

Having stayed at the Waddilove establishment at Baildon on several occasions I had been highly amused one night when Bertie had drawn back long folding doors to reveal his extensive wardrobe and shelf upon shelf of hats for every occasion. I had warned him to 'go steady' on clothing for our Arctic adventure. In the event, he arrived at Grimsby Town railway station laden down with gear, including three dozen pairs of socks. Oh yes, I'd already met Nanny at Baildon. 'Now, master Philip, if you're off to Arctic waters you'd best keep warm!' Fortunately he had heeded my warning about taking a silk dressing gown, highly spiced after-shave and slippers. I mean we didn't want those hardened trawlermen to think there was anything soft or sissy about two ex-army types!

The *Northern Sceptre*

The *Northern Sceptre*, the company's latest deep-sea trawler, was berthed on North Wall. Only seventy-two hours before she had returned to port with her fish pounds weighed down with a rich harvest from the sea. She had been refuelled with oil, her fresh-water tanks filled, rations put on board and below hatches she carried a hundred and ten tons of ice to preserve yet another catch from Arctic waters.

The top of the iron stove in the forecastle was almost red hot when Bertie and I went aboard. Within only a short while the ship's carpenter had fixed wooden blocks to the small table. It wasn't until we were underway that I discovered that every time the ship rolled, so my typewriter carriage would lift and I'd be typing everything in CAPITALS. Soon we'd fixed strappings for the two BBC Midget Tape Recorders, batteries, battery charger and converter, and stowed our somewhat sparse clothing. We, trying to look like seamen, wore thick new pullovers, stout trousers and canvas shoes. But let me now quote a little from the Feature programme:

> When the *Sceptre*'s crew arrive to be signed on by the ship's husband, they come in cars or by taxi as they bring their gear and bedding with them. They're all smartly dressed in lounge suits or good quality sportswear before they change into more serviceable clothing aboard ship.
>
> A voyage of twenty days or more for twenty men of varying responsibilities, varying ages and of varying character. Their names are entered in the book.
>
> Walter John Saxby, skipper, age 33, … Maurice Edward Coll, mate, age 25, Cyril Pidgeon, deck-hand, 19, … Albert Gray, cook, aged 56, Joseph Sidney Dalton, wireless operator, aged 45, … and, finally the two spare hands.
>
> The crews go below to stow their gear. Some bring a crate of milk aboard. That goes aft below the crews' washroom and showers. Richard Oldershaw, the decky-trimmer, brings oranges and lots of magazines. The chief engineer likes bacon – six pounds of it. And the skipper? A rubber foam mattress. He'll need it before this trip is over. As for Sparks, he'll unpack later. His first job is to test the Marconi transmitters and receivers in the Radio Room; the echo-sounders for tracing fish on the bed of the ocean, the radar housed in the Chart Room, before we leave at high water. The skipper slides back the armour-plate window on the bridge as he calls down to those on deck.
>
> 'Stand by your ropes fore and aft; standby the telegraph!'

A few more quietly spoken words of command and the *Northern Sceptre* is nosing through the Lock Pits and into the river, the morning sun shining on the gleaming white superstructure of the deep-sea trawler.

'South east by east!'

'South east by east, skipper!'

Sparkling waters spray out from either side of the ship's bows as Sid Dalton makes contact with Humber Radio.

'We're now leaving Humber bound for Bear Island. Have you anything for me, please? Over!'

Abeam of Spurn Light Vessel, the ship's log is 'streamed and set'. We'll have clocked up some three thousand nautical miles before this trip is over!'

With Bertie on deck and myself capturing the sound of the rotating Radar Scanner high above the bridge roof whilst we are in still waters, we are recording and noting, recording and noting. Tubby, the bosun, is up forrard to tidy all the tackle in the net room with Dick and young Brian, the decky-learner. A tear, however small, in the nets, and the combined force of water and weight of fish soon make a gaping hole – and that means a loss of catch and a loss in the crews' earnings. Tubby lends Brian a wooden needle, twine and an experienced hand.

'First a side knot, then ... over there. And bring that piece together.'

Bertie and I go about our business as unobtrusively as possible; the crew about theirs. They are soon less aware of our presence, of the microphones. The experience brings us together.

'Been to sea before, Twev?' enquires Tubby. 'Mind those steel floats, Bertie!' warns the mate. Yes, I've chosen some good shipmates for this trip. We keep in touch now with Wick Radio. What has Wick to say?

'Gale warning, Friday, zero 4.55 Greenwich Time. South easterly gale imminent sea areas Iceland and Bailey, veering westerly in Bailey ...' I'm not worried. Sid's just told me we aren't going that way!

There is a worried look on Bertie's face a little later, however, when it's time for the skipper to issue 'Bond' – cigarettes, tobacco, chocolate. We are offered, of all things, a packet of bath cubes each. Should we take them?

'You'll want to be rid of a different sort of "perfume" by the time we get down to fishing!'

That night, Bertie and I are offered the loan of a dressing gown each and one or two more home comforts as we join some of those 'Off

Watch' in the mess room. 'Pidge' asks one of the old hands what it was like in the days *he* first put to sea.

'Well, we had all the ashes to heave over th' side even when it was blowing a livin' gale, and all our lamps to trim. No oil-burning ships in them days!'

A loud guffaw at the next question: 'Washing an' shaving? We had one bowl, just one. None of your fancy showers and such. And if cook was using bowl for soaking peas in, you went dirty, I can tell you!'

Dick had been at Dunkirk. Tubby had been adopted by fifty school children whilst he was serving in a mine-layer. Sparks did wartime service in rescue tugs at Dunkirk and, four years later was towing sections of the Mulberry harbour over to the Normandy beaches. John Saxby spent several years in armed trawlers doing convoy work. We were to sail over the spot where his brother went down with all hands whilst on the Russian convoy route.

At latitude sixty-six degrees, thirty minutes North, Sid Dalton allowed me to send a cable via Wick Radio. The postmistress at Slimbridge gave it to the local constable, who cycled around one or two Gloucestershire lanes before he caught up with Margaret, who was now

Our 'recording/editing' cabin aboard ship

staying there.

'Have crossed that Arctic Circle. Love you. Trevor.' She kissed the constable for both of us.

Ten o'clock on the morning of the sixth day out and the *Sceptre* lies between the first and second gully on the East Side of Bear Island, just visible on the horizon. We have reached the fishing grounds. At a depth of one hundred fathoms and with the 'Kingfisher' giving an audible click to denote fish concentrations on the luminous screen, John Saxby gives the order to shoot the first trawl. At two hundred and fifty fathoms, the correct amount of steel trawl cable has been paid out.

'She's all square. Skipper!' The *Sceptre* tows her trawl at around four knots. It'll be an hour and a half, maybe two hours before they begin to haul in.

There is time for me to make Radio contact with those Norwegians who man the Weather Station on Bear Island. Four men and a steward.

'The polar bears do what?' I ask.

'Step off the passing ice-floes?' Are they having me on or is this something for *Northern Naturalist*? I begin to record a tape or two as we go back to the start of our conversation. Louis Aldreas speaks well and in fluent English. He tells me about the white Arctic foxes on the island, which they feed with cake and with eggs. He goes on to describe the many sea birds which nest there. From the Radio Room I can see Bear Island quite clearly.

Bertie remains on deck as they begin to haul in the trawl. There is a mass of foaming bubbles some fifty yards behind the ship's stern as the trawl bag 'breaks water', jumping all of six feet above the surface of the sea. The gulls become even noisier as the wet nets sparkle in the Arctic sun and water streams off black oilskins. It happens again and again.

Bit by bit, we noted and recorded the whole process, including the cleaning and washing of the fish before they are stored below. Funny, but when the crew invited Bertie and me to try our hand at gutting some enormous cod, my sharp knife just would *not* slit its gullet! Had the fish really swallowed that long wooden fisherman's needle I found inside? Or were those lowered eyes and faces standing in the deck pounds hoping *we'd* swallow it all!

Cook took only the heads from the very first cod brought aboard. He left them in a basket outside his galley. Three days later, with only the addition of some onion and herbs, there was fish soup on the menu. And what soup!

It was on that day that Bertie decided to try out a bath cube or two and freshen up. It was a bit close with the roaring fire, which the crew kept stocking up for us during the night, rustling in and out of the forecastle in oilskins with lots of 'shushes' as they grabbed the hot handle of the poker. I asked the skipper if a bath was in order, Bertie first. It was a fresh-water hip type of bath, which Bertie clambered into. The *Radio Times* had lent me a rather good camera for the voyage. I told my shipmate I'd take a photo. I knew his current girlfriend had seen everything, but I thought Nanny might be amused. He posed with a loo brush held aloft above his head, whilst I carefully lined up the sort of shot that Nanny could approve of now that Bertie was a big boy.

'OK. Hold it!'

Sid Dalton had been on the ship's bridge when I'd asked John about taking a bath. 'Hold it' was the pre-arranged signal for Sid to sling in a very large cod from the other side of the door. It landed, 'plop' right in the bath water. Bertie was very sporting. He joined in the laughter as he grabbed the slimy tail, but then jumped up saying, 'But it's moving – it's still moving!'

Well, perhaps he *did* have something to complain about. Not like the time when he was staying with us in Cheshire. Margaret heard the sudden shout and woke me up. 'It's Bertie,' she cried, rushing into the guest room.

Our guest was standing up in bed and sort of 'spread-eagled' across the back wall.

'Take it away,' he yelled. 'Take it away!'

Eventually I noticed a daddy longlegs. 'This?'

'Yes, *that*! It's ... It's all of s-six inches l-l-o-n-g!'

I never did show Nanny the picture I'd taken of Bertie and the fish in the ship's bath!

I have only one frightening memory of my voyage to the Arctic and that was self-induced, like Bertie's 'flying beastie'! The fishing hadn't been at all good to begin with, and Skipper John had even forbidden any of us to shave.

'Cut your beard and you cut your luck!' he'd pronounced. This seemed strange coming from a young man who knew all about the latest Navigational and Electronic fishing aids. I'd seen John hour after hour at the helm and noticed that his ankles were so swollen he couldn't untie his shoes. After two or three days of this, Sid Dalton, as a much older man, persuaded John to take to his bunk for a few hours. Sid did likewise, after he'd quite satisfied himself that this particular 'spare hand' could hold the course we were on and would keep a steady helm in the wheelhouse.

There were Dutch, German, English and Russian trawlers in the vicinity. We'd been keeping station with a large Russian trawler – and not far from her own territorial waters, either. After half an hour or so, I suddenly noticed that the Russian ship, trailing her trawl a long way behind her stern, had altered course. We looked set to part her valuable nets within the next ten minutes or so. I darted into the Radio Room. No sign of Sid. Then I began sounding the ship's hooter. Surely someone would come. It was George Mussell, the chief engineer, who upbraided me for wasting pressure.

'Collision course my eye. She's a good two mile away!' There followed a few untrawlerman-like words. Not that they use bad language or blaspheme – they daren't. They are too close to death and to their Maker. But I didn't argue with George. 'Mussell' was an appropriate name for him.

The fair-haired, quietly spoken mate, Maurice Coll, was the only crew member we recorded in anger. With young 'Pidge' at the powerful winches, Maurice was supervising the hauling up of the trawl; the steel cables taut and straining as they snaked over the gallows wheels, fore and aft, and onto two stout cable drums. Perhaps Maurice had noticed a change in the sound of the winch motors. If a cable snags on an underwater obstacle and parts, the 'whip' can slice through a steel stanchion, or far more easily through a crew member.

'Hold it!' Maurice yelled. The winchman didn't hear.

'Hold – the – bloody – trawl!' bellowed the mate, leaping across to 'Pidge'. In the silence which followed, Maurice turned and saw us – still recording.

'I er, I mean DO hold it!'

When we arrived back in Grimsby, considering ourselves seasoned sailors, we gave a party for the *Sceptre*'s crew and for their wives or girlfriends, and played back that bit of the recording.

The BBC sent Margaret over in a staff car, which was to bring both of us back to Cheshire. It was good to be home – yet sad to bid goodbye to those trawlermen who had shared at least a small part of their lives with us. They didn't forget Bertie. They sent him fish until the following summer. And straw basses kept arriving at our home too, via the railway, always it seemed on hot days and just when Margaret and I were setting off on another job. Still, we became quite popular with some of the neighbours.

I haven't really been what you would call 'to sea' since those Grimsby days. When I was aboard our boat, *Cleo* on Lake Windermere and standing at the helm in her wheelhouse, I would sometimes think of that journey to the Arctic and of the men who gave me a rare experience besides some excellent recordings. Not that MV *Cleo* is quite like the *Northern Sceptre*. Our boat was named after our Siamese cat and was built in 1979. She's sea-going, 14 tonnes in all and her length would just fit nicely into one the *Sceptre*'s fish pounds below decks.

After listening to and editing many reels of tape with our BBC Recording Department, I sent a finished script off to Henry Reed, the composer. He also listened to all of the Actuality Recordings we'd made at sea and then wrote a very appropriate score, which was recorded by the BBC Northern Orchestra for our feature, *Arctic Trawler*. The right sort of voice for speaking the narration belonged to actor John Slater.

And so it was broadcast. However, I got into trouble with the then Post Master General's department, because accompanying two or three of the photos I'd hopefully taken for the *Radio Times*, was an article in which I had made mention of Bertie's 'Music While You Gut' broadcasts from the *Sceptre*.

'It is clearly understood that Shipping Frequencies are to be used only for normal traffic and not for the broadcast of music …' was the gist of the letter I received.

What that department didn't know was that after a day or two, ship by ship in a large area of the Arctic circle would pick up and pipe Bertie's broadcasts to their own crew members, besides transmitting the programme from their own aerials further afield.

A national newspaper gave us a complimentary write-up on *Arctic Trawler*, adding it was a pity that the BBC had not done the programme for Television. We couldn't have done it for Television, not in that way. It had far more 'colour' on radio than would have been evident on a TV screen, and none of the intimacy, which is essentially Radio.

But Television was something I now had to think about – and it loomed in the not too distant future!

12

Back to School

It was Bertha Lonsdale, adapter and author of many good plays and serials from the North, who suggested we might do a series of features on *Other Children's Schools*. She would go ahead, make contacts, visit the place herself, come back, write the script and only then would I join her when we went to record. I never had any trouble in going away with Bertha – only with my wife. For *Afternoon Out* the BBC would book her into hotels in her professional name, Margaret Potter. Then, a few weeks later when it came to the recordings, a booking would be made in the name of Mr & Mrs Trevor Hill. We got some old-fashioned looks a time or two I can tell you, for things were different in the 1950s, and quite a few people knew that I was the person in charge of *Children's Hour* in the North of England.

Bertha, a remarkable Yorkshirewoman, certainly got around the North region despite a deformity of both feet – something which had not responded to surgery when she was a small child. As it was, she couldn't move without the aid of surgical boots and callipers – at least, not until she underwent major surgery in her early fifties, and only then did she dispense with high-laced boots and don a pair of silk stockings for the first time in he life. Before that event, which was noted in *The Lancet*, I cannot say that *anything* held Bertha back. She walked the boots off me at many a school up and down the country. On St Bees headland, this keen ornithologist had scrambled over the rocks with field glasses at the ready even before a hotel breakfast. Whilst at Lancaster School, we were recording on the river bridge one bleak winter's day when I turned to ask the small fur-clad figure, who always carried her scriptboard and stop-watch, if she thought the interview had gone OK. But Bertha was missing. Two masters and three schoolboys found her lying in a snow-drift at the bottom of the steep riverbank.

'But why didn't you shout to us?' I asked in anguish.

'What and spoil a good recording?'

Bertha's format was to have a jolly good pupil return to the school in question, and be taken round by the present-day head boy or girl. The distinguished former pupil would also narrate the programme, linking scenes from the school's history. The staff and pupils always enjoyed this part of the proceedings after I'd held on-the-spot auditions and then rehearsed the chosen few in their respective roles. It was only in later years, when I came to direct that most talented and amusing actor, Ian McKellen, in a serialisation of *Fame is the Spur*, that he told me how awed and impressed he had been when we did Bolton Grammar School. It seems that the headmaster had introduced me by saying I used to make all the sound effects on *ITMA*. Ian wished *he'd* been cast for one of the parts when we were recording at his school.

'Anyhow, I and some of the other junior boys hid behind a hedge and watched,' he said.

In all, we would spend three or four days at each venue, so I'd got to know several schools and their heads quite well by the time I got back from my arctic adventure to find there'd been a phone call from the firm of W.H. Smith and Son. Would I contact their director of publicity, Sydney Hyde? That call led to another series of broadcasts over several years. This long-established firm of newsagents and booksellers came to the conclusion that they should introduce young people to those who actually wrote and published newspapers, books, magazines and poetry. And so we began a *Young Person's Forum on Books*. I suggested Manchester Grammar School for a pilot programme, but Eric James, then headmaster, wasn't so keen on his school taking part in anything but *Top of the Form* – or so it seemed to me. I therefore suggested Bolton Grammar School to Sydney Hyde since they had a most lively and amusing head in F.R. Poskitt. He accepted. We asked the school to submit a list of questions that the pupils would like to put to a panel concerning literature in its widest terms. Sydney and his team selected what they hoped would be the right people to answer the sort of questions received. It worked well at Bolton.

We included Frank Singleton, that great editor of the *Bolton Evening News* and look-alike Mr Pickwick, in the team. After each recording of *Young Person's Forum on Books* had taken place, the distinguished panel would be whisked away to a suitable hotel for their overnight accommodation – but before that, came the dinner. Frank Singleton personally supervised the preparation of the main dish in the kitchen of the Bolton hotel. It was only when I saw him with his sleeves rolled up, that I recognised in him a much younger man who at 200 Oxford Street during the war had been one of the main editors on *Radio Newsreel.*

If only the BBC could have recorded the conversation that took place at some of those dinners! Alas, there is the law of libel, but there was also some of the liveliest, wittiest and well-informed conversation it was ever my pleasure to hear. Elizabeth Pakenham, L.A.G. Strong, Keith Waterhouse, L.P. Hartley, John Braine, Gwyn Thomas, Hammond Innes, Hugh Ross Williamson, Rupert Hart-Davies, Richard Church, and Laurie Lee. Believe me, we took some of the best literary minds with us back to school.

At one place, an anxious headmaster had taken me aside before the dinner, asking that on no account, should he be seated next to the headmistress of the girl's department. I passed this message on to Sydney Hyde.

'Why ever not?' he enquired.

'Well the man said he would probably bite her!' I replied. Mind you that headmaster had a point. I sat next to the lady in question myself that night. As the long dinner came to a close, I thanked her for her company and said that perhaps we might meet again. She looked me straight in the face as she declared, 'Oh, and do you consider that likely?' I wanted to bite her myself.

We had a panel in sparkling form at Repton School, with Margharita Laski who was to become a fairly regular member of our panel, Robert Henriques the novelist and Ivor Brown as our chairman. I soon discovered that Lord David Cecil and Lady Violet Bonham-Carter did well together on a panel, except that Lady Vi *would* turn away from the microphone on the table in front of her in order to look into Lord David's eyes when answering a question and seeking his opinion. She complained to me at one dinner, saying, 'I really do not know what your BBC engineers do to my voice. I heard the last book broadcast. I sounded as if I had walked away as I was speaking and then walked back again!' I told the good lady that short of fixing her up with the sort of microphone chest-set that New York telephonists appeared to use in all the 'B' movies I'd ever seen, there was little our engineers *could* do.

'A chest set! Ah, now that *is* a good idea, Mr Hill!'

I really think, upon mature reflection, that I would have withheld my feelings a little more had I realised at the time that I was speaking to one of the BBC's Board of Governors!

The liveliest chairman we had for several years was undoubtedly Lionel Hale. One of the most wickedly amusing of men, too. After a somewhat heavy set of questions had arrived in from one school in the south of England, we chose our panel accordingly. The dinner proved a pretty staid affair, mainly because some of the senior school staff were present and wouldn't let their hair down, although Sydney kept the wine waiter on his toes. The panel retired to bed unusually early, but Lionel and publisher Marcus Morris decided to give the hotel porter the list of papers which should be on the breakfast table the following morning.

I can still see the distinguished figure of Ivor Brown tucking into egg and bacon and *Robin*, John Connell thoroughly engrossed in a teenage girls' magazine, whilst our pet poet, John Betjeman declared, 'Oh, how jolly. Do you know, it is simply *ages* since I have seen the *Beano*!'

To some preparatory schools, we'd take personalities like Noel Streatfeild and George Cansdale. Funny, but none of the rest of the panel wanted to touch, let alone hold, the snake that George invariably travelled around with in a Gladstone bag when we went by train.

Also on train journeys to junior schools, I often had the pleasure of travelling just with W.E. Johns in a first-class compartment all to ourselves. We had much to discuss with our mutual interest in 'Biggles', and he was always fascinated by the way Bertha Lonsdale adapted his stories, inventing minor characters herself for those chapters in which 'Ginger' often went off entirely on his own. The author thoroughly approved and so I never discussed with him the sort of mistakes in storyline we sometimes came across in dramatising his highly successful books.

We were, ourselves, almost caught out once but saved with only minutes to airtime by the observant Jack Watson in the title role. He suddenly realised that in the instalment we were about to broadcast, he and Bertie were about to give chase to Von Stalhein in an aircraft which didn't exist on this deserted island. I still relish the story in which Biggles and Co down an enemy aircraft by dropping a crate of corned beef on it from some unspecified altitude above. W.E. Johns' books were the very stuff of radio. To other members of the team he would always want to talk about things like Income Tax, but to me it was a different story.

We were a little disappointed by the rather uninspired questions that the gentlemen of Eton put to our panel, but greatly impressed by the quality of the cucumber sandwiches, which we enjoyed with Dr Birley in his study.

When it came to *A Young Persons' Forum on Books* at Harrogate Girls' College, Sydney Hyde kindly invited Margaret to be present at the recording and at the dinner, since he had invariably stayed with us when it came to editing each recording at the BBC studios. W.H. Smith and Son always booked the shorthand writers who take down every word in parliament for *Hansard*. The transcript they provided made my job of editing all the easier. On the occasion of the Harrogate programme, a very charming and very ancient classics mistress had been temporarily taken out of retirement, although the whiff of lavender remained. She was placed at dinner next to Hugh Cudlipp. On Hugh's other side was my wife, who heard some of the conversation.

'Tell me, Mr Cudlipp,' said the classics lady with a wide-eyed expression, 'Is it true that you are – a Socialist?'

Mr Cudlipp owned up immediately. There was a little gasp.

'Do you know, I have *never* sat next to a Socialist before!'

I particularly remember our visit to Tenbury Wells. It transpired that the headmaster of the Choir School was such a devotee of *Sooty* that Sunday Services and all else were not allowed to interfere. We had arrived in the city around noon that day and been taken straight to a very select country club hotel, distinguished, we were to discover, by the number of retired gentlefolk who sat sipping their light sherries and reading in the columned hall awaiting their luncheon. As Lady Barlow, better known as the distinguished actress and speaker of verse, Margaret Rawlings, ascended the wide oak staircase trailing her mink-lined mackintosh, Sydney Hyde called to her, 'What will you have, Margaret?'

That strong voice of purely modulated purple velvet replied, 'I am going to have a pee, Syd-ney, and then I shall have a l-a-r-g-e b-randy!'

Copies of *The Field, The Times,* and *The Tatler* suddenly rattled and several sherries were spilled as Lady Barlow then continued her stately ascent.

13

'Tell the Customers Who You Are – and Get on With It!'

Whilst I'd been away fishing, Margaret had been commissioned to write a sequel to the *Island Of Moressa* serial. Now, *The Silver Jet* had been accepted by the BBC in London and was scheduled to be broadcast in the November. As soon as *Arctic Trawler* went out over the airwaves – and I loved the *Radio Times* billing and what came after the narrator's credit: 'John Slater is now appearing in Dry Rot at the Whitehall Theatre' (thank God we had none of that aboard) – I turned my attention not only to that message about book programmes from W. H. Smith and Son, but also to an official memoranda from the BBC's Staff Training Department in London, which informed me that I was to attend a television course in November 1954. Since this meant I wouldn't be free to do any radio production work for the whole of that month, all six episodes of *The Silver Jet* were recorded at almost the speed of sound, with Desmond Carrington as Dick, the intrepid hero, and Bryan Forbes as Dave, his cockney ex-batman.

There was also a quick sprint across into Wales and to the Liverpool University Salmon Observation chamber on the River Dee, for *Northern Naturalist*, then off to Lime Grove and that television production course. I don't recall much about it now, except that the course students were expected to make programmes on 'closed circuit' at the end of the four weeks.

For my production exercise, I wrote a two-hander 'drama' entitled, *Masquerade*. Staff Training allowed us something like £15 for incidental costs incurred, so I managed to persuade John Slater and Ivan Samson (Colonel Sallis in all our *Bunkle* serials from Manchester) to learn rather longish lines and then to come and take part 'just for the experience'. Oh yes, and there was the short scene with 'partygoers' at the start of it all, including my shipmate, Bertie, and his recently reunited girl friend, Panje. Quite a stunner. She turned up with a small dog under her arm and brazenly informed the Lime Grove commissionaire that I'd said she and the animal were to be allowed into Studio 'D'! In the next few years, I was to be the instigator of dogs making regular appearances from BBC Television Studios.

Long after *Masquerade*, John Slater avowed that this is why he eventually came to be cast as a policeman in *Z Cars*. I'm quite positive that for my 'exercise' it was Sammy who played the role of the policeman. *Z Cars* came about for John purely because he happened to be a very fine actor. What did stand out about *Masquerade* was the studio set. That was done for me by the then master of TV design, Roy Oxley of *1984* fame. I felt quite pleased with our achievement – until I saw the production exercise by Margaret Dale and what she had accomplished with just two dancers and one drum. And I hurried back North again.

Someone in the BBC, and I cannot remember who was to blame for this, considered that as I'd announced for the Home Service and Light Programme besides doing quite a lot of the daily 'ad lib' on *Children's Hour*, I should appear in front of the cameras – or was it that my recent Course Report concluded I'd do less harm in front than behind? In any event, I made my TV debut in February 1955 at precisely 5.35 p.m. from St George's Hall, Liverpool.

Willie Cave was the director and he'd got together some of the antique musical instruments from the Rushworth and Dreaper collection. I'd suggested that Joyce Palin should appear with me as she could play a number of stringed instruments and keyboards. And so it was that a certain Dr J. E. Wallace took us and the viewers on this tour of Ancient Musical Instruments. The Liverpool firm had some publicity photos taken of the occasion. They show rather large BBC cameras mounted on *very* large sort of bicycle wheels. I know because later, I proudly took a friend into Rushworth and Dreapers just to *prove* I'd been on the telly. Not that it convinced him entirely. Lovely display but every caption above photographs of me read, 'Trevor Howard introduces some of our Collection on BBC Television'.

Of course following my debut the offers came in thick and fast – all from inside the BBC. Being a member of staff no one had to *pay* me to appear! By the better weather in April, I was out there in person to *Meet The Speedway Riders* at Belle Vue racetrack, Manchester. Derek Burrell-

Davis, our fully-fledged television director in the north was directing that day. He didn't allow me to be killed, and I'm glad about that, because many years later Derek was to return north as the head of Network Centre at New Broadcasting House and to open a few windows and a lot of doors which allowed creative staff to flourish again, for he headed an excellent management team. Derek was a showman in the best sense. Perhaps that is why, at no danger to his person, he thought it would be a good idea that day at Belle Vue if, after I'd interviewed some of the speedway aces and we'd seen a lot of close-ups of engines and things, I should join the top riders in a final race.

There was only time after the last interview for me to don a crash helmet, goggles and a leather top, more for disguise than anything else, but no time to pull something more serviceable over a pair of flannel trousers. Oh yes, and I now had to remember it wasn't Mary Malcolm I was to hand back to at Lime Grove after all, but Macdonald Hobley. I wrote that down on the palm of my left hand, then goggles on and away. Several laps later and I somehow managed to pull up at a pre-arranged line. Speedway bikes don't have brakes. I took a hand-mic from BBC colleague Michael Barton who was the OB floor manager that day. Fine, but I couldn't let go of the handlebars with my left hand in order to lift the goggles and reveal the face of the Phantom Rider, because with that hand I was holding in the clutch, with the engine still racing away under me.

I somehow 'wiped away' the goggles and, by luck, even remembered to hand back to the right announcer in London. But having done so, I then saw Michael giving me the 'string it out' sign. He then signalled more frantically. What! Go round the circuit *again*? As I did so, weaving a way through the speedway aces, down came the rain. Water shot up from the ruts made by countless racing-bike wheels. The BBC never did agree to pay for my new pair of flannels. To make matters worse, when I got back home after a hot shower and a couple of stiff ones, I was reminded by a certain party that I'd faithfully promised *never* to ride a motorbike again, though I'd never said anything about 'on television'.

Well, Margaret *had* seen what happened with my lovely German DKW machine in Hamburg. On the way back to lunch one day, she was sitting in the BFN staff bus and I was following behind at a respectful distance. At the Stefanplats tram crossing, the narrow front tyre of the motorbike slipped into a deepish rut in the tram points. Margaret saw me tip over the handlebars and straight under the wheels of a passing Büssing diesel lorry and trailer. What she didn't see, was that I slid on the cobbles and straight out the far side, with only holes in the elbows of an army-issue leather jerkin to show for the experience.

A week after my first and last speedway race, I was *Behind The Scenes* at Blackpool circus to do interviews with some of the acts as they came out of the ring. I know my friend Barney Colehan wouldn't let me endanger life and limb. Good programme, exciting acts – particularly the American circus family. Father, in a deep stetson, did some remarkable tricks with a lethal bull-whip. He'd pluck a cigarette from the red lips of his shapely wife at fifteen feet without disturbing a single sequin, and then tear off a chocolate wrapper held by his daughter from even further away. Oh no, not the beautiful daughter. I could hardly bear to watch. Even the clean-cut son stood upright and real cool, an apple perched on his head, as father did his William Tell bit, slicing the fruit clean in half without so much as ruffling a hair of his heir's head.

When the family finished their Act, they came backstage to thunderous applause. I was now to be holding a pencil and scriptboard. Barney's idea was that, with the crack of the whip, the pencil should fly from my grasp. In the event, the tip of the whip caught the edge of the BBC lighting stand. The pencil still shot away from my grasp, but quite suddenly, my thumb felt numb. Very numb. With never a falter I conducted a brilliant interview with the American circus stars and only complained after the programme had finished. I showed my thumb nail to the beautiful daughter. She didn't kiss it better, she kissed me. I decided it had been worth it. The thumb nail fell off the next day.

From then on, better insured and prepared, I covered such diverse Outside Television Broadcasts as racing at Oulton Park, interviewing another great Amercian driver Harry Schell, and getting into something of a muddle when interviewing the Ferrari Team and discovering that almost every Italian mechanic I spoke to answered to that name, it being more common than'Smith'.

I think I first appeared with Ray Lakeland as my director, at a large factory belonging to the Dunlop organisation. There was a lot for me to learn and to mug up. Ray made you do your homework. We were covering the making of a tennis racket, a cricket bat, and a new line in crossbows. I also had to interview a well-known sporting personality in each of those three fields of sport. Holding together all those bits of lamination which go to make up a tennis racket can be tricky. At rehearsal, talking straight to camera and holding the bits to another camera for close-up shots, I found a convenient bench to lean against. On the live transmission, the floor manager or someone 'struck' (removed) that bench. I went to lean back, managed to recover my balance, but inadvertently said, 'Sorry, darling!' No, not to Ray! I knew Margaret would be watching on the TV set owned by our nice nextdoor neighbours.

I got another of those floor manager signs towards the end of the Slazenger programme. He looked to be pulling at an imaginary bow-string. He did it twice so I wound up my star cricketer interview before we'd really finished, put down all the bits of cricket bat and quickly crossed to the bow-making area of the factory floor, noticing that two BBC cameras were trying to race me to it. This part of the programme went on far longer than had been planned – or rehearsed. It later transpired that the floor manager's sign was supposed to mean, 'String it out. We are under-running'.

I suggested that Ray Lakeland's own son, Paul, should be in vision with me at the York Railway museum for *Trains of All Ages*. It proved a good suggestion. Young Paul asked all the right sort of questions on a rehearsal which went swimmingly. Fortunately, we had Don McKay of 'Mac' as our senior BBC cameraman at York because shortly after the live transmission began, so the enormous amount of television lighting required to cover such large areas began to take a toll on the Yorkshire Electricity Board's power cables. First the little transmission light went out as I was confidently talking to Camera 3, so I turned and continued to Camera 2. That suddenly went out as Paul was asking the curator how passengers managed to accommodate their stove-pipe hats in the early days of railway travel. From then on Mac, on his single camera. 'conducted' us from behind his viewfinder, pointing out where to go next when certain items couldn't be covered as planned, signalling when other things would have to be brought towards the camera – small things, not engines. As Ray Lakeland didn't have a spare camera for 'credits' at the conclusion of the programme, I spoke them and signed off. I know at least one person thoroughly enjoyed watching this televised occasion. I was invited to stay with Robert Patterson and Mary for the night. I'd done so many programmes from Pat's place up the road, that instead of signing off from the Railway Museum, York, I'd given a nice plug to the Castle Museum instead!

The Royal Yorkshire Show was to be honoured by the presence of BBC TV cameras. Again, it was Ray Lakeland directing the coverage over several days. My task was to be in the commentary box whilst the Royal Canadian Mounted Police went through their paces, and then I was to interview one of the riders in vision.

I'd been South for a couple of days beforehand in order to see the

Mounties on part of their tour of the United Kingdom. They'd been jolly helpful in filling me in on their history and on their duties in modern-day Canada. By the time I arrived at the Yorkshire Show I felt pretty confident. Ray rehearsed my interview on camera during a pause in the day's activities, ready for their televised performance on the following afternoon. All went well – except I noticed that the events seemed to be running rather late. Would they be appearing in the showring at 5.30 p.m. precisely the next day as advertised in the *Radio Times*? When Ray said he'd sort things out, I relaxed again. He came back to say he'd had words with the show organisers.

As I climbed up the tall scaffold tower to the BBC commentary box the following afternoon, so I met the debonair and very professional Dorian Williams. He had arrived early to cover the evening jumping events. And just as well. At 5.30 p.m. that day, things were running so late that Children's Television had show jumping until 5.55 p.m. expertly described by Dorian Williams. At around 6.30 that evening, when this event *should* have been taking place from the Yorkshire Show, according to the *Radio Times*, the Canadian Royal Mounted Police were coming on. I distinctly remember Ray's instructions to me over the headphones as I sat in the BBC commentary box.

'Tell the customers who you are, say what's happened, and get on with it!'

14

Another Side to the Camera

The one area of the BBC in which you'd find women in most of the top posts in the 1950s and 1960s, was in departments connected with broadcasting for children. Until I was appointed to succeed Gwen Pain in the north of England, all the regional children's radio heads were women. It was whilst attending the television production course at Lime Grove that I first met the remarkable person who, in my opinion, was the architect of television programmes for children. Freda Lingstrom had been in Schools Broadcasting. Now, she very successfully ran her department, providing a daily programme for young viewers. Freda reminded me of Nan Macdonald in the sort of standards she maintained and in what she expected of her staff. Her deputy was Ursula Eason, a former wartime head of programmes in Belfast, who still did a lot of production work herself and was responsible for starting special programmes for the hard of hearing. I both liked and admired Freda and Ursula. Each taught us a lot about television, could be tough when necessary, and each was good company in a predominantly male organisation.

It was Ursula who suggested that I might like to direct a programme or two with Ross Salmon, an ex-naval officer who had a thing about the Wild West – and in the West of England of all places. He kept a small beef herd which he'd round up for the benefit of the film camera, assisted by a hired hand. So down I went to Dorset with a cameraman and on 16 mm mute film we shot scenes on the edge of the Downs which were to be later used in conjunction with a studio-produced live transmission. I did several of the Ross Salmon programmes from the Shepherd's Bush TV Theatre, later used for *Wogan*, so that Ross in full cowboy regalia could have an invited audience to see his show. But it was Studio E, Lime Grove, which really meant 'Children's Television'. It had a good-sized floor space for those days and could quite easily accommodate the three or four separate studio items which went to make up the daily programme.

When Ursula was about to go on an extended holiday, I was attached to the staff of Children's Television for a while and took over some of the programmes which she had been working on, besides thinking up a few of my own. It is largely thanks to Rosemary Gill, who was then Ursula's production secretary, that I managed not to dent the department's image too badly, for Rosemary took me under her experienced wing. Only a few days before Ursula departed on that spell of leave she and Rosemary were doing the final programme in a series called *Our Port*. A model-maker named Kim Allen showed young viewers the sort of buildings that would be required for a large port installation, and more importantly how to make such models. The best received each week were shown on the screen and added to the large studio model of dockland with its waterways, cranes, building and jetties. With expert lighting, those scale models made by young viewers looked just like the real thing when seen on a studio monitor.

I watched Ursula rehearsing the final programme with her camera crew and noticed how carefully she lined up each shot in order to show everything to advantage. Just after she and her team had gone for tea, however, so 'Mum', as Freda was affectionately known, came down from her office. At one side of the studio was a large table on which were a number of discarded models.

'There will be a lot of disappointed children,' remarked Freda. With that she got me to add one more model building here, a cluster there. I was careful to note where each one went. As soon as Freda left the studio, so I cleared all her 'additions' from the set. The transmission went well. Then came a call to the Control gallery. Miss Lingstrom would like to see me. We had a nice chat and I even began to relax as Freda asked me about my trip to the Arctic. It wasn't until I was leaving her office that she said. 'Why did you remove those extra models?' It was the type of question Nan always used to ask.

'Because Ursula had carefully rehearsed all her shots and some of those things would have blocked them!'

I got quite a warm smile from Freda. 'Well, that is a very valid reason!' I can't say I was quite so lucky on other occasions. Calls to the gallery from 'Mum' became something of a regular occurrence.

When I thought to myself that she might do well to take me on as a permanent member of her department in view of the programme I'd just done, I was invariably wrong.

'I liked that Polish wood-carver you found. I take it he *was* only carving those guardsmen with their busbies out of *safety* matches!'

Freda wasn't going to allow her young viewers to take chances with anything we showed them. At other times my mistakes showed all too plainly on the screen but, sometimes when I was summoned, it was to be told about the better parts of the programme. And if I thought that Freda had a bit of a 'thing' about rather a lot of things, then she completely knocked the wind from my sails when I tentatively suggested that much of the film I had taken from the salmon spawning chamber on the River Dee, could make good television. I'd already been told by Rosemary that 'Mum' wouldn't allow any form of fishing to be shown as she considered it cruel, but the idea of salmon spawning was accepted straight away. And not only accepted, Freda's brief was that this part of nature should be explained *in detail*.

Dr J.W. Jones of Liverpool University had not only sat and got saturated filming those salmon hour after hour in his underwater chamber, but between hefty colds he'd proved himself to be a very good off-the-cuff broadcaster. I had already used him in two or three of the *Northern Naturalist* programmes on radio. Together, we edited his film at Lime Grove. It wasn't until the afternoon of the broadcast that we both realised he couldn't 'talk to camera'. I couldn't let him sit and read a script in vision either.

'Then get someone to interview Dr Jones. They can talk together as they watch the film,' declared Freda. Until that day, all viewers saw from the Lime Grove continuity studio were the BBC announcers in vision. Now it was my friend from 200 Oxford Street days, Mary Malcolm, who talked so encouragingly to Jack Jones as if she'd been with him throughout the whole life-cycle of a salmon.

When it came to a programme about Scouting, which I got Jack Cox, then editor of *Boy's Own Paper*, to introduce from Studio E, it happened to be an extremely hot August afternoon – even more so under all the studio lights. The self same Mary Malcolm was announcing that day, but not from Continuity, she would be with us in our studio. As we came towards the end of my scouting programme, so I released a camera in order to cover her in-vision close. As I lined her up, I noticed Mary was looking as elegantly delightful and cool as usual. She was wearing a bolero jacket over a sunsuit. With clever studio lighting, the viewers saw some of the Rover Scouts from Gilwell Park in silhouette through the canvas of their tent as they rested on the latest type of light-weight beds. Outside, a spiral of smoke rose from the wood fire. A cool night scene. Closer examination would have shown a multitude of wilting leaves on branches of trees brought into the studio, besides a wilting floor-crew in all that heat. Just as I told the studio hands to 'roll captions', so the heat got the better of Mary and she quickly removed the bolero part of her summer outfit. A moment later she appeared to the nation as if dressed in only her birthday suit, the camera showing all bare shoulders. A quarter of an inch lower and her strapless sun top *would* have been in view! Freda Lingstrom didn't let this pass without comment. Funny but nowadays I don't think I would get away with my programme title, either. I'd called this epic *Camping in Comfort*.

* * *

If I tended towards a wish to do television drama, then it was because Freda had Shaun Sutton on her staff. He would do really marvellous mini-dramas, often period pieces, within a twenty by twenty foot area of studio space, only bits of scenery, a small but talented cast besides splendid 'smoking cannon' and other exciting things manufactured by Jack Kine of the BBC's Special Effects department.

A day's Children's Television from Studio E might start with only five feet of floor space for a recital directed by John Hunter-Blair. He'd vacate the producer's chair up in the Control Gallery when the next item came on, perhaps a piece about sport. A bit more of the available studio space would then be taken up with something like *How To Paint* with artist Mervyn Levi, and then came Episode 5 of Shaun's current drama serial as he took over in the Gallery. In later times, Shaun was to get *Z Cars* and other serials into the ratings, to be instrumental in the prestige achieved by *Play For Today*, and many co-productions with the television services of other countries, and to so successfully lead a large creative department when he became head of BBC television drama. Whilst in that job, Shaun managed to make time to adapt two of Hugh Walpole's novels for me, *Rogue Herries* and *Judith Paris* as part of a twelve-episode *Herries Chronicle* as the Radio 4 Sunday evening serial. When we'd first met I didn't realise he was Westmoreland born and bred, although I'd done several programmes with a much older man from that part of the North region, besides enjoying several of the novels he'd written. He was Graham Sutton whom we'd chosen as the 'distinguished old boy' when

The poster distributed throughout BAOR for our Children's series

Rosemary Fry, aged 9, sent me her cartoon of ‘The Mouse Who Wanted the Moon’ having heard mine

BBC Radio NEW SEASON

NORTH WEST (BBC Radio Manchester: page 70) 16-22 January 1982 Price 25p

Radio Times

Family portraits

Their names echo through the pages of history – six 'Great Families of Britain'. Radio 4's new series traces the stories of the Russells, Hamiltons, Howards, Fitzgeralds, Percys and Mostyns. Back feature: The Russells of Woburn

Cover for the 'Great Families of Britain' series I did with Alison Plowden and John Julius Norwich – 1982

The 1988 launch of Wallace Grevatt's definitive book on the BBC *Children's Hour* as published by The Book Guild

Reunited in Hamburg in 2001 with a *real* musician in the person of Axel Alexander

he did a history of St Bees school. It took a long time before it dawned on me that Graham and Shaun were father and son.

During the time I was attached to Freda's department, I was delighted to catch up with the splendid Cliff Michelmore again. He'd already done that sports programme for me on radio. Now, from Studio E, Cliff introduced my *Sport on Stilts*. I imagine they allowed me a bit more studio floor space for that item. All I really remember about it is that, on this occasion, Pru was the Vision Mixer – the person who sat right next to the producer and cut from one camera to another, mixed between cameras and did the fade-ups and fade-outs. Dear Pru (they all seemed to have names like that), she was so cock-sure of her mixing capabilities that she spent a lot of the time knitting – yes, knitting – *and* looking like Madame Lefarge watching trainee producers like me go to the guillotine. Pru's most spectacular moment came when she had to intercut Cameras 1, 2 and 3 to show close-ups of a ball being dribbled by stilts across the floor.

'Oh, brilliant, darling, bloody brilliant!' declared our Lighting Supervisor. In her determination to get a cardigan finished, Pru was late each time she cut to those shots. All the viewers saw that day were three bits of Studio E floor! Rosemary Gill was of the opinion that dear Pru should get knitted. And so was I.

Rosemary helped and assisted a lot of the guest producers (the word 'director' didn't come into use until much later), and back in the office she never seemed unduly upset by anything – or if she was then out came the bottom drawer of her desk. Resting her pretty feet on this, Rosemary would play a mouth organ until calm was restored once again. She rushed around and organised a marvellous selection of film clips from library stock for the final programme I did during that first stint at Lime Grove. It was all about the dangers connected with swimming and sailing. I got Lieutenant Commander Douglas V. Duff to introduce the programme for me. I chose an appropriate title for it too – *Out Of Your Depth*.

On arriving back North, there were a few more OBs to do with Ray Lakeland. The RSPCA Animal Rescue Unit in Liverpool made exciting viewing – at least, the way Ray handled his cameras. I started the live transmission by talking to some people and their pets in the RSPCA clinic. (The particular pet I talked *with* was an African grey parrot.) Then came the great call. A poor cat was stranded high up on the roof of a city building. A second BBC Outside Broadcast unit was already there as a brave rescuer went up a long ladder and the rescued came safely down. Well, not *exactly*. Having got to know 'Mum', I'd said to Ray we really could not allow a poor moggie to be taken up and plonked by a chimney as darkness fell just so we could televise it being rescued. In the event, viewers caught just the merest glimpse of a fear-filled cat's eye peering round the chimney stack, then Ray handled the actual rescue all in long-shot. It had been arranged that poor puss would be handed to me, then I would turn to camera to show in close-up that all was well.

The intrepid RSPCA officer from the Animal Rescue Unit descended from the high building with his back to camera. As I stood at the bottom of the ladder, so he handed me the stuffed cat we'd used. This, I quickly secreted inside my duffle coat in exchange for a real cat whilst Ray had cut to show the relieved faces of the crowd that had gathered to watch. Millions of homes must have echoed to the sighs of relief as I then held pussy aloft for all to see. It was at that very moment the little bugger bit me – just to underline the fact that he had no intention of being thrust under anyone's coat again. Not even for the BBC.

Having survived the dangers of the speedway track, the accident at the circus with that bull-whip, and being bitten by a cat – and in vision too – I decided it was probably a lot safer to remain on the other side of the camera. I also had a series of my own to produce from Lime Grove. Freda Lingstrom had accepted my idea for a follow-up to *Our Port*. How about a similar programme – again with Kim Allen as the expert model-maker, on getting to the moon and, once there, building a space-port? A call to Professor Bernard Lovell at Jodrell Bank, and I had one of his staff from Manchester University Department of Radio Astronomy lined up to introduce each programme. When Freda first saw Dr Roger Jennison, or 'Clifton Jennison' as he liked to be called, she was under the impression that he was an actor. With those very bright, darting eyes, a small beard and all that youthful enthusiasm, he not only looked but sounded like a slightly mad scientist.

With Roger's expert knowledge concerning space and the necessary hardware to get us successfully launched, we took off for the moon in February 1956. We were right on target too! Over six programmes, models made by young viewers came pouring into the BBC, hundreds of them, brilliantly made, launching pads, earth station control centres, fuel stores, rockets of all shapes and designs, lunar exploration vehicles, and a complex of living accommodation and workshops to be assembled from cargo-carrying rockets on and under the surface of the moon – well, just a part of the surface. The section created by Kim Allen and some of his own staff, assisted by BBC Scenic Workshops, took up thirty-two feet of Studio E, and that was just the diameter. A special film studio mobile

Our final 'Port' before a bit of a storm!

Kim's own model

selection of the best made by young viewers!

Prof. Roger Jennison and Kim Allen invite young viewers to make models for our 'Space Port'

crane was hired in order that a BBC television camera could reach across the section and show our 'moon' and the models in close-up.

Harrods were so impressed by the standard of the models constructed by our young viewers that they displayed them on a smaller section of the moon which the BBC made for the Earl's Court Radio and Television Show that year. *Space Port* became one of the main attractions. Roger Jennison became something of a TV personality within the run of the series, and was a great success at Earl's Court, especially when he turned up one day with 'Conker', his dog. The only let-down was a letter to Freda. I am fairly sure it came from the Astronomer Royal. He took Children's Television to task for putting such ideas as men in space into the heads of our young and impressionable viewers. And as for reaching the moon! Even as the gentleman wrote, I imagine the Russians knew precisely how and when they would be putting the first man into space, for that event occurred only a few years later. Does television encourage the young to make such intricate models these days? It now appears to be all paper and paint!

Working from the Lime Grove studios meant I'd have the guiding hand of Rosemary Gill to assist me, but once we started *Space Port*, it was Denness Roylance of Northern *Children's Hour* who took on the additional task of becoming my Production Secretary, organising the hundred and one things in the weeks leading up to doing a six-part series and then sitting by my side in the Control Gallery and 'calling the shots' as the show went on. Denness took to it as if she'd been on this side of broadcasting since the day Logie Baird started it all.

Once *Space Port* was completed, we said goodbye to the experienced and helpful camera crews and technicians at Lime Grove because, from now on, we were to be using properly equipped studios in the North. For several months, the BBC in Manchester had been building up its own studio crews and production facilities, besides enlarging the TV OB Unit which still covered all programmes as 'Outside Broadcasts' even when we operated, as we often did, from inside a radio studio with lighting and cameras.

The week *Space Port* reached for the stars saw the television launch of someone who, as I've already told you, was to sparkle as a star of television for many a year, Violet Carson. Her TV debut, in *Bran Tub*, was on February 23rd 1956, from the Manchester Playhouse studio. I too went 'solo' that day as a producer for BBC North television and was now put in control of both Radio and TV programmes for children when they originated from the North. Since the BBC's Holme Moss transmitter had just opened, I was able to 'opt-out' and to do television programmes purely on a regional basis, besides contributing programmes which could be seen nationally.

We had our own signature tune for *Children's Hour*, 'Northern Lights', and in the North I had several young people to announce my radio programmes. Besides introducing the teenage magazine, *Out of School*, Judith Chalmers was also announcing for me the *Children's Hour* music show with an audience at the Playhouse, *At Home With Doris and Vi* which featured Vi Carson and Doris Gambell with the BBC Northern Variety orchestra conducted by Alyn Ainsworth. Perhaps Judith was the person to announce for me on television as well. She made her TV debut on April 17th 1956 when we celebrated our new-found television 'opt-out' freedom by doing a variety programme from the recently acquired Dickenson Road studio in Manchester. She introduced a young man named Ian Sutcliffe and his 'Midget Marionettes' and Violet Carson who was very much as home with *Songs At The Piano*. A couple of weeks later and for another 'opt-out' Judith was introducing Eddie King and Jo Day, *Telewise and Sound Foolish* and, more to her own liking I suspect, Cyril Washbrook and Cliff Gladwin who demonstrated batting and bowling and *without* smashing a camera lens. Surprising, really, that Cyril agreed to take part in a programme I had anything to do with since he was that same cricketer I'd rushed away from in the middle of that interview from the Slazenger factory, leaving a trail of bits of bat and Mr Washbrook looking, well, slightly startled by it all!

I always had a lot of support and encouragement from my head of programmes at that time, Bryan Cave-Brown-Cave. It was Bryan who suggested he invite Freda Lingstrom to visit Manchester, to see our Dickenson Road studios and advise on the sort of programmes we might provide for her department besides those we might do just for viewers in the North. Whilst Freda was never very keen on a magazine-type series of programmes, she did give her blessing when I suggested we might go ahead and see if we could do in vision the sort of Saturday magazine programme we did on radio with *Out of School*.

It was on Sunday 7th May 1956 that *Children's Television Club* literally set sail – and it has certainly clocked up a remarkable number of nautical miles since that date for, despite what else may have been written and said on the subject, this was surely the beginning of *Blue Peter*. That very first programme featured the *Royal Iris* steamer at Wallasey on the River Mersey. Judith Chalmers greeted viewers in the North at the foot of the ship's gangway and then we cast off from shore and set sail down river with out television OB Unit transmitting signals to shore using a sound and vision link. Aboard, I had a shipful of youngsters, Wilfred and Mabel Pickles to conduct interviews with the likes of Deck-boy Clegg and the captain of the *Royal Iris* from the bridge whilst, below decks, Judith introduced the musical items provided by the whole of the Merseyside Youth Orchestra who also sailed with us. By Jove! Marvellous this TV, *and* coming to you 'live'.

I had BBC Studio Manager Bill Slater with me to do the vision mixing. Perhaps this gave him a taste for the sea because, in later years, when head of television drama serials, Bill was to produce *The Onedin Line* which is still in my own Top Ten when it comes to BBC productions. For our Engineering Manager that day, the programme didn't rate much above the bottom twenty. When we had docked and the credits faded with the ending of our signature tune 'Ballet Of The Bells', Harry Cox, who had a gammy leg, almost swiped me with his walking stick.

'What a complete waste,' he said, getting a firmer grip on the ship's rail. 'You had all that scenery' his stick swept through the air, 'All that casting-off and arriving alongside, the journey down river and you used the whole damn thing as just a floating studio!'

Apart from some enthusiastic passengers pointing out a few of the landmarks to Wilfred during one point in the transmission, Harry was right. Another lesson learnt. But *Children's Television Club* survived and went on to become a regular programme from the Dickenson Road studios where, each month, we had a group of youngsters in the programme with Wilfred, Mabel and Judith. One time there would be a kiln in the studio and someone to show them how to 'throw' pottery, decorate and fire it. A Blackpool confectionery company brought an entire rock-making plant with them, and the youngsters in the studio put the initials of the programme 'CTV' into the sticks of Blackpool rock. Peter Butterworth, who'd worked with me from Lime Grove, came once or twice and did some of his lovely knockabout comedy routines, whilst, on film, I'd feature such events as the 1956 Scout Go-Kart finals with Sir Len Hutton to present the prizes. Oh yes, and Dr Roger Jennison kindly lent us 'Conker'. He was the first dog to be seen regularly in a children's television series – and he got his share of fan mail.

I cannot claim that 'Conker' was as well behaved as some of the Blue Peter canines in later years. He enjoyed the rock-making – or at least, the rock-licking – but kept dashing off to jump up and lick some of the young club members who were sitting at tables before coming back to Judith who was holding the large, sticky confection. On this occasion 'Conker' provided one of the funniest endings yet seen on TV in the 1950s.

After that experience our regular Floor Manager at Dickenson Road, Johnny Day, kept 'Conker' at bay behind the scenes and at a pre-arranged point in the programme would 'hand him on'. In point of fact, Johnny was invariably 'in vision', so much so that Wilfred said, 'Oh, heck! Let the chap come on like it was planned and we can see all of him, not just a hand and a bit of an elbow.'

Johnny Day ! Now *there* was a BBC Floor Manager. He could deal with anyone and with anything. He had pictures of Macmillan, Adlai Stevenson, Vivien Leigh and others of that celebrated ilk hanging in his office walls most proclaiming 'To Johnny with Love' – and not all signed by the same hand, either! He was often asked for when the Right Hon. Harold Macmillan was going to speak to the nation on television. Johnny's 'line', which I heard myself on several unforgettable occasions, went like this. 'Now don't you take no notice of them out there, mate. Soon as th' red light comes on an' I give you your cue, you just give 'em the old one-two, eh?' So unlike 'Auntie's' usual manner – yet so very effective.

In the former days of television's *Picture Page*, Ms Joan Gilbert used to rely heavily on our Johnny. The time they had a master baker on the show the presenter kept forgetting what all those utensils he used were called. Just before transmission she asked for the umpteenth time what 'this thing' was. Johnny sighed – and told her. As the master baker was about to make a series of holes in some dough, Joan picked up 'the thing' with spikes on the end and declared to the nation, 'Ah, and I know what *this* is. This is your crumpet puncture!'

As *Children's Television Club* progressed, so did Johnny Day's length of appearance on the screen. He got to actually speaking. 'Enjoying ourselves, are we?' he'd enquire as he brought 'Conker' to centre stage. Always a neat dresser, Johnny became nothing short of sartorially elegant. I'd congratulated him at the end of one transmission, but perhaps I overdid it a bit, because a look came into our Floor Manager's eyes. Never slow, was Johnny. He opened his mouth – and I knew what he was about to say. But I beat him to it. 'And if you are now going to ask to be paid for appearing in vision, I'll kill you!'

I was jolly sorry when Johnny and the BBC parted company. Nothing to do with Equity or non-payment of a fee, I assure you. In later times I was to meet a Wing Commander, who moored next to MV *Cleo* for a season on Lake Windermere. He knew I was something to do with the

Mary, Robert Patterson and my godson, Grahame, so '*Let's Get Weaving*'

BBC and asked if I knew a chap named Day – J. Day. Turned out that Johnny had been i/c Stores at some wartime RAF depot. 'Remarkable chap, Day. Could scrounge anything you asked for or even hinted at,' said the Wingco.

Johnny had been a particular tower of strength and support to me right from the day we started *Let's Get Weaving*, my first network series for children's television from Manchester. This featured our very good friends from the Castle Museum, York, Robert and Mary Patterson together with their young son, Grahame. Besides being the museum curator, Robert was one of the world authorities on wool and the history of wool. Johnny didn't have to scrounge an ancient handloom or any other paraphernalia. That was provided by the Pattersons. 'Pat' also made up a very simple hand-loom which viewers could easily make for themselves and we had several thousand leaflets printed for *Let's Get Weaving.*

Until this series, all children's programmes seen nationally throughout the British Isles were introduced by the BBC's television announcers from London. I asked Ursula about using Judith Chalmers – but that was a matter for the TV Presentation Department. Rex Moorefoot was in charge. Yes, he would willingly see Judith if I could book a vision circuit and control line between Manchester and London. I couldn't. The Post Office hadn't many vision circuits in the mid 1950s

'Then let her first appearance on national TV be her audition!' declared Rex.

Before that first appearance, Denness Roylance and I made sure Judith had signed and returned her contract for the full series. The first programme went very well. Judith announced it, then took part as the 'novice', spinning then weaving the wool collected from hedgerows. A couple of days later, an eager young voice was phoning me at home. How was I? How was Margaret? Er, had we heard anything from Lime Grove? I got on to Mr Moorefoot. Oh, hadn't the message been passed on? Yes, yes, a splendid young girl. His Presentation staff liked her style too. I had but one problem in launching Judith as the first regular BBC television announcer outside London. She would choose dresses and a set of pearls which made her look as if she had left her teens years ago!

We were to do quite a few more programmes with Pat Patterson and

Judith Chalmers' TV debut as the first BBC announcer outside London in 'Let's Get Weaving' from Dickenson Road, Manchester

with the celebrated Castle Museum, York. *Then And Now* was a journey back through time, showing everything from the earliest butter-churning and apple-corer, washing machine and vacuum cleaner, demonstrating that there is really very little new when it comes to household utensils and farming implements. We used the museum again when Margaret had her idea of a late evening programme about the history of Valentine cards accepted for St Valentine's Day. The museum's Victorian parlour provided our main setting. We made the most of it. One of the museum staff played 'Boots', whose Valentine card to the daughter of the starchy head-of-household was discovered by him. She, poor maiden, did a long backward staggering faint when Boots, in caption, was told, 'Darken not my door again!' We filmed it with the sort of overlaps and jumps in action which occurred in the very early days of cinematography. My cameraman colleague, Gerry Pullen, even rocked the tripod of the camera a bit, whilst his assistant increased and decreased the lens aperture to give a sort of 'early film' effect. And when the film was edited and we got to the stage of cutting the negative, we carefully rolled this in a deep box containing coarse string in order to give the finished product an authentic 'scratched' effect. I admit it. I *was* a bit put out when the then television Controller of Programmes wrote to say how much he'd enjoyed watching, *Be My Valentine* – but added, 'A pity Archives didn't have a better copy of that splendid old silent film you used!'

* * *

When Welsh whizz-kid Donald Baverstock suddenly took over as the Controller he just about killed off BBC Children's Television as we knew it. 'Too bloody middle-class, boyo!' is precisely what he told me. He may have had a point. It was a criticism regularly levelled at radio's *Children's Hour*. Perhaps our radio drama came into this category, yet, when I tried to inject a different sort of play into the schedules, I wasn't at all popular with our young listeners. I'd read a novel all about 'Cement Street School', one of the new 1950s comprehensives, found an adapter and went ahead with this as a serial. It was almost entirely the children from areas like Moss Side, Manchester, the Liverpool housing estates, and the poorer parts of Leeds who sent in their protests.

'Why can't we have those plays where people have nice things to eat?'

'When can we hear *Bunkle* again with Colonel and Mrs de Salis?'

'I don't like plays about poor people!'

I can't say that any of the books I adapted for *Jackanory* dealt with either the middle or upper classes, but stories are one thing, drama is another. However, *Children's Hour* had a least another year or so to run before Frank Gillard was to take on the role of axeman.

Donald Baverstock, a protégé of another of the small band of women executives in the BBC, Grace Wyndham Goldie, had done great things with *Tonight*, and with Cliff Michelmore, Cynthia Judah, Trevor Philpot and with my fellow 'Old Haberdasher' and Calvert houseman, Alan Whicker. Alan made his TV debut on this remarkable ladder of television journalism. I was to put a Liverpool group of lads into their first television series. *Dance And Skylark* featured The Spinners introduced by an old salt who was the expert on sea-shanties, Stan Hugill. The only trouble with Stan was that even his scholarly published work on this art-form contained 'edits' on some of the lyrics. Stan was a man for the original and so I spent a lot of time on re-takes and edits, and on trying to stop Tony, Mick, Hughie and Cliff from falling about laughing as Stan repeatedly forgot himself with nautical language which was anything but 'middle-class'.

I had a nasty moment in later years sitting comfortably at home watching *Sooty*. We'd recorded the programme earlier that week but within the first two minutes, something went wrong with one of the props – and Sooty's dad uttered a naughty word. As soon as the Sunday teatime transmission began, I realised that TV Centre was transmitting the first 'Take'! Remembering names and telephone numbers has never been a strong point; luckily I remembered TV Presentation's number in London. I was fortunate that Derek Ball, a former Manchester Studio Manager, was on duty. Even whilst I spoke so the *Sooty* programme faded from the screen and up went a caption with some music. A few moments later a voice-over said, 'Well, sorry we lost *Sooty*. So as not to spoil your enjoyment, we'll begin the programme again!' And they did, from the start of 'Take 2' without any naughty word. There'll be more about my friend Sooty later.

It was Donald Baverstock who decided that whilst *Tonight* and the team took a well earned break, it's placing should be filled by a series on Museums – 'not a stuffy-blooming series, boyo!' I think *Brush Off The Dust* was Donald's title as well. Guess where my edition sprang from? The one member of the *Tonight* team who didn't get a holiday break that year was Fyfe Robertson. But in getting him to open the series from the Castle Museum, what I hadn't realised was that Fyfe had not worked to TV cameras before – all those items he did so well were done on *film* where each shot would be set-up then done before a break and then another set-up for the next shot. He therefore found it difficult having to talk to one TV camera and to carry on, turning to another showing, perhaps, a close-up and *without* any breaks. I did some camera and lighting rehearsals at York the day before the celebrated interviewer arrived. Matters weren't helped when I suggested to Pat that he stand in for Fyfe Robertson. Effecting a somewhat dubious Scots accent, Pat's first question to my OB Floor Manager – standing in for Robert Patterson the museum curator – was, 'But why HAVE a museum, Mr Patterson?'

That same evening, the real Fyfe Robertson was speaking to me over the phone. I was telling him that we were going to feature the Edwardian pub in the new museum 'Street' and that to add to the warm glow at the counter, cast by practical bat-wing gas burners, he and the curator would end the televised proceedings by taking a drink with others who'd been in the programme. Was there a particular brand of Scotch he liked? That lilting voice, whose owner I'd yet to meet in person, said, 'Are you a drinking man, Mr Hill?' In those days, I wasn't really. 'Then it must be a Malt. And you know why? Ten minutes later I did. Ten minutes later I knew a lot more about the ancient art of whisky, so poetically described to the uninitiated. Although I say so myself – and I often do lately – it was a splendid programme from York and a good time was had by all, especially *after* we finished all the recordings that night. It wasn't the Post Master General's minions who spoilt things this time; it was HM Customs and Excise. They'd seen a copy of that day's *Yorkshire Post*. On NO account was the BBC to sell whisky and other intoxicants – even at 1910 prices, which we *had* done on the programme.

'The Castle Museum according to our records has no Licence!'

* * *

Petty officialdom wasn't the norm, thank God. If we went around shouting 'We are the BBC' then we deserved an occasional put-down. Once television really got going there was sometimes a change in attitudes by authorities and organisations which had had a visit from the few loud mouths – often 'visiting' directors, researchers and film crews, coming to work in the region for just one short item, who put a minor dent in the BBC's image. Having done that they left. We had to make amends. Rarely was the door shut to us for long. Public broadcasting and public relations go hand-in-hand.

I know that Margaret and I were very surprised by a visit from Granada TV to our home when the company were doing a drama series entitled

The Villains. A fresh-faced young Richard Everett knocked on the front door one day.

'Good morning,' he said, 'I'm from Granada. We are looking for locations in this area and feel your house would be ideal if we could turn one part of it into a village store!'

'Good morning to you, Richard,' replied Margaret. 'My husband and I, he works for the BBC by the way, we have spent the last seven years in trying to make this place *not* look like the village store – which it was when we bought it!'

Granada's Outside Broadcast unit and staff were splendid. A lot of things transpired. Jenny, the make-up assistant was the wife of Paul, one of our BBC Manchester design assistants, whilst Margaret and I had worked with at least half the cast in this episode of *The Villains*, so our bathroom soon became 'Make-Up'. Granada Design did a grand job on the front of the Queen Anne house, making it look so *much* like a village store that between breaking for their lunch and getting back again to put the finishing touches, we'd had several van drivers asking for 'Ten

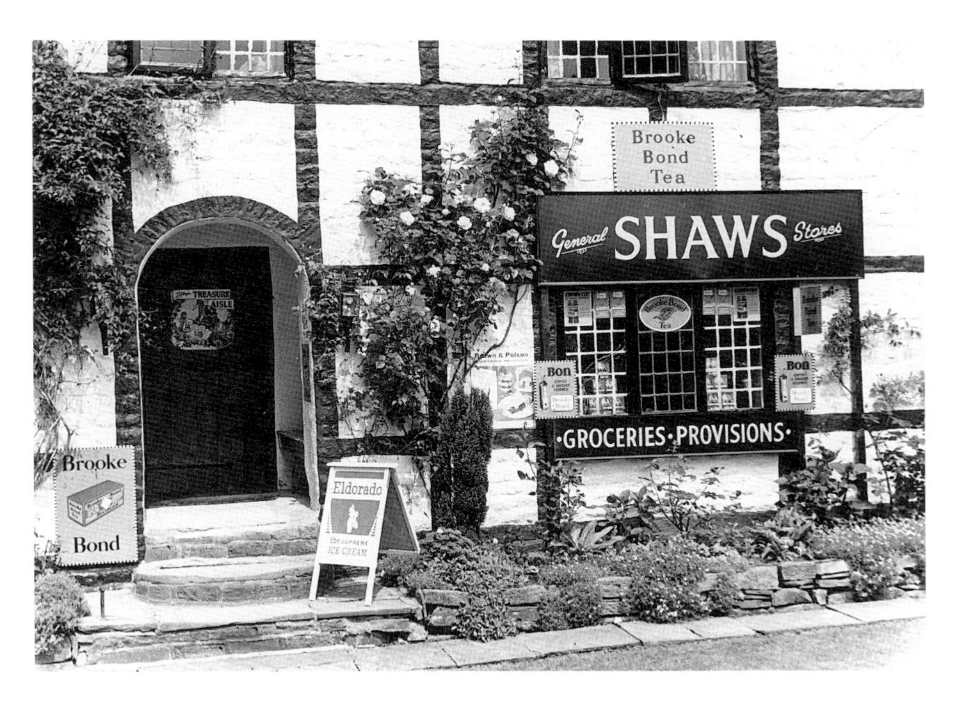

Granada Television changes our home to a grocery store for *The Villains*

Players, please!' And when it was all over and I came back from work, our leaded window panes had been carefully cleaned and there wasn't so much as a fag-end left behind. By post came a nice 'thank you' letter besides a framed photo 'Shaws – Groceries and Provisions'.

Again on the subject of public relations, I thought that the headmaster of Cheethams School, Manchester, now the School of Music, had been jolly co-operative and understanding when I went to discuss a programme of music and carols for Christmas Day. The programme was to lead up to the Queen's televised message to the nation that year. In the school grounds I'd noticed a genuine Roman milestone and as we sat at top table for lunch in the Elizabethan school hall, I suddenly had an idea for a visual treatment to the music master's arrangement of 'We Three Kings'. He'd scored this for voices accompanied by finger-bells and tabor, to be played in a very Eastern rhythm. I looked down at the long floor of the hall. It was stone. 'Er, d'you think I could dump two or three tons of sand in here?'

Harry Vickers was always helpful. He didn't choke on the school pudding, he merely said, 'Why not?' when I explained my idea. Later I 'auditioned' bare feet. Gerry Littlewood the talented music master was one who 'passed'. On Christmas morning, 1961, viewers saw just the footprints of the three Kings in the desert sand, a palm tree I had hired, and that genuine Roman milestone. I met that nice headmaster again around Easter time when some of the choir from Cheethams came in to our Dickenson Road studios to be 'sailors' in my televised series with The Spinners.

'We still have it down.' said Harry Vickers, looking keenly at me. 'You know, sand. *Lots* of it!' Was he kidding?

I was genuinely worried when he went on to tell me that one of the Chippendale chairs in the Governors' Room had been damaged. It must have been knocked by one of our heavy camera dollys. I assured Mr Vickers that we were well insured and that a chair of such value should be sent to an expert – and no expense spared. It turned out that Mr Littlewood had already seen to it. He came to Cheetham's as woodwork master. That he also happened to possess remarkable musical skills was just a bonus.

* * *

A big bonus for us in Children's Programmes, North, was a visit to the Isle of Man two or three times a year where every possible help and assistance was always readily available. Mind you the authorities couldn't do a lot for me the year I planned a short feature on Manx kippers. Evidently fish aren't entirely stupid. They must have read the *Radio Times* billing because not one single herring came anywhere near Mananin's Isle until a full two weeks after the BBC had departed those shores.

There was always a bit of rivalry between south and north of Watford in programme making and before ITV came along to provide the keen edge of competition, so London and the Regions would strive to 'go one better' on the sort of series which would be London-based yet, 'with your facilities, will travel'. Such a series was *Children's Caravan*, dreamed up by Freda Lingstrom and Ursula Eason unless I'm mistaken. That was a travelling show as the title implies and it certainly had some pretty snappy openings from different venues. Since we'd be having both radio and TV OB facilities over in the Isle of Man during the summer to cover the TT Races I suggested we should do *Children's Caravan* from Douglas.

'Grab your audience in the first minute!' With that maxim in mind, I got in touch with Sir Joseph Qualtrough who was an ideal PR man besides being Speaker in the Manx Parliament. He put me in touch with the Town Clerk, the Manx police and the fire brigade. 'I'll show London a thing or two,' I thought. Apart from having to employ the entire Manx steam packet dock labour force on double-time rates in order to unload the London-based caravan on that Sunday morning it cost us precisely nothing for facilities when we came into the homes of the nation at the start of the programme. A large stretch of Douglas Promenade was closed to traffic at 5 p.m. that day as the Manx fire engine came roaring along, bells all a-clang, to pull up with a screech of tyres right in front of the Villa Marina. Up shot the fire ladder with our presenter leaping up it and then on to the flat roof of the covered garden walk. 'Hello and welcome ...' beamed Jeremy Glidt in breathless tones.

I'd planned another bit of breathless viewing and pace to some of the more sedate juggling and balancing acts which were taking part in the Big Top below. I'd asked TT rider Geoff Duke to make s surprise appearance. He came literally roaring along the flat rook of the garden walk as if he was taking part in the Manx Grand Prix.

Another chap I got mobile that day was a young singer. I liked him and I liked his voice, also the fact that he was game to get astride a smaller motorcycle and come riding into shot along the Villa Marina garden paths, keeping in time with the orchestra playing over a hundred yards away, as he sang one of the latest 'hits'. This was nothing compared to the antics he later got up to in all those 'Carry On' films – or in the New York production of *Barnum*. A great performer was Jim Dale.

Whilst still on wheels there were those early morning practices on the TT course. We used to get up very early to watch, especially if Geoff Duke was riding. For several seasons my assistant Denness Roylance would be helping with the broadcast commentaries on the TT and Grand Prix races. She'd take useful lap-timings during those dawn practices when the circuit roads were closed for this purpose. We were up at Bradda Head one coolish morning with Denness wearing a nice bright coat she'd bought for her Isle of Man visit that year. As one motorcyclist came roaring into sight, so Denness stepped out with millboard and stop-watch in order to identify the rider. A few minutes later, the Ace himself, Geoff Duke, pulled into the pits asking what was up. Nothing! Then why had the Course Stewards put up that red flag on Bradda? Truth to tell several of the TT riders whistled 'The Red Flag' every time they saw our Denness during the actual race week.

Denness really demonstrated her devotion to BBC duties some two or three years later. I was filming for a *Jackanory* series on Manx folk tales and songs. The final programme was to end with the Manx storyteller, Marian Norris, standing atop some harbour steps at Douglas. The ever helpful Manx Tourist Board had fixed us up with a rather powerful and splendid speedboat belonging to Mr Manx Ice cream in person. The boat's propellers just idled close to the jetty steps as Marian ascended. A gentle touch of the throttle and the camera crew, myself and Denness eased gently away to reveal Marian as she reached the top of the steps. Then, in the setting sun, her figure was to grow smaller and smaller as we sped out to sea and she waved 'goodbye'.

It nearly *was* goodbye! Above the roar of the speedboat's engines, I heard Denness shout. The next moment, a steamer's siren was blasting our eardrums. Looking round quickly I got a very close look at the churning propellers of the great ship as she too backed out of Douglas harbour. Even the owner at the helm of the speedboat had been concentrating on Marian on the quayside! We managed to avert disaster and prevent camera and cameraman lurching overboard as we skidded sideways upon an enormous wash. Denness stopped timing the final 'Take', and then calmly enquired, 'Is that the end of Shot 92?'

15

'We Can't Have Sex With Sooty'

As we came out of the tobacconist's shop on Lord Street, Southport, sudden recognition spread across the cheeky young face of the Lancashire day-tripper. Sprinting around the passing traffic he made a bee-line for Harry Corbett. 'I know what YOU do, Mister!' he exclaimed in genuine delight, 'You put your hand up Sooty!'

'Fame at last,' muttered Harry.

The BBC's Audition Report of May 2nd 1952 explained the rudiments of his act in slightly more genteel terms: 'Very pleasant fair-haired youngish man with hand puppet.' And against his name, his type of act was described as 'Magician'.

* * *

One of Harry Corbett's neighbours in the Yorkshire village of Guiseley was Barney Colehan then producing radio's *Have A Go* and, from time to time, Harry had been the pianist. He asked about the chances of getting an audition for television and Barney immediately phoned the person who was organising amateur acts that same week for the Radio Industries Exhibition from the City Hall, Manchester. Sorry, they were fully booked – but then came a call back. Someone had dropped out. Mr Corbett could be auditioned tomorrow afternoon.

As I've already mentioned, Violet Carson always said that what brought her success wasn't so much a question of talent as being in the right place at the right time and being able to show what you can do in front of the right person. Friday, May 2nd 1952 was Harry Corbett's lucky day. He'd been auditioned then asked to stay on until 6 p.m. when the best acts seen that day would be shown on closed circuit television at the City Hall for the benefit of visitors and exhibitors alike.

As Harry appeared, so did BBC light entertainment producer, Eric Fawcett, just off the London train to prepare for a live Saturday evening transmission gleaned from the best acts of the whole week. He stood by one of the cameras, still in his overcoat, watching the young man assist a glove-puppet with some magic tricks.

'I must have that for tomorrow night!' he declared. What proved to be even more helpful to Harry was the excellent advice Eric gave him. He told him to alter the facial character of the glove puppet in order to make it Harry's own design, give it a name and above all to register both the name *and* the design! His final words before departing were, 'Oh, and twelve and a half minutes is far too long. Get your act down to four and half!'

Harry and his wife got to work. They made several alterations to the bear's features including sewing on black eyebrows and blacking the ears until the name 'Sooty' suggested itself to them. The following evening Sooty made his debut. Introduced by Harry Corbett, he appeared in a puff of smoke and at once delighted the viewers with some of his own tricks which included 'manufacturing' a golden hamster and then demonstrating his musical skills on the xylophone – or rather Harry's musical skills.

* * *

By the tender age of seven, Harry was showing an interest in the upright piano at home in Yorkshire. His mother sat with him for one or two hours almost every day, then she and Harry's father paid for one of the best teachers in the area. The day came when they knew he'd need a really good instrument and so off to Bradford where Harry was told he could choose any piano. He chose wisely – a Steinway Grand no less. Not easily come by in the 1920s with only the weekly proceeds of their fish and chip shop to support the Corbett family and quite a few of their customers working 'short time' at the mills or endeavouring to exist on the dole! From the age of eleven, Harry's musical talents began to flourish as he achieved a manual dexterity which, in the years ahead, was to make him known to a far wider audience both at home and abroad than many a concert pianist. That had been the goal to strive for as he practised, played at various local concerts, then went back to the long routine of practising again. However, only gradually at first, deafness was setting in.

Harry began to play a different kind of music by joining his younger brother, Leslie, who played a pretty good alto and tenor sax. They called themselves 'The Rhythmists' and the louder they played the better for the one member of the band. By the time he was sixteen, Harry had taken up an engineering apprenticeship with the electrical firm of Crompton Parkinson. Then came another interest besides music. The young lady in his life, Marjorie Hodgson, worked for Harry's already famous uncle. Fish 'n' chips must have been very much a family affair – they certainly made Harry Ramsden's fortune. His richly carpeted emporium, with never a whiff of frying oils, was more than just a landmark on the Ilkley to Otley road in Yorkshire. It became a 'must'. The large car park boasted many Rolls and Bentley owners among the clièntele who either queued at the take-away counters, or sat in the opulent comfort of the large restaurant with its crystal chandeliers.

One of the waitresses was Miss Hodgson, far more of an attraction to young nephew Harry than his uncle's fare. According to an article in a woman's magazine written in the years ahead when Harry Corbett was far better known than Harry Ramsden, the ardent suitor would roar up on a cold winter's night to Ramsden's on his motorbike, 'wearing a large pair of furry gloves'.

'Then I must have been gripping the handlebars with Sooty on one hand and Sweep on the other,' explained Harry, 'only in those days, neither had even been thought of.'

It was Marjorie who consoled Harry in his increasing deafness. Instead of raising her voice, as many people do, she helped him to lip read. She also suggested that if he had to give up playing the piano, then why not turn to something else he could do with his hands, conjuring! In 1944, Marjorie and Harry were married, and so was his brother Leslie to the girl of *his* choice, Muriel, in a joint ceremony.

A few years later and now with their sons, David and Peter, the family were on holiday in Blackpool. One morning Harry decided to take young David by tram to the North Pier leaving Marjorie back at the digs with Peter who was still a baby. It was when they got back that Harry first mentioned about the teddy-bear glove puppet he'd seen in the joke and novelty shop. After he'd mentioned it several times, Marjorie said the magic words which were to completely alter their lives, 'Oh, go on love. If you want it, have it! Er, how much is it?' It cost precisely 7/6d.

By this time Harry was an engineer surveyor with an insurance company and managed to get by with a hearing aid. He could also hear sufficiently well to play piano from time to time at the Royal Hotel, Ilkley and at other functions but as his deafness increased so he turned to entertaining as a conjurer. The small bear would be ideal in assisting Harry to produce cigarettes, coins and billiard balls as part of the act. But then the situation changed. It was now Harry who acted as 'stooge' to the teddy bear who popped up from inside a soft felt hat. Next, there was a small conjurer's table draped in black and from behind this the small glove puppet went from strength to strength, finding chosen cards, whispering to Harry and only to Harry about their audience, and generally making magic combined with a clever mix of mischief and mayhem. What is more, the small bear didn't have to whisper as loudly since Harry had heard of a celebrated surgeon in Edinburgh. Simpson Hall did a fenestration operation, first on Harry's left ear and, later, on his right ear. Now he no longer required to be 'wired up' for sound. His magic act around the north of England grew in popularity. 'That bear's nothing short of wonderful,' they'd say to Harry.

Those watching television that Saturday in 1952 thought so too, a verdict echoed by most of the Sunday papers. The Corbetts waited for the offers to roll in. Two months later, nothing.

In the meantime, Harry had written to the head of Children's Programmes, Television, at Lime Grove, London, enclosing copies of the press reports on Sooty's debut. When the two met, the voice of experience and caution spoke as Freda Lingstrom pointed out that, although he might be asked to do several engagements, and in spite of the very favourable press reaction, Harry should certainly not think of giving up his job.

There followed the offer of six fortnightly appearances on *Saturday Special* with the entertainer Peter Butterworth. But Saturday was a working day for the employees of Harry's firm, especially the surveyors. Could he take six alternate Saturdays off work in lieu of holidays? No! It was engineering *or* television. In the firm's view Corbett couldn't mix the two. Harry was in a dilemma. What should he do? A series on TV, even a short one, might do wonders. Marjorie was quite sure of one thing. 'If you don't do these dates then you'll only spend the rest of your life wondering what *might* have been,' was her advice. His salary at that time was £12 a week, not a bad wage; the *Saturday Special* fee plus expenses was twelve guineas per show. On a fortnightly basis that worked out at £6 6s a week. Taking a deep breath, Harry Corbett and Sooty decided to turn professional.

Within days of their appearance on the show, a man from Barnsley wrote and asked Harry for the sole rights to manufacture Sooty xylophones. Next, the large toy firm of Chad Valley came along asking to market the glove puppet, then it was Butlins Holiday Camps and the large city stores who began to book him. Eric Fawcett's advice had begun to pay off.

Had Harry remained with the firm he might, by 1957, have been earning as much as £15 a week allowing for promotion. As it was, in that year Sooty was bringing in £1,000 a week – and fifty years ago, *that* was indeed a star's salary!

I firmly believe the old adage that behind many a successful man there is a woman. Harry and Marjorie Corbett, together, made a success of our friend Sooty. Come to think about it, three very well-known men in showbusiness married wives with certain things about them in common! Beryl Formby, Mabel Pickles and Marjorie Corbett had very similar colouring, each was northern born and bred, and each gave a lot of help and assistance to their respective husbands in their business affairs.

Marjorie and Mabel I knew very well and am fortunate to have counted them as friends of long standing. I only worked with the Formbys on two or three occasions, the last time with George when he starred in the stage musical, *Zip Goes A Million* which opened at the Palace Theatre, Manchester. I attended several of the rehearsals and noticed Beryl backstage. She would help the scene hands to rock the boat in one of the most spectacular storm scenes to be staged. Sadly, she seemed to rock the boat long after the scene was over.

Shortly after the musical opened to very good reviews and business at the box office, I took the Formbys to lunch in order to discuss the broadcast I was to do with George. For some reason, as I drove them back towards their hotel a heated back-seat row was going strong. I turned into Peter Street. The Midland Hotel was only at the top and I'd be leaving them there. As we passed Henley's car showrooms, George cut Beryl short by asking me to stop a moment. You could in those days. He hurried across to peer into one of the showroom bays. There, sparkling and immaculate, was a brand new Daimler coupé in two tones of brown. Beryl caught up with us as I discreetly asked the showroom assistant to get hold of Mr George White one of the main directors. He ran the Manchester part of the firm's operation with Ann Roylance as his faithful assistant – her sister, Denness, being mine at the BBC.

As Mr White joined us, so Mrs Formby was telling Mr Formby that maybe it was very nice but they had quite enough cars already! Mr Formby rather pointedly addressed his remarks to George White. It seemed his mind was already made up as he said, 'Er, but we'd need two of them, same colour!' Ah, now I got the picture. His and Hers. He'd be able to go happily off on his own, she could jolly well go off on *her* own. At least that is how I interpreted it. But it was really Harry Corbett who was to give *me* a taste for cars well above my station in life.

There came a time when we were asked if I would write and direct a series of Road Safety films featuring Sooty and Co, and we made an appointment to visit the Chief Constable of Middlesbrough and his committee who were to be the sponsors. I drove across to Guiseley in my new Triumph Herald. As Harry had done a late show the night before, he asked if I would drive him up to Middlesbrough in his car whilst he a had a bit of a 'zizz'. He was a great 'zizzer', so there was I driving a gleaming Bentley with every care and attention, the side only being let down by the affluent owner with Sooty snoring away in the back seat. At our meeting with the Chief Constable, we took the decision to form Guiseley Films, then I chauffeured the newly appointed Managing Director and chief shareholder back to his home.

The warm glow of unaccustomed affluence which wrapped itself around me that day abruptly evaporated the moment I got into my own car to make the return journey across the Pennines. The vehicle seemed to have four flat tyres, no suspension, a coffee-grinder under the bonnet and a few major faults besides. In a short while I was back to see George White. Perhaps he had a third or even a fourth-hand Jaguar? Sooty has a lot to answer for as I was often to remind him – although I was honoured in the 1990s to be introduced by Yorkshire Television as 'the man who did for Sooty what Brian Epstein did for the Beatles'!

After a major heart attack, and then a minor one, Harry was to hand over to his son, Matthew, while he and Marjorie confined themselves to only local and far less demanding theatre work with Sooty. Marjorie became very much a part of their act. In a remarkably life-like polar bear skin, and doing some clever and delightful mime, she appeared as 'Cuddles'. At times her glasses tended to steam up a bit inside the polar bear's head. In a routine with Harry on stage reading a book to Sooty, Cuddles was supposed to pass silently behind them on a small scooter with the audience screaming, 'There's a polar bear!' followed by the 'Oh-no-there-isn't' routine.

On one occasion when really 'steamed up', Cuddles lost her sense of direction, scooting past in front of Harry and ending up patting a blank wall in an effort to 'exit stage left'! Always the professional, Harry paused, looked up from the book and with Sooty holding paws apart in an expression of startled anticipation exclaimed, 'Are you in trouble, polar bear?'

Anyhow I hope I'll not be in trouble when my friend Sooty carefully dons those black-rimmed glasses of his, does his famous 'double-take' as he reads what I've written about him, then hits me on the head with that hammer you used to see on BBC TV many years ago. At the end of one of the early shows we did together, Harry was supposed to hide an egg under a school cap he was wearing and when Sooty couldn't find it he was to hit Harry with his hammer and break it, the show ending with Harry raising the cap and egg streaming down his face. In the event, Marjorie brought a couple of eggs from the fridge at home. On transmission Sooty hit Harry not once, not twice, but repeatedly and when Harry raised the school cap an undamaged egg dropped out.

It turned out that young David and Matthew had asked Mum to hard-boil some eggs before she and Harry left the next day for the studio. Marjorie had picked up one of those by accident. No wonder Harry had literally gone 'bonkers' with that hammer, whose days were already numbered. Mind you, when Harry and his furry little friend were presented to the Queen and Prince Philip at the British Industries Fair at Earls Court, Her Majesty did ask Mr Corbett if Sooty had bonked him on the head that morning. To the unexpected enjoyment of those present, Sooty quelled Prince Philip's roar of laughter by squirting him firmly in the royal face with his famous water pistol.

* * *

Shortly after becoming Sooty's producer in 1956, I was told very firmly by Freda Lingstrom that the hammer was 'out'. It appears that a very young fan of our Sunday tea-time show had popped up from behind grandad's newspaper saying, 'Bonk, I'm Sooty!' – only it wasn't a balsa wood hammer he used. A very upset Harry not only went in person to commiserate with granddad, who was a bit poorly in the local hospital, but to help make amends he ordered Sooty to give a separate show in each of the four wards that day. So the hammer was never used again and I was warned to 'watch it'. Just before November 5th 1957, Freda's second-in-command at Lime Grove, Ursula Eason, got wind that we intended to have some fireworks in the next show. I'd been all the way to Half Moon Street in Huddersfield just to see Mr Greenhaulgh, the kind and helpful boss of the Standard Firework Company. To make quite sure it was 'Safety First' hadn't Mr Greenhaulgh let off one of his special offerings in his own office and before my very eyes? When I'd first gone in, the managing director was wearing a crisp white shirt; by the time he'd finished demonstrating a range of safe, coloured smoke, it had turned a not-so-delicate dirty pink. But as Ursula cautioned, whilst Harry would not have suggested or shown Sooty doing anything which was dangerous, the fact of seeing Sooty handle a firework on the screen might encourage children to play with them.

I thought Harry might have made a far better case had he not replied to Ms Eason's letter stating that Sooty wasn't going to let off any fireworks. Not at all. He was (and I quote) 'simply going to get some gunpowder mixed in with the November 5th toffee he'd be cooking over a gas ring, and this would have gone off with a bang as the pay-off to the show!'

I particularly liked Harry's PS: 'Anyway, I shall have to scrape around for something else quickly, and if it is not up to standard you will know why! (sulk).' My friend, Mr Greenhaulgh, liked the 'up to standard' bit.

The early 'Sooty' shows I did with Harry were always 'live' as part of family entertainment on Sunday Children's Television, although there was one occasion when Sooty stayed up late in order to do a live performance for German television and entirely in that language. Sooty's dad was particularly good and fluent, after learning and re-learning his lines. Whilst the transmission was in progress I heard the German station manager, who was in overall charge of a whole evening's entertainment from the BBC declare,' Ah, but ziss is vonderful. Soo-ty mit the Bradford accent, ja?'

Most times things went entirely as planned, well, almost. But not always. The week we did *Sooty's Magic Fountains* was particularly hairy. We'd been relegated to a small scene-store which had a presumptuous 'Studio B' written in superior lettering upon the door. The BBC Northern Orchestra were rehearsing and giving a live televised concert later that same day from the much larger and better equipped 'Studio A' at Dickenson Road, Manchester. This disused church had, until the BBC bought it, been the home of Mancunian Films wherein Frank Randall had done most of his screen burping, old Mother Riley had stormed at daughter Kitty, and Joseph Locke had sung in those big close-ups of Irish eyes.

Sooty's magic fountains were designed as usual by the highly inventive Harry Corbett with the aid of his engineering background, and executed by the redoubtable and often dour Bill Garrett, Harry's full-time property maker and qualified engineer. Bill, assisted by Leslie Corbett who always manipulated Sweep and also did Sweep's 'voice' so imaginatively, were underneath the stage set manipulating a set of taps which fed the jets of the miniature fountains in Sooty's stage extravaganza. One George Barber, a never-to-be-forgotten stage-hand from our very beginnings of TV in the north, was always i/c water, gas and certain categories of special effects. He gave Bill a feed from the nearest available water supply to the studio – the 'Gents'. At around 4 p.m. that day I was wailing from the Control Gallery, 'Can I *please* see a picture?' For nearly two hours we'd been struggling to get things set up, the fountains working with the correct water pressure, and to start a camera rehearsal. We were on the air in precisely one hour. Bit by bit we did a stop-and-start rehearsal. Unfortunately, the BBC Northern Orchestra finished theirs and, quite logically I suppose, so Sooty's magic fountains failed to 'spurt' in direct proportion to some seventy musicians. I informed George that on NO account was anyone else to use the Gents. They'd have to go down the road to the pub we used at lunchtime – or just wait!

In those days there was always a long pause in studio time for our TV cameras to 'line up'. Ours occurred whilst I was endeavouring to restore water pressure and some order out of chaos. We still hadn't had a complete run-through of the show. When the time came, however, the fountains worked a treat spurting to their respective and pre-determined heights in precise time to the waltz tune which Sooty played on his gleaming electronic organ.

I then saw a perspiring Harry. 'Great, just great,' I exclaimed. (This was a phrase I'd acquired since coming to work in television.) But Harry was a perfectionist. 'It'll be even better at 5 p.m.,' he sighed. Marjorie, there to assist as always, handed him a lit cigarette.

'But that was it, Harry. That wasn't the run-through!'

He looked up at the studio clock. We'd come off the air just two minutes ago.

The following morning at our Programme Review Board, at which nice things were mostly said only if the producer was present, my revered friend and always encouraging head of programmes, Bryan Cave-Brown-Cave said, 'I enjoyed it. A pity about the string showing!'

'No, no. Not string. Those were miniature jets of water, *real* water, Bryan.' I should have added real *sweat*, tears and water.

Not content with thinking up plots and situations, seeing to props with Marjorie, an excellent needlewoman, acting as full-time wardrobe mistress to Sooty, Sweep, Butch the snarling bulldog, Ramsbottom the philosophical Yorkshire snake, Kipper the cat, who kept falling asleep, hence the name, and other minor supporting cast, Harry would rehearse all the routines for each show at Guiseley. Sometimes I'd join them there a few days before the Sunday TV show if I needed to script the camera shots. Occasionally these rehearsals were cut short and Harry would shoot off North, South, East and West in order to do one-man stage shows for the National Children's Homes. He'd often have short lunch-time engagements in once place, followed by an evening show at another place. One day, busy until the very last minute in his rehearsal rooms, he realised he was cutting things a bit fine, changed, waved to Marjorie and sped off. Forty miles on he realised he'd forgotten something – something important. Pulling up at a telephone kiosk he luckily got through to home and asked Marjorie to arrange a taxi, pronto. Within seconds of its arrival, Marjorie was handing a small suitcase to the driver. 'Well, and where's the fare, then?'

'He's in there,' she replied. 'And please hurry!' A hour later Harry was able to appear at his function *with* Sooty.

After a particularly heavy spate of personal appearances Harry finished the week by doing a stage show somewhere approximating Lands End on the Friday night with yet another show at somewhere like John-o-Groats the following evening, and then drove straight down to Manchester for his live show on Sunday afternoon. He arrived on his knees and, like the character 'Kipper', almost nodded off himself during transmission.

That caused Tiff No. 1 in our working relationship. Tiff No. 2 was later and became known nationwide, so read on folks.

Doing Sooty, if you will pardon the expression, was generally more a sort of dedicated fun than work, a feeling which so often ran through the whole team from call-boy to Harry himself. It had become exciting as well as fun the early 1960s. We were now far more adventurous and ambitious for the annual run of the Sooty TV series. I was given a far larger budget which enabled me to pre-film more complicated sequences and trick effects. Occasionally we filmed the whole programme. And then came the day when we could telerecord a studio programme, first on film and later, marvel of marvels, on tape. I was later even allowed to cut the tape – with a charge levied against my budget for each edit I made!

But filming on location gave us some of the best shows. *Sooty on Safari* became a three-part screen 'epic' filmed on location at Chester Zoo with the utmost co-operation from one of Sooty's firmest fans, George Mottershead, the founder and director of the zoological gardens. Among George's many inspirations was the making of a waterway around the zoo grounds and enclosures. One stretch, with an island as a background on which roamed and swung real live gibbons, became the Zambesi river

The Sooty Circus

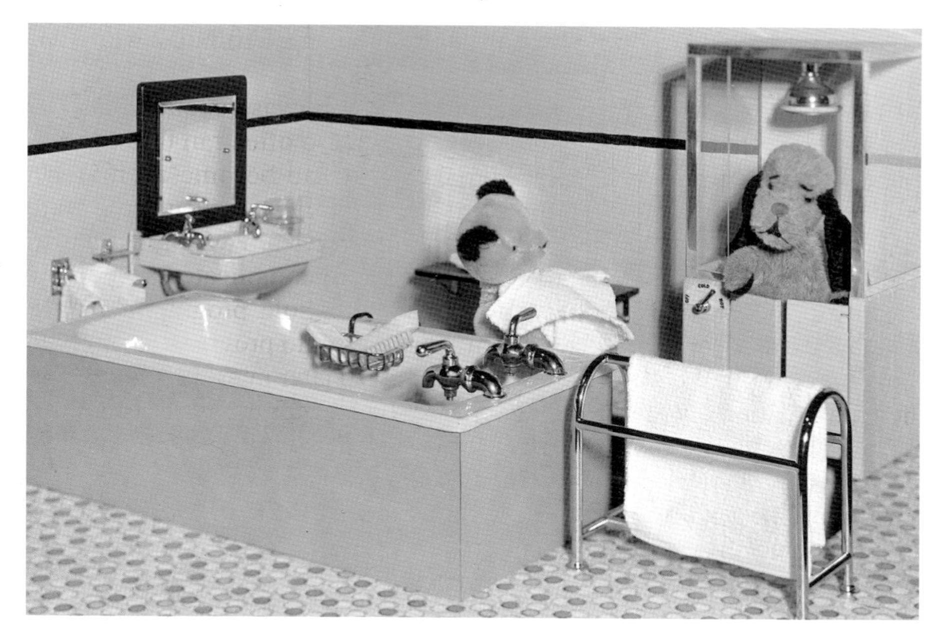

Making a clean Sweep!

up which paddled the intrepid explorer before landing on the island in order to discover its darkest secrets. Harry had miniature pith helmets complete with leather chin straps and brass buckles made by the firm of Christie's. They were complete even to a miniature on the inside crown of the hat maker's label.

We lost one reel of film which had just been put into a can carefully sealed with camera tape and the camera re-loaded. The can was snatched from the grasp of the assistant by an inquisitive gibbon who managed to unstick the tape, a feat in itself, and then to festoon our precious undeveloped reel of film amongst the upper branches of a tree.

But before we reached darkest Africa there had been the departure from Blackpool airport aboard a real transport plane. The owners of the company operating the aircraft had gone to the trouble of having the words, 'Sooty's Safari' emblazoned on the large fuselage and at no extra cost to us. Of course Sooty and Sweep got aboard OK, then took a great interest in the aircraft's cockpit and controls whilst poor panting Harry, also in tropical kit, brought up the rear carrying pots, pans, blankets, water bottles and a lot more besides. He had to make a sudden run for it as 'Sooty's Safari' sprang to life and began to taxi down the runway passing a sign which read 'To Africa'. The next moment a sprinting gasping Harry was running back the way he'd come with a large two-engined cargo plane gaining on him with Sooty at the controls, or rather, now slightly out of control!

We got a lot of acclaim from our audience and from the press. One of the national newspapers wondered how we had managed to show Sooty literally muzzle to muzzle with a large evil-eyed black panther. George Mottershead's assistant, Reg Bloom, assured us that we'd all be quite safe filming inside the enclosure with the beast and *not* through bars! Indeed, for a panther it looked quite docile – decidedly too docile by half for our purposes. His eyes blinked as he lay stretched out on the large branch of a fallen tree his tail occasionally twitching.

We began filming with Sooty popping up from behind a portable palm frond and Sweep, carrying a miniature movie-camera and tripod, not a paws-length away. You are either lucky or jolly unlucky with animals, *and* with children when it comes to programme making! We were extremely lucky that summer's afternoon, but not before we'd wasted a lot of footage whilst waiting for that panther to show at least *some* passing interest in us. Sooty even donned those glasses for a closer inspection of nature in the raw. Suddenly, the black panther's muzzle creased back in a snarl revealing sharp, gleaming teeth. In popped

Sooty's head. A quick shifty and out again. And for that shot Harry had the presence of mind to move his wrist right up to the lower part of the panther's jaw in order that the camera wouldn't show anything other than Sooty's upper half.

'How Did They Do It?' proclaimed a national newspaper. I wondered that myself at the time of filming. 'What made it suddenly come to life and snarl so savagely?' I enquired of Reg. 'You'd do the same if I tweaked your tail,' replied George's helpful assistant.

BBC budgets don't allow for lost rehearsal time or for waiting for panthers to perform whilst costly film footage is slipping past the camera gate, yet people have and will always imagine that those in TV not only spend but waste thousands particularly in the BBC where, according to the misinformed, licence money is there to be wasted. You should have asked Marjorie Corbett, a very good business manager, about the budgets we had in those days. What appeared to be costly and sometimes even extravagant was often achieved almost entirely through goodwill. It was there to be used, not misused. In what I now know to have been the heyday of *Sooty* with Harry Corbett at the helm, that stalwart of BBC television, Bill Cotton Jnr, was near the top in the Light Entertainment TV department and many of our discussions about the *Sooty* show and budgets were as much with him as with Children's Television. For *The Shirley Bassey Show*, his department had received precisely the same sort of goodwill afforded me by those running Blackpool airport and by the managing director of that cargo-carrying company. I think it was the staff at either a civil or an RAF aerodrome who had happily arranged or rearranged some of the landing lights to spell out the title for *The Shirley Bassey Show*.

As so often happens poor old 'Auntie' was once again accused of wasting vast sums of public money on unwarranted and unpardonable extravagance.

Mind you, I know I went too far myself on one occasion over the business of extravagance. For *Sooty The Fireman*, Bill Garrett had painstakingly spent weeks of his engineering skills and Harry's money in making an exact replica of a 'Dennis' design fire-engine. The turntable revolved, the ladder raised, ran out, then back again and lowered at the touch of a Sooty-sized lever. There were even fire hoses to scale and replicas of two London-type fireman's helmets.

The fire station was something Hamley's would have been pleased to stock, even to the highly-polished fireman's pole and when I saw it all one evening in Harry's rehearsal room and prop store, I was

After many years together, Sooty now decides to shoot his Producer!

Waving a magic wand, Sooty and Harry arrive aboard MV *Cleo*

flabbergasted, even knowing Bill's skill and painstaking attention to the smallest detail.

Two days later we were filming with the fire engine and its one bear and one dog crew as it sped through town on a call. Most of us will end up lying prostrate in a vehicle travelling at a more funereal pace. Harry, however, had already spent quite a bit of his working life lying on top of a BBC film truck with just an arm protruding through the stand holding a model car, boat or plane in order to get real moving backgrounds to the action.

My quite unforgivable *faux pas* came when we were rehearsing *Sooty The Fireman* in the studio. Looking around the fire station set in order to work out some of the camera angles and shots, I noticed something missing. Bill was adjusting the small searchlight he'd made, and we were expecting our publicity officer and a 'stills' photographer any moment. I checked again. 'It's fine, everything's fine, Bill, the uniforms even the leather belts but wouldn't Sooty and Sweep be carrying firemen's axes in those holsters?'

Mr Garrett, always a man of few words, pulled himself up to his full five feet and fixed me with a look that instantly withered. 'You think ah've 'ad time to 'and-forge bloody *axes*?'

In all the studio and location filming we did on *Sooty* in the twelve years we were together, boy and bear, we were excellently and most professionally served by Arthur Smith, one of the nicest lighting cameramen in the business assisted by John Buttery who, in later years, was to devise and produce *Screen Test* and *Film Buff Of The Year*. Graham Turner on sound and Gordon Entwistle as electrician made up our tireless technical team. On occasion we had the debonair Gerry Pullen as cameraman. Like Arthur, he'd come to us via Eric Barrow's National Film Agency in Manchester. We learnt a lot from them, especially patience.

There were often excited and lengthy phone calls from Sooty's dad when he and Marjorie were on tour and those nine months or so of stage appearances were coming to an end. 'I've been thinking about our next TV series …'. Harry would give us an outline for various programmes. He'd ask Margaret to script an idea of his, for by now she was writing part of each season's *Sooty* brochure, on sale to the theatre audiences. We'd begin to laugh at various ideas. Harry's enthusiasm was highly contagious. Perhaps I'd suggest another story progression. Leslie could be relied upon to add to it and to work out suitable 'business' some of which he only revealed on 'the day'. Meanwhile, Bill managed to make most of the ideas work in practical terms of glove puppets and props, even to a special radio-controlled frame over which Sweep was placed so that not only could he be seen going up in a balloon but, thanks to Bill, he was able to wave, look down at the receding ground and clutch his head between his paws.

Marjorie's contribution was not only confined to manipulation and costume. In between long tours and the pressure of an annual TV series she kept a well-ordered and happy home for Harry, for David, who was to become a deputy headmaster, and for Peter, better known in later times as Matthew. Having taken over the mantle from Harry, he was to give Sooty a different dimension which was to cater so well for a later day and age of television viewers and family theatre audiences. Oh yes, and I mustn't forget 'Timothy Corbett'! When David went off to study at the Central School of Speech and Drama, the hefty lad had to take up ballet – or so he informed his parents and a hilarious and cheeky younger brother. By the end of that first term Timothy was able to greet David's return with, 'Hello, twinkle toes!' Not bad for a budgie.

There was a special occasion for Harry, Sooty and for me at the Café Royal, London, in July 1961 when Sooty received the National Television Award for the best children's programme. It was the night that those awards were also presented to Violet Carson and to Tony Warren. I must say I was a bit annoyed with Auntie that evening. Because Harry had a long-term contract with her, he wasn't allowed to appear with Sooty on ITV who were covering the Awards that year.

In Harry's own estimation the greatest unsolicited tribute paid to him occurred one Sunday lunchtime in the West Yorkshire village of Esholt, now famous for its locations for *Emmerdale Farm*. As Harry was having a quiet pint in the comfort of the Commercial Inn, one of the locals ambled across to him. A man of a few words, it seemed. 'Ah'll not waste thy time an' ah'll not waste mine. Suffice to say thee stuff's acceptable!' Basic comment, like the remark that young lad made to Harry on Lord Street, Southport – which brings me to what became the great television talking point for one whole week in the 1960s.

* * *

The seeds were sown that summer's day. I'd chosen Southport for filming *Sooty's Holiday Snaps* mainly because of Councillor Mae Bamber, a former Lord Mayor of that celebrated watering place besides being a good friend of the BBC over the years and, indeed, a contributor to the early days of North Regional radio programmes. I knew Mae would enjoy playing the role of 'the lady in the deckchair' who, according to our script, was to be the centre of a holiday-snap sequence with the tide getting nearer and nearer as Sooty's lens kept following birds (the feathered variety) and other beach scene distractions. We had a good morning's 'shoot' except that my own attention hadn't wandered far enough to see that one somewhat heavy Jaguar was slowly sinking into the notorious Southport sands. But councillor Bamber was at hand. She spoke to someone who called up the Beach Patrol and they hauled the car out. I rather fancy Arthur Smith would have liked to film it disappearing altogether as a pay-off to *Holiday Snaps* with Harry and Sooty waving 'Bye, bye, everyone. Bye, Bye!' As it was, down came the deluge, not just a shower.

Arthur and the film unit returned to base whilst Harry and I stayed behind to take Mae for a well-earned drink. As I was thanking her Harry began to doodle on a glass-mat. I saw Mae into a taxi for a lunch appointment she had that day then returned to the hotel bar. 'There,' exclaimed Harry, 'What do you think of that?' He pushed his glass-mat across to me. On it was the drawing of an innocent looking bear with long curly eyelashes and positively Jayne Russell appendages. He saw my expression and burst into laughter. 'Sooty's girlfriend?' 'Over my dead body!'

It was now almost two years later, and the Easter weekend of 1965. I was clearing bracken from the wood behind our home in Pott Shrigley, Cheshire. A nice peaceful occupation with the first signs of spring and the knowledge that, within a few weeks, the whole of that wooded slope down to our garden would be a carpet of bluebells.

I heard Margaret's cupped-hand call from below. 'It's the *Daily Mail* … Douglas M-a-r-l-b-o-r-o-u-g-h!'

I should have said I was out.

Mr Marlborough came straight to the point, having got my home phone number from our press officer Vernon Noble. 'Is it true you won't let Sooty have a girlfriend?'

I didn't know what he was asking about. Mr Marlborough briefly explained. It appeared that Ray Nunn, a reporter then on *Woman's Mirror* had recently done a routine interview with Harry Corbett and wondered if any new puppet characters would be appearing in the next BBC series. Harry replied that he'd toyed with the idea of a girlfriend a year or two back but that his producer, Trevor Hill, was against it on the grounds that sex would be creeping into the Sunday teatime programme. Ahhh, realisation began to dawn. That glass-mat and my comment, 'Over my dead body.' Douglas Marlborough laughed with me. 'Why shouldn't Sooty have a girlfriend?' was his next question.

I don't recall my precise words, as I wasn't taking the *Daily Mail*'s enquiry seriously, but I do know I explained that with the present set-up of Harry in the middle with Sooty and Sweep on either side helping or hindering him, we had an ideal triangle and a formula which had proved successful with large TV audiences both at home and abroad. Besides, in my experience, four to six year olds might think it a bit silly. Yes, we did have other characters from time to time but the idea of a girlfriend had never cropped up in any discussions, only on a glass-mat.

I went back to the woods whilst the *Mail* and Marlborough's friend, Martin Jackson of the *Express* went to town on the story for the following morning. The *Mail* wrote:

> Mr Hill, 39 married, no children, produces the puppet show from BBC's Manchester studios. He said, 'I may be old fashioned but I feel it is wrong to introduce a girlfriend. It is introducing a human relationship. Teddy bears are sexless.

The *Express* story was bannered:

Sooty Mustn't Have A Girlfriend

whilst a few days later, the *Sun* proclaimed:

Sooty will get his sex life, so there

Emmwood's cartoon in the *Mail*, a copy of which I still treasure, shows a cowering little bear on the edge of a dark wood completely overshadowed by a macho Bruno. 'I know sex and satire is out for telly Teddy Bears, doll, but I ain't Sooty.'

Within the space of that very odd week the issue had been ventilated at some length on the ITV *Eamonn Andrews Show*, on radio's more reserved *Any Questions?* and then on the Sabbath day *The Sunday Times* did me the honour of referring to me as 'this Reithian character'. I should add that all this time we were negotiating a new contract with Harry Corbett. The *Mail* quoted him as saying, 'no girlfriend, no new BBC series.'

Copies of BBC correspondence were reaching Huw Wheldon, Michael Peacock and Bill Cotton Jnr, whilst Harry was writing to Douglas Marlborough saying that although he appreciated all the valuable publicity, what, in the first place, had been a bit of a giggle, was now getting out of hand and making things difficult for him and the BBC.

Next, Roger Woddis went into print and stated that there was encouraging news for all those uptight citizens who had campaigned long and ardently against filth on BBC television. Sooty was *not* to have a girlfriend. What is more (shock horror), Mr Woddis had been rather worried of late by Andy Pandy. Only recently Andy and 'a friend' called Looby Loo had hidden inside a cupboard, leaving what happened behind closed doors to childish imagination. As he so rightly wrote, 'this kind of leering suggestiveness is only calculated to inflate the baser instincts of the BBC's under fives audience!'

Well after all that I took the view that it would be a terrible waste of national interest in Sooty's lifestyle if he *didn't* have a girlfriend. Behind closed doors we got to talking about a panda. She'd be called 'Soo' and would be a bit of a natterer. To be perfectly truthful, I thought Harry was being somewhat chauvinistic when he suggested that Marjorie should do Soo's voice, adding, 'Well, she's a good little natterer.' And so, Soo was introduced later in that 1965 BBC television series, with lines like, 'Oh, Mr Corbett, Sooty's taken the last of the sweets! Oh, Mr Corbett, Sweep's slid-did-did down the bannister. Oooooh, Mr Corbett, why have they left me at the t-o-p of this dark t-o-w-e-r ...?'

What had the *Mirror* to say about all this? Yes I wondered about that too. Searching through the 'Sooty' press cuttings I've kept, I came across their story about Sooty and a girlfriend, but it took some finding. You see it is dated 17th June 1968 (three years later), saying that Sooty's television romance would blossom on ITV at 4.30 p.m. on July 30th, the BBC having disapproved of introducing sex into a children's programme. Not only the BBC!

Allowing Soo into the 1965 BBC series was yet another wrong decision on my part according to Maurice Wiggin in *The Sunday Times*. He took me to task for having given way to the forces of reaction and wondered how long it would be before I let Sweep have a queer boyfriend.

A week after that dressing down there was a meeting of the BBC Governors and the Board of Management in Manchester, to which some of the senior staff were invited. Over an informal drink my then Director General, Hugh Greene, came over to me. A very tall man. Bending, he discreetly said, 'I think you were wrong not to let Sooty have his girlfriend.'

Our BBC Governor for Wales took a different stand. In anything but a murmur, Dame Anne Godwin declared, 'We can't have sex with Sooty!' And quite right too, madam. A few years later, I was to wave 'Bye, bye' to Sooty – only on a professional basis, you understand, as he and Harry went to work for Thames Television, but I wouldn't have missed a moment of this Sooty Saga – not for the world.

Sooty and Sweep rehearse Pinky and Perky
to the accompaniment of one their records

16

On Location (Bangkok, Hong Kong and Norway)

Some of the very best moments during my working life with the BBC were spent filming on location with a small BBC team – and I do mean 'small'. Much as I enjoyed creating electronic pictures this always involved a large number of people even in putting just one 'talking head' onto the TV screen, but to be allowed to make a programme entirely on film was something I always relished. One of the first was on 35 mm film, a luxury in the 1950s, albeit in black and white. No colour in those days and yet black and white had a sharpness about it, also a 'depth' to the picture which isn't always so noticeable when filming in colour. Thirty-five mm film was expensive, however, and BBC budgets invariably small, so you really only sold an idea if you could back it up with a detailed shooting script and the promise of a shooting ratio of 2:1. Rarely attainable, that meant for every two feet of expensive film stock that went through the camera gate one foot would end up being shown, the other ending up on the Cutting Room floor.

I'd come across the American greetings card company, Rust Craft, and was shown round their factory in Leeds. Soon I was working on the script for *A Greeting For Christmas*, the story of a card selected in a shop by the camera itself to send to a friend. The film camera then traced this particular choice right back to the designer and then followed the whole process of manufacture. Now I wouldn't wish you to have the impression that something *always* went wrong when I had a hand in it. No, not always – but quite often. Gerry Pullen and his camera put a lot of 'sparkle' into my story of a Christmas card – if you'll pardon the pun, and so anxious were the greetings card firm to let their distributors know

A Greeting for Christmas

that the BBC had just made a programme with them that they enclosed a note to this effect to their national network of wholesalers and retailers. As a result, the BBC received a written complaint from a rival company and so my first film for television was kept off the screen for a full year until the following December.

Still, being shot on 35 mm it lost none of its sparkle and, what is more, when it was eventually screened it came as something of a surprise. When you have spent many days in editing a film you soon become bored as you run through it time and time again cutting, re-joining, the film editor marking all the 'Fades', 'Mixes' and other information for the film laboratories who will process the cut negative and produce a show-print. Seeing this for the first time in a pristine state can sometimes rekindle a little of the original enthusiasm and excitement.

Having seen just what Gerry had achieved with his camera and with his clever lighting for *A Greeting For Christmas*, it was agreed to let us tackle a far bigger film project, the story of the Britannia turbo-prop aircraft, 'Speedbird 933', which made special flights from Tokyo to London via Hong Kong and Bangkok, bringing children of various nationalities back after the holidays to their schools in the United Kingdom.

BOAC and their chief press officer, T. Ivan Pyle, were all for the idea but there was a major snag – and not the sort we could overcome with TV production and the Unions in later years. I wanted to begin the film with one of the Britannia fleet being serviced in one of the giant hangars of BOAC's Headquarters Building at London airport. No problem. I also needed to film on the aircraft flight deck, particularly on the outward journey and several times on the return trip, using the aircraft's own electricity supply for our mobile lighting since the sort of batteries we used were very heavy. On the understanding that once 'Speedbird 933' left London Airport for the Far East there would be a BBC film crew of G. Pullen and T. Hill, *and no others*. Because of available space, we went ahead with the project.

Gerry took along two 16 mm lightweight cameras without any synchronised sound and only a modest amount of lighting equipment for 'interiors'. I took two BBC tape recorders, improvements on those which Bertie and I had with us in the Arctic. It would be left to our BBC film

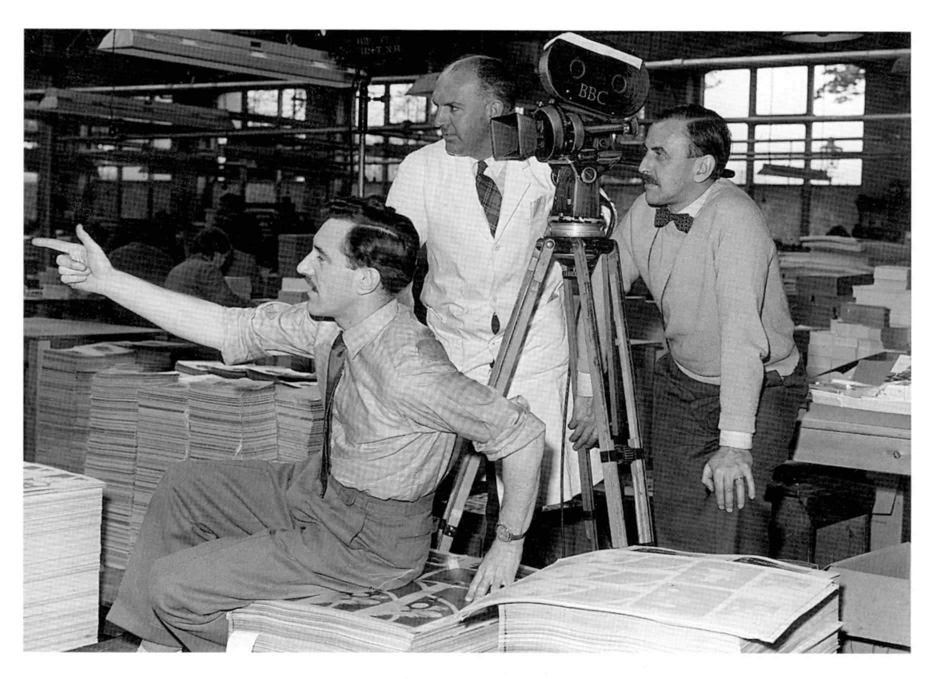

Trevor directing at the printing works

unit editors to hopefully fit 'wild-track' recordings of the sound to picture upon our return. Even with the minimum of equipment and staff, BOAC had to remove two seats in the first-class cabin accommodation in order to allow us to keep cameras and recorders 'at the ready'. We were joined by 'Tip' Pyle as he was known and by journalist Barbara Cooper. In making programmes there is very definitely a thing called 'continuity', and you cannot fool some of the audience even some of the time. We used to get letters about *Children's Hour* plays, like this one: 'How come Biggles jumped into a 15 cwt Austin truck which revved up its engine, and next we heard him change gear and drive off inside a Morris van?'

It's far more of a hazard when filming. Even a large film crew of precisely two cannot be in more than one place at one time, so on the outward journey from London we filmed a lot of the flight deck material with the crew talking as if they were on the journey *back* with school children aboard. What is more, BOAC had to schedule the same captain and flight deck officers for the return trip to ensure we kept continuity. I took my hat off to the young man in Flight Control at London Airport. He had the task of making up the Flight Board which showed the precise movement of every aircraft operated by all BOAC's services as if it was on the day 'Speedbird 933' left Tokyo. He even made up information to include minor delays. In the finished film we kept cutting back to Flight Control as they monitored our return.

Once Gerry had filmed the captain and crew bringing us safely down at Kai Tak airport, Hong Kong, we then had to cut to 'exterior' shots showing the same aircraft as seen from the long runway as it made its landing approach, and then, from the Control Tower as it touched down. In order to achieve this without having a second film crew on terra firma, the captains of other Britannia aircraft approaching Kai Tak, the Nine Dragons, would be filmed coming in and recorded, taking care to identify themselves to our specific requirement. The first time I took a recording from the Tower, it went like this:

Captain: Hong Kong Tower! Jet Speedbird er … er …

Radio operator's voice (slightly off mic): We are pretending to be 'Speedbird 933' today, sir!

I didn't blame them. Having seen what goes on from the flight deck, all those safety checks, switches, even coming in through such a small gap between the mountains petrified me.

Janet Cantopher records for my Radio version of 'Speedbird 933' with Gerry Pullen now recording rather than filming

Mrs Parthong describes Thailand's most sacred shrine to me

Above: A B.O.A.C. Bristol Britannia turbo-prop airliner photographed on the apron at London Airport North. In the foreground is the statute of Alcock and Brown who made the first non-stop flight across the Atlantic in 1919.
Left: A 2-man Film Unit take on a rickshaw Recordist in Hong Kong

We filmed young Michael Lamb as he spent his last day and night at home in Hong Kong before the long journey and the start of a new school term in England. Twelve hundred miles away, on the outskirts of Bangkok, eleven year old Janet Cantopher was filmed as she got ready to leave her family and home.

To me Bangkok in the year 1959 seemed precisely like the Bangkok of Anna Leonowens and the King of Siam in the previous century. Our hotel in Sarawangsi Street had lace anti-macassars on the high-back chairs and could have been vacated only that day by Queen Victoria herself. In fact as we drove from the airport to our hotel, I saw a bronze of Anna's King suspended by his royal neck which was wound round with thick chain-link to take the weight since the pedestal was undergoing repairs. The very next day I noticed a discreet awning had been erected over the scaffolding. Rather a nice touch.

In Bangkok, Gerry and I were to meet the remarkable man who was BOAC's representative in Thailand. I later learnt from Jim Steer, BOAC's Far Eastern Manager, that this Thai employee had never drawn one *tical* of his salary from the company, since he considered it an honour to work for BOAC. He spoke no English so his charming wife acted as translator. Shortly after we were introduced he got her to say to me, 'I marry my wife because she is one quarter English. I learn to love her later!' Her husband owned several of Thailand's newspapers and radio stations. Besides wealth he also had great influence – as we were shortly to discover.

We had a full day off whilst in Bangkok. Well, not exactly. In the morning we sailed down one of the *klongs* or waterways with dwellings on stilts liberally scattered atop the mud banks. I noticed pictures of the King and Queen of Siam in almost every shack – and a lot of their subjects happily washing their black hair and causing the murky waters of the river to look even darker by contrast with the foam and bubbles such hair-washing created. I think washing up liquid must have recently arrived in the city. That and an incredible amount of toothpaste, for those not washing hair were happily cleaning teeth. No wonder the Thais must surely be one of the most beautiful races on earth, even in old age when the women put up their grey hair in order to give them added height and stature. Gerry lost no time in capturing all this with his film camera. I think his previous employers had asked if he'd be prepared to shoot off a reel or two of backgrounds in colour for them. We made one trip round the floating market then repeated the journey as Gerry peered through his viewfinder and finished by photographing the beautiful Temple of Dawn.

I really wondered if I should say anything to him. I mean, here was a very experienced film cameraman, commissioned in the services, and terribly but terribly bright – yet surely that round black disc on the end of the camera lens *must* have obscured all those pretty pictures? It had!

For the third time round that morning, Gerry removed the lens cap from his camera. As for me, well my busman's holiday started that afternoon when the wife of BOAC's Thailand representative took me to one of the city's landmarks, the Wat Phra Keo or temple of the Emerald Buddha. As she was recording an interview with me, so some noisy tourists clattered down the temple steps, talking and laughing loudly. The same thing happened a second time. When teatime was over, however, it had been arranged for me and my tape recorder to have entry to the leading monastery – away from noisy tourists and the sounds of traffic. I followed the day in the life of one young English-speaking priest. It ended with him in his cell, hanging his saffron-coloured robe on a hook, placing the begging bowl beside a wafer thin mattress and then, to my astonishment, he produced a tape recorder of his own. 'With this I rehearse again and again so that I can make a Number One prayer to Buddha!' he declared.

The final recordings I made were in the city's main temple at the sacred shrine of Buddha. The awe-inspiring figure had different clothing and jewels for each of the four seasons of the year. When the temple monks began their service they chanted not in their own tongue but in Latin, for Anna's King had decreed it and his word was still law in Siam.

There was to be yet another surprise for my two-man film crew when we returned late that evening to bathe and change at our hotel. Awaiting us was an invitation to attend a private performance by the royal dancers at the palace. I simply mentioned to Gerry that of course we would not be taking a camera or a tape recorder on this occasion. 'Hardly form, old boy, hardly form,' he replied as he put an immaculate knot in his black tie. You really could take him *anywhere* – as I often did!

Our influential Thai friend and his wife were there in person to receive us as we arrived at the palace. He took us through to a columned courtyard where resplendently attired servants stood at a respectful distance in the cool of the evening. Our host indicated the small wooden block placed some two or three feet in front of a row of chairs. Oh well, this is where we get the proverbial 'chop' – some minor indiscretion on my part, I supposed! As I was led forward by his wife she smiled and said quietly, 'My husband thinks you will like to stand upon that sometimes during the performance and film the feet of the royal dancers!'

The occasion seemed all the more unreal when, the following day, on our second visit to the palace BOAC's man in Dreamland – er, in Thailand – spoke to me in English for the first and only time. I was quite quite sure he said to me, 'The revolution breaks out tomorrow!' It did.

As we drove to the airport at dawn on that Monday morning *en route* to Hong Kong, tanks and lorries stood in front of the clusters of multi-tiered Siamese roofs and golden *chedis*, the rising sun transforming the spires into columns of molten light. 'Tip' had been nonplussed about the revolution. 'Ah, yes. We've been holding a booking for the man at the top. An enormous "excess baggage" bill for him and for his family, so we informed the FO that something was in the wind. They must be chucking him out within the next twenty-four hours!'

On reaching Hong Kong I immediately wired BBC Television News. 'Have cameraman, Hong Kong. Do you wish cover Bangkok revolution?' On checking with Thai Airways, I then discovered that all their airports were closed until further notice. Fortunately when the BBC wired back they didn't say 'Yes'.

The 'revolution' appeared to have been a great success. The one government figure complete with family and possessions left the country, a few rifles were fired into the air by the troops who were sitting in their trucks to protect the palace, and the revered King and his chief ministers declared a public holiday until further notice. It was still going strong when we stopped at Bangkok airport on our return journey to the UK.

Our remarkable Thai friend was there with his wife to greet us and to give me a large basket of pomelo, a sort of grapefruit which I'd thoroughly enjoyed, whilst Gerry was presented with something called shrimp bread all to himself. We took a meal in the VIP lounge before rejoining 'Speedbird 933'. Gerry Pullen was a gourmet, as I discovered when he made me order *and* partake of bird's nest soup aboard a floating restaurant at Aberdeen, Hong Kong, and again when he insisted we ate in a different French restaurant every night whilst we were filming at the International Children's School at Fontainebleu, France another year. That project took over two full weeks, but my stomach took over a month to recover.

* * *

For fear of having to tackle smoked reindeer's head, I left Gerry behind when Margaret and I went further afield to make a couple of films for the BBC in Norway. The first one would have interested him because *What's*

Cooking was about Norwegian pottery. It ended with us filming a meal during which the guests were served very appetising dishes cooked and presented on the fire-proof pottery of Stravangerflint where the film was made. He would certainly have approved of that meal, cooked and served at the Norwegian School of Catering at the Solar Strand Hotel, Stavanger.

For the other film, *Bread and Cheese*, it was mostly a case of sandwiches 'oppe i fjellet', which simply means 'up the mountain', so I had a less fussy lot with me, cameraman Bob Sleigh (yes, really) and assistant, Gordon Entwistle, plus a sound recordist. The Norwegians provided electricians, for as they said in answer to my telex on this subject, 'Yes, we have the man for lighting the people!'

My BBC film colleagues arrived all the way from England in a BBC Film Unit truck which had already had a thorough service before leaving home-base, but having wound its way from the port of Bergen and up through all those steep mountain passes to Voss in central Norway, I thought it best for the vehicle to have a further check before we got cracking over some pretty rocky terrain. Accordingly we took the film truck to a local garage.

'Good morning,' beamed our Gordon, 'Would you mind having a look at this?'

All the Norwegians I've ever met – and I've met a good few over the years – have always been helpful and so polite. The young fair-haired garage mechanic walked round our truck not once but twice.

'Yes, yes,' he said, 'It is very nice!'

Gordon then invited him to 'examine it'. This he then proceeded to do most carefully. Poking his head from under the chassis he addressed Gordon, our driver-cum-assistant cameraman. Gordon taught that mechanic a new English phrase as he shot from under the vehicle, visibly shaken. 'There is only one … bolt holding the steering together! The other three have fallen out of the plate somewhere on the journey up here I suppose!'

The Norwegian garage had the sort of spares for English vehicles which evidently drop to pieces upon Norwegian roads.

Our good friend, Trygve Fitje, the man from the Tourist Board in Voss, had not only assembled a lot of the 'properties' we required for Margaret's story but also several young Norwegian lads one of whom, hopefully, would be the 'star' of our film, *Bread and Cheese*. This was to be the story of a young boy who, for the very first time, is taken by his elder brother up to one of the highest mountain streams to fish, and of the adventures which befall the wide-eyed youngster once it is discovered that they have left their bread and cheese back in the village and so 'Nils' sets off on his own to get it. All we required for our script was a seven or eight year old who could climb a thirty-foot Norwegian pine, run 'oppe i fjellet', and 'down i fjellet', fall into a fast-flowing river and, if Trygve could possibly find one for us, ride a fjord pony bareback up the mountain. I had also added that a tendency not to tire too easily would be an asset.

We auditioned some half a dozen youngsters who were tested for the part of 'Nils' after the outline of the story had been explained and translated to them – though the 'river episode' never entered the conversation at this stage. They weren't bad some of them, but not quite 'Superboy'. We all felt a bit deflated as we took a glass or two during lunch. As he drained his, so the man from the Tourist Board quite suddenly exclaimed, '*Atle Slettemark*!'

Now *that*, I thought to myself, is a wonderful expletive for the next time we find next to nothing holding our steering together. I repeated the phrase, not once but twice. '*Ja*,' replied a now cheerful Trygve. 'He is

Atle Slettemark as 'Nils' thinks a pony would certainly help him on his journey back to the mountain

most keen on the athletics. And I am quite sure his parents will not mind if *he* falls into the river!' Atle was shortly produced, all four foot of him. He did a test and accepted the star role the moment Trygve's translation of the plot got to the bit about having to fall into water and to ride a pony bareback.

We soon made another discovery about the BBC film truck of ours. It would only go 'oppe i fjellet' in reverse gear without coming to a shuddering halt. Within a day or two we'd got things to a fine art. Atle would stand in the back poised to spring and as we progressed backwards so he'd leap off, hold open gates across the mountain tracks, then run alongside and be hauled aboard again. But even in reverse that truck only went so far up the steep mountain slopes. We had to lug the film equipment including a heavy camera tripod the last mile and a half.

Atle spoke no English but I soon discovered that he did a lot better without the aid of an interpreter, so we left Herr Fitje to get on with his duties in the town of Voss, meeting each evening at our hotel so that he could give our Norwegian star any notes about the following day's shooting schedule. He patently enjoyed being collected in my Jaguar each morning. Sitting in the back he would wave to friends who were off to school whilst *he* was making a film!

In order to demonstrate tiredness to Atle one day up the mountain I panted like a St Bernard, held up a thumb and said, 'OK?' He nodded, as our attention then turned to sorting out camera angles for the sequence in which Nils is lost in the mountain forest having left the path in order to take a short cut down to the village. To find out the lie of the land, he wearily climbs that tall pine tree.

When ready for a 'take' we called him. Atle was now a good half a mile down the forest slope but returning to us at a fair old trot and panting like a hungry hound after the scent. Taking a deep breath it was he who now held up a thumb. 'OK?' We started filming right away.

Our Norwegian star made a point of carrying the shot board as we moved around. On this we chalked things like, 'Scene 12. Take 1'. He'd watched Gordon 'clap it' for synchronised sound many times during the course of making our film. On the last day up the mountain he'd watched me stumbling a bit as we traversed a slanting rock. In those days I smoked. He came forward, took the cigarette from my lips and 'clap' – it was firmly extinguished in the jaws of the clapper-board.

Atle Slettemark was to leave the village on the outskirts of Voss for the first time in his young life to spend a fortnight's holiday with Margaret and me in Cheshire. He travelled to England together with the young son of the managing director of the Norwegian pottery firm, Trygve Brekke. The son's English was excellent and we took them both around and about as much as possible during their stay. The 'Tivoli' as they called the Blackpool Pleasure Beach was a great success and a further day had to be spent on things which whirled round and round and zoomed up and down. By contrast, I found the Olympic-size swimming pool a nice quiet relaxation – until I spied two familiar figures on the Olympic-height diving board. Atle was astride the other's shoulders as they did a 'dead man's fall' into the water. He'd survived the river at Voss, but would I be sending a telegram to his parents in Voss, 'Sorry, young son drowned Blackpool Baths?'

A baths attendant took two lads aside after their second or third 'dead man's fall' from that height. I relaxed, but not for long. A motorway was another new experience. 'Atle wants to know can we go one hundred miles an hour in this Jag-u-ar car of yours?' We could – and we did. Once in London for five days there was an immediate request to visit the Chamber of Horrors and to have several peeps behind curtains which revealed severed heads and unattached limbs. Although she did not wish to accompany us to the Chamber, Margaret then had to listen to graphic descriptions. Madame Tussauds and the contents of the Science Museum provided some pretty wide-eyed expressions but were nothing to the joys of the Circle Line which we travelled several times, until two adults insisted on coming up for air. When we did so we felt rather as moles must feel in seeing daylight for the first time in what seemed like days.

We thought Atle's gasp would never end the night we took them to see Cinerama for the first time and *How The Wild West Was Won*. He leaned forward from the front row, centre circle, forgetting the large blob of ice-cream balancing on the end of a cornet. In the heat and excitement, it slipped off and down to the darkness below – only to be followed by a woman's sudden scream as it landed on the back of her neck. It required all my strength to restrain young Mr Slettemark from leaning over to see for himself where his ice-cream had come to rest.

We were shown a copy of a Norwegian newspaper when we were back in that country a year later. The article had to be translated for us. It dealt with 'Voss Boy's Dream Holiday' according to the headline. We had taken him to see a polo match one Saturday whilst he was with us in Cheshire. The newspaper article began by quoting some of Atle Slettemark's impressions: 'In England they play golf on horseback!'

* * *

Strange how one thing does indeed lead to another. After the film on Norwegian pottery had been shown on BBC television, Margaret and I were invited to go and see the Burslem firm of Royal Doulton with a view to making a film for them. I had explained that I was a member of the BBC's staff not a freelance. To my surprise my Head of Programmes, Bob Stead, encouraged me to go ahead and explore the possibility of doing a film for a commercial company since, in the BBC management's view, it would be further experience. Just two reasonable clauses: I'd have to assemble an outside film crew and equipment and I would be required to take 'leave of absence', a sort of sabbatical.

Margaret came to my assistance with the script for *Focus On Fine China* which we shot in very glorious Technicolor and with no worries about 'ratios' or, indeed, certain other costs. Apart from one brief reference to the illustrious founder of this distinguished firm together with a shot of his bronze bust with cherry blossom gently wafting in foreground and a brief shot of the firm's namestamp on the foot of an exquisite piece of their bone china tableware, there was no other advertising for Royal Doulton. 'Fine English china speaks for itself' – as we got Deryck Guyler to say in the English commentary to a background of suitable music composed by Henry Reed. That cherry blossom, by the way. We have to hold a lot of 'dingleberry' (foliage held in front of the camera to mask road signs and the like) in frame whilst filming. On this occasion it was to obscure a rusty drainpipe outside the Burslem factory.

The Central Office of Information took over the distribution of *Focus On Fine China* once the film commentary had been done in a dozen or more different languages. I later heard from a BOAC chap I'd met whilst doing 'Speedbird 933'. He'd seen our film which was being screened daily at the British Pavilion during Expo 70. That was in Tokyo. Yes, we certainly got around a bit!

17

Pinky And Perky

On Tuesday February 26th 1957, when Barney Colehan first featured two little pigs in BBC Television's *It's Up To You* they were billed and introduced as 'Pinky and Porky'. We phoned Barney who said, 'You and Margaret ought to meet their creators, Jan and Vlasta Dalibor. What with your radio musical cartoons, the four of you will doubtless have a lot in common.'

That same summer off went Margaret and myself to Heysham Head, Morecombe. We not only enjoyed the afternoon matinee, we also attended that evening's performance of their 1957 show. Almost at the bottom of the billing we noted: 'Pinky and Porky – the twin piglets'.

That night we sat in the Dalibors' caravan on the headland enclosure as we talked not only about the above but also about their beautifully designed and manipulated 'Mr Frog' who played his saxophone to a then 'pop' record in such a clever and imaginative fashion. It was also then we were to learn that Jan, a former Czech university lecturer in Art, and his wife Vlasta had fled their own country when the Communists had taken control, and had come to Yorkshire. Jan's first job in England was as a stone-breaker in a Tadcaster quarry. Next, this man of only slight build was to be working away underground at Fryston Colliery – yet still managing to practise his skills at sculpting the faces of his string puppets, whilst Vlasta, with equal skill, did the finishing work and made the imaginative and colourful individual costumes for each of their characters.

Their own lives were to change when Jan won a National Coal Board competition by doing a sculpture – no, not in stone, but in a tablet of soap! With the cash award the Dalibors now decided to take advantage of their joint creative skills and that puppetry should become their chosen profession. That very first evening together at Morecombe turned out just as Barney Colehan, bless him, had predicted. The Dalibors now brought out a file of cuttings from the *Radio Times*. They had kept nearly every billing and illustration from our *Cameo Cartoons*. We knew we had met kindred spirits.

Next morning I sent off a memo to Owen Reed, that genial, warm and intellectual man whom I'd previously met and briefly worked with when I was in Bristol and he was Head of Radio Drama there. Owen, as I've already explained, had by now taken over from Freda Lingstrom as Head of BBC Children's Programmes, Television, bringing with him a slightly more adventurous approach to the output. Under Owen's creative leadership, drama was to flower in the type and standard of Sunday teatime serials which came to the screen. Right now, however, he expressed his interest in the Dalibors. 'Anything in it for us?' he enquired.

I didn't take Owen to see them in a sand-show but to a theatre in Blackpool, for now they had a London agent working for them. 'Splendid technicians operating splendid puppets,' declared Owen as I drove him back to my home in Cheshire for the night after we'd seen the show. 'And a first-class cabaret act – for the *stage*,' I added. We both wondered how best they might be used by the BBC. It looked very likely to me that the experienced TV puppet man at Lime Grove, Gordon Murray, who was already on Owen's staff, would be taking on the Dalibors. There was talk of Alan Melville being approached to write and to appear with the various puppets, since both the Dalibors had strong continental accents. What is more, they also had their hands full of strings in manipulating their clever creations.

What turned the tide in our favour was the fact that Gordon considered that because of cameras and lighting, the Dalibors would now need to work from a 'high bridge', using far longer strings, and not the sort they used in their theatre act. It was at this point that Jan asked if he might join forces with me and Margaret in Manchester. I'd experience of glove puppets but not of marionettes. As things turned out, I was extremely grateful to Owen Reed for giving this idea his blessing.

We began working on something akin to a radio *Cameo Cartoon*. A 'Teletoon' is how we eventually billed it. It featured just the two little pigs, in order that Jan and Vlasta could do all the necessary manipulation themselves. When it came to that all-important design registration for Pinky and Porky, it turned out that the latter was the trade name for a brand of sausages! How unfeeling can you get. At about three o'clock one morning, a voice said, 'Dar-ling!' I was almost awake when for the first time – but certainly not for the last – I heard the names 'Pinky and *Perky*'.

By April 1958 Margaret and I had worked out a storyline and I'd completed a shooting script. The story itself told by a narrator, would also become one of my radio cartoons, since I would ask Henry Reed to compose a musical score. This, I could charge to my annual Radio Budget. Part of the script went like this:

INSERT SET	MUSIC	'Moonlit Night'
Painted scene of cottage roof, with practical chimney pot smoking. brightly shining in sky above	(Cue 6)	Begins with 'Dancing Moonbeams' Phrase

CUE

NARRATOR: Soon, the moon had risen in the clear night sky. And snug inside their beds lay Pinky and Perky, tired but happy, happy because they had a home of their own – at last.

MIX to:

Cottage interior,
Pinky and Perky in their
beds. Moonlight streaming
through lattice window.

CUT to:

Close Up. Perky sleeping.
His mouth opens and closes
as he snores. Each time
the bobble of his night-cap
rises and falls.

(Music – Segues to a 'Lullaby' based on melody of the Signature Tune)

Then, of course, this tranquil scene is loudly interrupted by a certain 'Mr Frog' croaking and a lot of other countryside-at-night 'noises off'.

Whilst Jan was busy making extra props for filming the story including, for 'close-ups', carving several additional Pig's trotters, viz 'trotter holding oil can' (used on 'Mr Frog'), 'trotter holding feather duster', 'trotter with spade', et cetera, so Vlasta had been busy making night gowns and night caps.

Filming would enable us to work shot by shot and to end up, when edited, with far more movement and pace to the programme. Excluding the cost of the music but including film stock and processing charges, design and materials, artists' fees *and* expenses, I asked the Programme Organiser at Lime Grove for a total budget of £160. It was turned down as being too costly. Our senior TV designer in Manchester, Kenneth Lawson, found room to store the 'cottage sets' which he and his staff had constructed for us whilst Jan stored away, for the time being, a lot of extra 'trotters'.

In the week of my leaving with Gerry Pullen for the Far East to film 'Speedbird 933', so Children's Television gave us the go ahead for Pinky and Perky – not to use film but to make a pilot programme by a cheaper method, by telerecording. Our *Pinky and Perky Teletoon* was seen throughout the country on Sunday 20th October from 5.26 to 5.36 p.m.. It had charm but certainly lacked the sort of pace I could have achieved had we been given the financial resources for filming.

It was Marcel Stellman, one of the managers of Decca records, who put 'Pinky and Perky' on the road to television acclaim. The Gramophone Company couldn't easily prevent artists like the Dalibors miming commercial records within the confines of a theatre, but there existed very hard and fast rules for an organisation like the BBC. The Dalibors speeded up many of the recordings they used, copying them and editing on the tape. It was illegal for the BBC to make any mechanical reproduction of a commercial recording. Marcel Stellman reasoned with the Gramophone Company on the one hand whilst Mr Walford of the BBC Copyright Department made an approach on our behalf. EMI were the first company, after Decca, to agree whilst other including several of the American recording companies followed. I'd often wondered how Jack Jackson had managed to do his highly successful TV record show without breaking the law. But now and for the first time the BBC had official permission to copy and to edit commercial recordings for a proposed Pinky and Perky series. It was agreed by the BBC that the Dalibors would provide a 'package' for a pilot programme; the records, as selected by Marcel, all the puppets, properties and the script. The BBC in Manchester would provide the technical and design facilities, also the producer.

At a meeting I attended with their London agent, Norman Murray, the Dalibors asked for Margaret to script the storyline since she'd already done this for one of their ITV appearances. The BBC's TV Light Entertainment department agreed that this project now came under their auspices. Margaret's basic idea for the proposed series was the Pinky and Perky would be seen running a Radio Station, the one to be the disk jockey who put the records on the turntable, the other, the station engineer. And in the middle of the proposed mayhem would be BBC North regional announcer, Roger Moffat, who'd already had a great success in appearing with Sheila Buxton in *Make Way For Music*.

I talked to Jan about making two glove-puppet duplicates of Pinky and Perky which we could use at the Radio Station and thus avoid any 'strings' on this particular set apart from now being able to pick up such things as records! A variety of Dalibor puppet creations would then mime to various songs and types of music within situations which the writer and director would devise.

As a direct result of our *Pinky and Perky* agreement with the Gramophone Company the BBC at Dickenson Road, would soon be launching a series originally entitled *Hit Parade* and produced by Johnny Stewart. At the time Johnny hoped that the Dalibors might make and manipulate for him puppets which looked like some of the pop stars of the day, since it was highly unlikely that the more famous recording artists would agree to appear in person on his show. But not many recording stars have declined to appear on *Top Of The Pops*, as it was to be re-titled, since it began life at Dickenson Road, Manchester – as did many other highly successful TV series – Harry Worth and Val Doonican included.

Before all that happened, however, I had suggested we call our proposed puppet series *Pinky and Perky's Pop Parade*, courtesy of station P.O.P. I now had an appointment to meet and to discuss our ideas with the then Head of TV Light Entertainment. The very first time I waited outside HLE's office, I found myself absentmindedly humming the melody of 'A Nightingale Sang in Berkeley Square'. Was it because of the composer's name, Eric Maschwitz, was on his door? And even inside that office when the very nice and helpful man was discussing Pinky and Perky with me and beginning to solve all sorts or problems, like money, my thoughts wandered again. Fancy waking up each morning next to the one and only Hermione Gingold! I could imagine that when the butler brought in the silver salver with morning tea, she would enquire of her husband in that marvellous voice, 'Mil-erk, Eric?' – except that in the post-war radio series she did it was always 'Mil-erk, Ed-muuund?'

Mr and Mrs Maschwitz must have made a great team. He was

The first series 'Station P.O.P.' with Pinky, Perky and Roger Moffat

Backstage in Poppa Luigi's kitchen at the *Pop In*

Ship ahoy with John Slater as Captain Scuttle, and the two little piglets Pinky and Perky as Mates aboard the paddle steamship *Melodymaster*

certainly a great man to work to as head of a programme department as far as I was concerned, giving of his time, experience and advice. We got off to a good start when I asked for a modest budget allowance for a little filming. I had in mind the two principal dancers from the Northern School of Dance – or rather, just the shadows of these two human beings as they fall across the diminutive figures of the Whiskerley Sisters, three Dalibor mice. They would be sitting at their mouse-sized table within a small hole in the night club wainscot, as the macho man's shadow whispered sweet nothings to his dancing partner. This was all to be mimed and filmed to Ed Byrne's recording of 'Square Dance For Round Cats'. Eric liked this; he liked some of the other ideas we had that cost a bit of money too. And when we had completed these film sequences he tried them out on some of the London TV critics before we went ahead. Eric Maschwitz helped in so many ways to get *Pop Parade* off the ground.

Back north at Dickenson Road there were a lot of design conferences with Ken Lawson, with freelancer Paul Bernard who was responsible for all the set designs for the first TV series, and with our TV technicians. During this time Jan Dalibor took on Ronald Cryer and, later Philip and Elizabeth Rose as additional manipulators. Mainly they would work the glove versions I wanted of Pinky and Perky.

A large part of the filming budget went on 'Mumbles', a funky sort of tune by Johnny Bachelor. This would interrupt Roger Moffat, the station announcer, so he'd send off Perky at regular intervals to try to trace the source of this very strange sound. The Shell Oil Refinery at Stanlow provided one location, a Manchester dental surgeon and his surgery another, and the Corporation Cleansing Department lent me a drain-cleaning van for half a day's filming whilst Perky investigated a suspect drain or two – only to discover that the strange sound had been sucked up through the long tube and now appeared to be lodged inside the van's large storage tank!

It is an historical fact in the Annals of Broadcasting that the first Authorised Independent Radio Station in the UK came 'on air' on Sunday 28th February 1960. This was for an adult audience. In between announcing records, Station P.O.P.'s announcer began knitting pullovers for his two station assistants. We saw the wide-eyed and wide-hipped Prunella Pig with the voice of Ruth Olay 'Singing In The Rain', following a station weather forecast, Ambrose Cat and Midge Mouse who were 'Making Whoopee', and Rachel Rabbit and old George Hare in his bath chair with a then current hit, 'Little George'. The sax-playing and popular Mr Morton Frog mimed to 'Charlie Brown' to the delight of his television audience.

Come to think of it, there was really only one serious complaint during that first *Pinky and Perky* series. Midge Mouse went to town with 'Fings Ain't Wot They Used To Be' – only we'd speeded up the voice of vocalist Bill Cotton until he sounded as if his truss was almost up to his chin. Bill was soon on the phone to station P.O.P.

'Hello, mate! What can I do for you?' beamed Roger.

'Don't you "mate" me. That's my line, anyway! Wot you done wiv' my voice? Tryin' ter make a monkey out of me, eh, eh?'

Roger was nothing if not honest and direct in dealing with complaints. 'W-e-l-l, more of a mouse really!'

The man I'd first met and worked with when his Bandshow came to Hamburg was tickled pink when we'd invited him to 'phone in'. At that time his son, Bill Cotton Jnr, was making his way up the ladder in Eric's department and, in turn, was to be very helpful indeed with the *Pinky and Perky* series which were to follow, as was John Weekes from our Hamburg days. He became extremely skilled in the record 'speeding up-slowing down' process and sound editing which he did for me.

As *Pop Parade* progressed through a twelve-week run so quite a few viewers also took up knitting on behalf of the two pigs – even more on behalf of Roger Moffat since Perky, quite inadvertently of course, showed Roger up and in vision too by sticking a small trotter through a hole in the station announcer's cardigan. The series was later to be repeated in Children's Television time, omitting only a couple of programmes where our treatment of certain items was, perhaps, decidedly 'adult'. We'd also met with copyright clearance difficulties over a recording we had used of Peggy Lee. At that point Jan and Vlasta Dalibor took off smartly to do cabaret in Las Vegas and there met other American recording artists who almost implored them to mime to some of their current hits.

There were several things I learned from *Pop Parade*. We needed to be able to set the scenery and backgrounds for at least three individual numbers within the same operating area of the studio in order to save on the studio time allocated to the show. With Jan, I decided we should now work 'in the round'; a circular rostrum with a centre manipulation area and three cheese-like 'wedges'. The item would be performed and photographed on these and, once finished with, the area re-set and lighting adjustments made for the next three items we'd be rehearsing and then recording.

For our second television series with the Dalibors, we teamed up Pinky and Perky with John Slater in the role of 'Poppa Luigi', owner of the 'POP INN'. In order to allow for a lot more movement and action in this new series, we had the restaurant exterior and interior, and a behind-the-scenes kitchen set, including the rows of store cupboards in which the volatile Italian proprietor kept 'ze ingreediementa' for some of his culinary concoctions. Poppa Luigi also kept mice without being aware of it. Those cupboard doors for the kitchen were scaled to normal, human size. Our design department and scenic workshops, under Bob Dunscombe, made greatly enlarged versions of the cupboard interiors, so that Midge Mouse and the close-harmonising Whiskerley Sisters, miming to 'doctored' commercial recordings of groups like the King Sisters and the Clark Sisters, were scaled down to life-size mice.

In the alley-way outside the kitchen, Poppa Luigi's window box was done in precisely the same way, so that a life-size caterpillar and a lady-bird could be seen amongst giant-sized foliage and flower heads, hovered over by an inquisitive bumble-bee and other small winged creatures. Inside the restaurant itself at the serving counters Pinky and Perky worked an explosive espresso coffee machine and several other catering gadgets. There was a real juke box and then, in a corner of the café, a sort of cabaret area and a small dance floor.

I'd talked to Jan about making a new puppet which combined strings for the head and body, eye and mouth actions, but which had human arms and hands appearing from the folds of a satin cloak. Now, Wilbur Wolf could perform on the miniature white piano keyboard, his gloved fingers playing all the right notes too since they were the hands of a professional pianist. Wilbur could smoke a cigarette or cigar besides expertly shuffle, cut and deal – or misdeal – a hand or cards, for which I'd book a professional croupier instead of the pianist. But of course, Wilbur was always seen right up against the scenery since the human hands had to protrude through holes in the set whilst whoever owned the hands watched their actions on a small television monitor.

It was nearly always a case of having to use string puppets right up against or close to the scenery – until I remembered what I'd seen in use some years before at the Rust Craft Greetings Card factory. It was called an Ameise Retrak – an electric fork-lift truck. Why bother with high bridges, low bridges or with any puppet bridges for manipulation? Why not have a special platform built for the Dalibors and let them manipulate their string puppets mounted on a fork-lift? We found a local firm and a young careful driver. He could move that machine and its valuable load around our studio floor like a well-programmed robot *and* start off and stop without a visible jerk. This idea made a huge difference to our Lighting wizard Tommy Mottram who, until then, was always having to worry about puppet strings and shadows showing on the backgrounds. It also made a world of difference in the amount of movement we were now free to achieve; long tracking shots of 'Peaches' Puss, a slinky feline puppet, mincing along a mirrored hall miming to the voice of Miss Eartha Kitt.

We also had technical assistance, not only from the BBC in London who sent up special equipment as we required it, but also from our friends down the road from us in Manchester, Granada TV. As they were then operating on a Monday to Friday basis, with ABC covering the weekends, Granada often loaned us such things as an additional camera dolly over the weekend we did the Dalibor programmes, delivering and collecting their equipment too. Over the years I and other BBC colleagues certainly enjoyed a happy working relationship with Mr Bernstein's boys.

We became even more ambitious and adventurous with the third BBC series we did with the Dalibors. Margaret Potter had the idea of sending Pinky and Perky around the world on a musical voyage aboard the *Melodymaster*. This was a highly unusual rather Heath Robinson paddle-steamer presided over by a Cap'n Scuttle, or John Slater in the bewhiskered disguise of an ancient and often pig-puzzled mariner. To go with the captain, Jan and Vlasta created a 'blasted ship's parrot' who, of course, kept repeating himself, as parrots do. This one, however, was always on about buried treasure and his clues certainly proved useful in conjunction with Cap'n Scuttle's old map as the *Melodymaster* sailed from port to port, country to country.

What helped us enormously with this series was the inventiveness of a BBC technician in our Manchester engineering department. Ron Pearn designed and made his own version of electronic 'in-lay' and 'over-lay' – a system far superior to that invented by and used by the BBC in London. Of course, Auntie, bless her, wouldn't allow me to use Ron's bit of imaginative magic since it had not been officially tested and approved by Designs Department at HQ. Of course, I did use it right from the start since we recorded the whole programme in sections. Pearn's veritable pearl enabled us to do such things as ring Pinky's head within a ship's lifebelt as he sang the opening theme, or show a scene as if through a port hole without the difficulty of holding camera focus as between foreground and background. And now we could even 'wipe' from one part of action to another, and things like that.

In those days we had telecine facilities at Dickenson Road for playing in filmed extracts where required, but no studio back projection – that lovely facility which gives the impression of, say, driving along in a car, or flying in a plane. The car interior or plane cabin are stationary but photographed against a filmed background of passing buildings, trees, clouds, et cetera. As I say, we had no back projection so I brought along my own 16 mm American film projector with a shutter design which didn't appear to make the backgrounds 'roll' when seen by a television camera.

To give the appearance of being 'at sea' I got our young and enthusiastic designer for this nautical series, Tim Harvey, to construct our paddle-driven steamer so that the side which the camera saw was actually standing in just about three inches of studio tank water. The whole ship structure was mounted on a wheeled frame, and as the paddle rotated, it could be rolled forwards or backwards a few feet. With a hosepipe jet of water playing onto the bow section of the *Melodymaster* and a Strand 'cloud' machine projecting onto a sky-blue backcloth, it all looked quite realistic – and no one was sea-sick! A further nautical dimension was added by Norman Newell and EMI records who brought out a commercial LP of Pinky and Perky singing the sort of songs which we required for this series.

That studio water tank I mentioned was made up for us by the local metalworks in the village of Bollington, Cheshire – at a fraction of the cost quoted by some of the large firms the BBC dealt with for set construction. Whilst it was only inches deep near the hull of the *Melodymaster*, much nearer to camera the tank dropped to a depth of four feet and was fronted by a large panel of perspex. With advice and help from the British SubAqua Club, I put puppeteer Philip Rose into a genuine frogman's suit. Now he was able to operate some of Jan Dalibor's very clever rubber-coated puppets, designed and made for the occasion, literally under water. That went without a hitch – except for the very first time when the Floor Manager said to Philip without a sign of a smile, 'Take those headphones out of your helmet before you go under or you may be electrocuted!' Because of the distortion water causes to the human eye, it was difficult for Philip Rose to see what he was doing, even with a TV monitor directly in front of the perspex panel in the tank, so I had to give him verbal instructions from time to time over those headphones as he mimed a water puppet to various records, or when a seal or a fish had to pop up from beneath the waves as Pinky and Perky swabbed the decks, singing as they worked their passage.

Tim Harvey really excelled himself the time the *Melodymaster* and her crew left a foreign port in a great hurry. Cap'n Scuttle mistook a night of fireworks for the start of a revolution. Tim planned that some of his scenery and props, like a large bell-tower in the foreground, should be mounted on wheels. *That* moved away from camera in a zig-zag course as the *Melodymaster*, her stack belching black smoke, stood in point of fact quite motionless except for her paddle wheel pounding and thrashing through the water. Down in the 'Tim Harvey' engine room, Bertie, the baby elephant and chief engineer stoked away like mad, his trunk twined round the long-handled shovel whilst the main steam-pipe, already patched up with a bandage and 'bulging' in time to the get-away music, hissed and wheezed in accompaniment to the pounding of the ancient ship's engine.

To see our Scene Supervisor, Frank Taylor, and half a dozen of his stage hands pushing this, blowing that, making steam, directing an electric fan on the ship's smoke stack, was entertainment enough in itself. Those BBC staff at Dickenson Road were a marvellously talented and integrated team of technicians, engineers, electricians, make-up and wardrobe staff, carpenters and props men. We had our favourite scenic artist in Bob Dunscombe, and even a Pinky and Perky fan in the person of the studio fire officer who allowed his precious extinguishers to be used for spurts of steam – if pressed, something which applied to both!

In later years, it was no wonder that Tim Harvey was to win an award for his distinguished design contribution to the success of the celebrated drama series *I Claudius*. As a small memento of the *Melodymaster* series, I gave him the scale working model of the boat he had designed. It was radio-controlled and built for us by the BBC's Special Effects Department in London. We filmed the model in our Dickenson Road water tank. Whilst we never managed to achieve life-like streaks of 'lightning' for the storm scenes, that perspex panel in the tank gave us some wonderful underwater shots of the *Melodymaster*'s paddle wheel lifting clean out of the turbulent 'ocean' in a Force Ten gale. Yes, those *Pinky and Perky* series we did were certainly team efforts – with the emphasis on 'effort' from all concerned.

In a recent television documentary marking the 60th anniversary of Children's Broadcasting it was asserted that much of the pioneering work done on those early *Pinky and Perky* programmes by BBC staff in Manchester led to the emergence and success of such series as *The Muppets*. Well, I'm not going to argue with that.

18

Pause for Thought (Unforgettable Moments – and Some I'd Much Rather Forget)

Within days of becoming 'Youths In Training' in the employ of the British Broadcasting Corporation in 1942, our course members were taken to one of the BBC's most important wartime sanctums, London Control Room. Over this ruled the impressive and revered figure of C.F. Bottle, Engineer-in-Charge.

'I believe I know your brother-in-law, sir,' I said, by way of conversation.

'Oh, and how is that?'

I really should have given my reply a little more thought. 'He happens to be our butcher, sir!'

* * *

The BBC ceased relaying Big Ben 'live' the day the sound of a German 'buzz bomb' was clearly heard in the area of Westminster during a pause in those famous chimes. From then on those of us in Programme Engineering had to play recordings instead. Watching a studio wall clock ticking each second away before we lowered the pick-up on to the turntable every quarter of an hour, twenty-four hours of the day, was the worst job I ever had. 'Hobby' warned us of the consequences if this secret were to be exposed.

Guess who had a 'repeating groove' on the one transmission?

* * *

My teenage idea of a *Vogue* cover, Mrs Jo Grimes of Programme Engineering, was there in person in front of me at the control panel in a basement studio of 200 Oxford Street. I cannot remember who was introducing the programme at the microphone but I know I was playing the commercial records for this tribute to the composer on the occasion of his birthday.

'When you think about it, Jo,' I said as we played another of his compositions, 'we use one tune of his to introduce *Front Line Family*, another for *Workers' Playtime*, and then there's *In Town Tonight*! Don't forget he wrote that too, so why the dickens hasn't the old boy been given a knighthood?'

As I slid the final record into its sleeve, Mrs Grimes turned round in her chair and gave one of her dazzlingly beautiful smiles to the little man in the raincoat who'd slipped into our Control Cubicle shortly after we'd gone on the air. By way of introduction she said, 'Trevor is one of our new Junior Programme Engineers, Mr Coates!'

* * *

Not far along the same corridor was a larger studio which had a piano. My engineering colleague, Leonard Treblecock, who later thought to change that to 'Trevor Duncan' when he began composing, was sitting at the Steinway Grand. A very good pianist too, our Leonard. I was waiting for my next 'booking' to arrive in an adjoining studio, Leonard for his, so I'd dropped in for a chat. When the studio door opened I assumed it was my man who'd arrived to broadcast, for he remained at the door. I smiled and went over to escort him next door for the talk which had been booked in there. But he seemed in no hurry. In fact he came forward and asked Leonard to continue playing. My colleague obliged.

'D'you tinkle the keys, too?' Leonard enquired after a while.

'Yes … yes I do a little,' replied Benno Moiseiwitsch.

* * *

I envied the professional way in which Nan Macdonald could stand at the microphone and 'fill in' with no notes to hand, until it was precisely time for the North to join another region for the next part of *Children's Hour* that day. And better still, at ten minutes to six on Mondays, she would tell listeners what was in store for the whole week's listening without any proper script.

The first Monday after she had departed, I spent a good part of that morning writing 'What's On' out in full. Came ten to six and I went 'solo' on this for the very first time. Pages 1 and 2 of my script went quite well

'And then on Thursday at five p.m. we start with ...'

I turned over to read from Page 3 but all I saw in front of me was the studio table-top. The rest of the week had been left back in the office. From then on Pat Paull, my secretary, pinned the pages of the *Radio Times* together for me each Monday. I could rely on her.

* * *

All those London and Regional BBC staff responsible for running *Children's Hour* throughout the British Isles met twice annually once David Davis was in charge – one meeting at Broadcasting House, London, the other in the regions. It was North's turn shortly after I took over in Manchester. Margaret thought it would be nice to hold a party at our home the evening before so I'd get to know them all a little better.

'I bet most will only sip lemonade,' I said, having already seen one or two of these former teachers.

That night a solitary figure sat on the settle in our dining room away from all the laughter and chatter, holding a glass of orange. We were fast running out of wine – in fact of everything alcoholic. In passing the lady I happened to hold up the bottle and say, 'I don't suppose I can interest you in any of this?'

She peered at the label. 'Och, now, I'd go to th' devil himself for burgundy,' beamed Kathleen from Scotland.

Much later the phone rang. It was Kathleen, now from a Manchester Hotel. Had we found her gloves? Yes, I'd bring them in to the meeting tomorrow. Was she comfortable?

'Yes, yes, indeed. And *such* a nice bunch of boys here too. They're celebrating their win they tell me – and we're all enjoying a wee dram. But I'm sure *you* know all th' Manchester United laddies!'

* * *

I think it was after 'talking a bit posh' that Dave Morris, the northern comedian, first began to tease me in the BBC canteen. The producer of the popular *Dave Morris's Club Night* was Alick Hayes, who had done comedy series with the best in the land including Will Hay. It was Alick who said that Dave would like to write me into his show as 'the man from the Corporation' – not the BBC but from Local Government – who would always turn up to complain about one thing or another and was given lines like: 'But you see, Mr Morris, we must take the waste of water very seriously! I mean just look at that tap. It may appear only a 'drip' to you ...'

It wasn't until we were on live transmission that the highly experienced Dave would suddenly *add* lines like: 'Eh, Cedric, are you taking this in? He's on about "drips"!' Cedric was Joe Gladwin. Dave could never have imagined that in the years ahead his 'feed' would become a star character actor in many Television plays. But at least Joe Gladwin kept his hand in with comedy when delighting us with his performance as the poor, downtrodden husband of Kathy Staff in *The Last of the Summer Wine.*

As for my performances, well *Club Night* was recorded in Working Men's Clubs and so perhaps one of the members reported to Equity, the Actors' Union, that I was *not* a member. In any event I had to withdraw my unpaid services and so *my* short career as an actor came to an end.

* * *

'If I can assist you at all ...' a young Charles Groves enquired of Sir Thomas Beecham who was to take over and conduct the BBC Northern Orchestra that day.

'Most certainly,' replied the distinguished maestro. 'Here!'

With that, he was to hand Charles a portable Roberts radio. 'Take this into your Green Room and, from time to time, come out and tell me how Yorkshire are doing in the Test.'

That same portable was later to accompany Sir Thomas to the Free Trade Hall in Manchester. Philip Dobson, the BBC voice for such an occasion, had read all the Programme Notes he possessed on the work about to be performed at the start of the second half of the broadcast concert. Now he was rather frantically 'filling in' awaiting the moment the conductor stepped into view once again.

Sir Thomas, offstage, was interested to hear what Dobson was saying. His Roberts was in his hand. Still holding it he came just into view of some of the audience.

'And here *is* Sir Thomas,' announced Dobson with evident relief. On hearing that the maestro turned, came off and went towards his dressing room, making his own announcement.

'I think,' he declared, 'I shall change this waistcoat!'

* * *

Daphne Oxenford made a very good Scots housekeeper to Professor Selby in Margaret Potter's serial *The Mystery Of Bendreda*. The only time she sounded even slightly unsure of herself was when 'Dick' had to say somewhat urgently, 'But where *is* the professor, Maggie?'

Maggie *should* have replied, 'He's up at the Meteorological Office, sir!'

Daphne kept fluffing the line. She had him almost up the Matterhorn before she gave up trying and simply replied, 'Och, *you* know. He's up with yon weather man!'

* * *

It was always reassuring for a young producer to work with Charles Groves. And when he told me it would be all right for the composer Henry Reed to conduct the orchestra I said no more. After all Mr Reed *had* written the score for the cartoon I was producing. Instead of the tall, dark, romantic figure I had imagined from his music, what in fact arrived at the Milton Hall that day was a large jovial chap who could have been a happy, ruddy-faced fruit-grower.

'Ah, my sugar-plum!' was the greeting he gave to a lady in the second violins. That and a smacking kiss. 'W-e-l-l now, lads and lassies …'

The slight nasal quality in the voice reminded me of the Inventor in *Toytown*. Hitching up his trousers, Mr Reed got to work on 'Cue 1' but stopped abruptly at some very complicated writing of his for brass.

'Christ, Charles,' he bellowed. 'What's the matter with your i-r-o-n section today, eh?'

I sank from view in the glass-fronted Control Cubicle. Cue 2 required a lot of percussion *and* in very quick succession.

'Yers …' mused the composer as he studied his own arrangement for a moment or two. Then he beamed at the percussionist. 'Give it a try, shall we? If you can cope with *this* lot, then when we come to record we'll stick a feather duster up your backside and you can sweep th' studio floor at the same time I shouldn't wonder, eh, boys and girls?'

* * *

The receptionist at the Durham hotel assured me that she would inform me the moment the Dean and his wife arrived to take dinner with me. We were to discuss the proposed *For Thy Great Glory* broadcast from Durham Cathedral. No, we hadn't met before and, yes, I gathered he'd only recently been appointed and may not have been to this hotel before. I was telling the girl at the desk that they'd probably both be grey-haired. Then, as a further guess, I said what I thought Dean Wild's wife might be wearing. My voice trailed off as I noticed through the staircase bannisters a pair of very shapely legs standing quite still. Looking up, I saw the smartly dressed figure of a young and attractive woman. She leaned over the rail, smiled and discreetly said, 'I'm the lady with the pearls and the two-piece. Mr Hill?'

* * *

We'd left Philip Robinson doing his live commentary during the broadcast from Chester. Now, the Zoo's Director, George Mottershead, was with me in my car as we made for the polar bear enclosure and the next part of the programme. A BBC van was awaiting our arrival as arranged but instead of handing me the microphone and headphones, engineer Harold Eckersley was using them himself.

'Ah, but here comes Mr Hill so I will hand you over to him!'

Fortunately there was a certain look on Harold's face, so I didn't say anything flip like, 'Ta. And don't give up your daytime job!'

And just as well.

Shortly after we'd left Philip to talk to the nation, Broadcasting House in London was to lose contact with Chester Zoo. The Home Service announcer apologised, played some music, then said they would hand back to the Zoo again in the hope that the line had been restored.

Helpful Harold had heard all that as he waited in the OB van. He picked up the microphone and put himself on the air explaining he was waiting our arrival which should be at any moment now. Had there been silence again London would almost certainly have abandoned the broadcast. As it was, Harold saved the day. I wrote such a glowing memo to our Chief Engineer in Manchester about initiative and such-like.

'Thank you,' he replied, 'but BBC engineers are not permitted to broadcast. Eckersley will, of course, be reprimanded!'

Thankfully, dimwits like that didn't abound in BBC Broadcasting!

* * *

I congratulated my friend and colleague in the North, Ken Ford, on the splendid way in which he had chaired *Gardeners' Question Time* after the sudden death of Franklin Engelmann. I can't have been easy for Ken, for it was also one of those occasions on which the BBC Board of Management was attending a broadcast.

'I could have done with you there on the night,' said Ken.

'But what about the boss?' I enquired.

'Oh he was there all right. He just said before we started, "It'll probably be a disaster, but do your best old boy"!'

I sent Ken a telegram with precisely those words when, a long time after, the BBC at last allowed us to use Ken Ford as the chairman as well as the producer of this very popular radio series.

* * *

When television's version of *Young Artists* came into my area in the mid 1950s, I knew I'd have the pleasure of working again with the Programme's Editor, Cliff Michelmore, who was then on staff contract to the BBC. Cliff must have travelled miles seeing hundreds of youngsters. And not only singers and musicians, as with our regular radio series, for *All Your Own* included youngsters like David Coppin who made wonderful toy soldiers, Patrick Dean and Theresa Dunn who showed what the best of Irish dancing was like, and the young and diminutive Anne Hinchley from Manchester who clearly demonstrated that you don't need to be six feet tall to blow a post horn. There were even young farmers on *All Your Own* from time to time.

Cliff's assistant in those days was Joanna Symons, still as graceful and charming as in the war years when she greeted visitors as receptionist at 200 Oxford Street. I am quite sure it must have been Joanna who began the fashion amongst those in broadcasting and the theatre of calling everyone 'darling'. Well, it *does* help people like me who aren't very good at remembering names. Be that as it may, I'd found a particularly brilliant young pianist – almost in the class of the young John Ogden who'd performed in *Young Artists* from Manchester. Now as you will probably remember, darlings, the man who conducted all those interviews so well for *All Your Own* was the one and only Huw Wheldon. On this particular live broadcast I'd kept my young pianist until the very last. Huw was so taken with the lad, however, that he kept surveying the palm of his hand; a delightful habit of his, and thinking of something else to talk about. Over the Floor Manager's headphones I said, 'For goodness sake give him the 'wind-up' sign! We're running out of time!'

When my pianist eventually got down to doing what he did better than

My first *Jackanory* adaptation featured children from Pott Shrigley village school

Our *real* policeman stops the children on their night-time flit

most, it was almost time to close. 'Set them to "Fast" and ... Roll Captions!' I ordered from up in the Control Gallery. Then I turned to Cliff. 'If *only* that lovely Welsh wind-bag could have *stopped* talking,' I wailed in despair. The next moment as the roller caption sped up to the producer's screen credit, so a firm hand landed on my shoulder.

'No, hold it,' said Huw, who was right behind me. 'You worked hard on this. You deserve your credit!'

I knew he'd heard what I'd just said. I also know that it seemed only a short while later that Huw Wheldon, one of the nicest of men, became the Managing Director of BBC television. *And* I kept my job.

For that – and for one or two other things besides – he deserved his knighthood!

* * *

I'd auditioned the burly lad from Newton-le-Willows in 1962. He came along with a pal from the Library Theatre, Manchester, and amongst other things, he sang to a guitar. I didn't think much of that, but then he read to me. 'Young, keen and intelligent. Good timing and bags of attack' were the words I wrote on the Audition Report.

He was good in the role of Ted Fothergill in *Deadline For Danger*, a serial I did only a few weeks later. It was his debut. Then he played various parts in the *Homer Jackson* series which Margaret wrote.

After television's *Jackanory* had been going for some time I adapted two or three books myself including *Gumble's Yard*, a novel by the *Guardian* journalist and author, John Rowe Townsend. Now this called for 'good timing and bags of attack', from a storyteller – besides a genuine Northern accent. I knew just the chap. Oh yes, and we had just started to use the Autocue which meant that the actor didn't have to learn any of the lines off by heart. He could sit and relax in a comfy studio chair and just read the story off the Autocue screen.

The live transmission had gone well as we came to the end of the first episode of *Gumble's Yard*. 'Stand by for closing music and captions,' I said, and then something I'd neither said nor done on rehearsal. 'Track back on Camera 1.'

I couldn't for the life of me understand why my storyteller suddenly leant forward on the edge of his chair and a glazed look came into his eyes before he'd got to the end of his narrative. He slumped back, looking quite limp in that comfy chair we'd provided after we'd come off transmission, but rallied as I came down to the studio.

Colin Edwynn and Gillian Fleming-Williams; Dick Turpin and his 'double'

'God, you sod!' declared Colin Welland.

I'd quite forgotten that he was reading from Autocue – and that was fixed to the front of the retreating Camera 1.

* * *

The lady at the Writers' Summer School, Swanwick, evidently had it in for me the moment I finished my lecture. *Her* script had been accepted by the BBC, *and* she had been asked by *Woman's Hour* department in London to go for a voice test.

'But they *s*aid my voi*c*e wa*s*n't *s*uitable!'

She 'whistled' on every single 's' and 'c'. And that is what gave me the idea of becoming Deni*s* Decibel the *Nursery Sing Song* po*s*tman, who took to the air mo*s*t Tue*s*day*s*, with Mi*ss* Violet Car*s*on, on the BBC Home *S*ervi*c*e!

* * *

It wasn't until Wardrobe said she'd have to let out Dick Turpin's riding coat that I became suspicious.

We were filming as near as possible Margaret's *Escape* series, the true story of the celebrated Highwayman – only someone at TV Centre insisted that we should include the famous ride from London to York. That was never Dick Turpin. It was done by John Nevison in 1676 who got from Gad's Hill to York on horseback in just three and three-quarter hours.

Be that as it may, by good fortune it happened to snow heavily a day or two before we were to film the entirely legendary ride, so I was able to shoot the whole thing in snow as a sort of 'dream' sequence. This began with Turpin, astride Black Bess, plunging into view through a cloud of pink smoke. (Please do not adjust your set.) BBC Audio Supervisor, David Fleming-Williams, the best in the business, and his wife Gillian, another best who often rode at Badminton, invited Colin Edwynn to their stables in the hope that he might get to know Gillian's black mare 'Tilley' before we started filming. Having fallen off a time or two, cowardly Colin suggested that he'd do all the 'sitting-in-saddle-and-swaggering' close-up bits if Gillian would do all the hard riding as his 'double'. Which she did.

When it came to Turpin's famous 'leap over the toll-gate', which I'd arranged to stage at White Lodge, Tabley, Cheshire, David made sure that bales of peat were liberally strewn on the frozen cobbles over which Tilley would gallop before doing the high-jump. To ensure we missed none of the action and got it 'in one', I had three film cameras out that day. One at ground level, the second set to run in slow-motion for the actual 'leap', and the third to take in the whole scene.

Both Gill and David assured me there was no great danger. I thought it went off beautifully – but David did not. 'She missed her stride. We'll do another Take! And don't look so darned worried, granddad!' he added, putting an arm round my shoulder. Of course I was worried – *darned* worried since learning why that costume had to be let out. Dick Turpin was pregnant!

* * *

The broad river near Voss in central Norway looked very placid and seemed an ideal location for our film, *Bread And Cheese*, and that part of the story in which young 'Nils' is on his way down the mountain to the village to fetch lunch – but decides to take a short cut.

Two weeks later the river was in full spate after several days of torrential summer rain. The day before we were to film the sequence in which the boy falls in, I stood on the river bank. Above the roar of water came another roar. An old motorbike and side-car with English number plates came hurtling over the coarse grass and screeched to a halt. One long-haired hippy drove, the other sat with legs dangling over the side-car. Leaning over he plucked a stem of grass. This he chewed for a moment as he watched the fast flowing waters. A big grin spread across his face.

'Bloody duck wouldn't last long in *that* lot, eh, mate?' he said as he caught my eye. It turned out that he and his pal were from Maida Vale, London. When they knew what we were up to they promised to turn up the next day.

They did too – both of them in swimming trunks. Turning to Margaret, who felt she had to share the responsibility since she'd written the story, the taller of the two said, 'Not to worry, missus. Us'll not let little bugger drown, eh, Syd?'

With those reassuring words ringing in my ears I said a quick prayer, cued the cameraman and released the hold I had on young Atle Slettemark's wrists. The boy fell backwards from the rock, into camera shot and then dropped the ten feet or so into the turbulent water. I needn't have worried. Our star performer was out of that river, unaided before either of our new-found friends were in it.

* * *

For the weekly *Showcase* programme which I produced in the early 1950s, any interviews we did from theatres counted as being in the nature of a Press Interview. If the stars came to a studio in Broadcasting House, however, then fees were payable.

When the Oliviers opened in Manchester with *Caesar and Cleopatra* one week, to be followed by *Antony and Cleopatra*, the helpful manager of the Opera House, Tommy Appleby, suggested that I use his office to interview Laurence Olivier. The answer he gave to my one question on the difference between playing Shaw and Shakespeare, was a lesson in conciseness from a master practitioner of theatre. As a token of appreciation I thought to have flowers delivered to Vivien Leigh.

Later that same day I received her hand-written letter of thanks for the basket of her favourite lilies of the valley, together with a warm invitation to join them both the following day for a lunchtime drink. I was about to take my leave of them when the telephone rang in their suite at the Midland Hotel. Someone from the *Oldham Chronicle* would like to interview Laurence Olivier. He was asked to come up straight away. In walked a very young cub reporter who must have been greatly impressed by Humphrey Bogart, in belted mac with trilby set well back on his head.

We relieved him of the hat after a while as he took out notepad and pen. Was it their first visit to Manchester? Did they often do Shakespeare together? Had Mr Olivier appeared in Shakespeare films? Oh, what were they? Well, what parts did *he* take?

At this, Vivien Leigh moved quietly across the room to adjust the curtains at the window, her shoulders visibly shaking. The answers the young man received were far more than he deserved and were, above all,

Peter McEnery and Rosemary Leach in *Sons and Lovers*

a lesson in civility. When he and the hat departed, Laurence Olivier looked a little dazed. Had I, by any chance, a cigarette on me? I had.

'And *do* stay for another drink. I feel we *need* one. Why, even your lovely flowers are wilting!' observed the even lovelier Vivien Leigh.

Contrary to general belief, Auntie BBC kept a pretty tight hold on our expense claims. I submitted Dingley's receipted bill for Vivien Leigh's lillies of the valley, plus basket and delivery, to my regional executive who had to check and pass such claims before we were allowed to take them along to the BBC cashier.

Edward Mills looked aghast. 'Really, Hill,' he fumed. 'Five pounds for flowers! Couldn't you have taken her a bunch?'

'In my hot little hand?' I enquired.

* * *

Dr Crabbe was not the learned old fogey I had imagined when reading his fascinating article on Binaural Sound in the technical press. In point of fact James turned out to be a very enthusiastic and lively young man just up the road from us at Manchester University. And sound reproduction was only his hobby. His daytime work and research was as a bio-chemist dealing with reproduction of a rather different kind – that of male sperm.

Thanks to Duncan Thomas and to his equally go-ahead successor, Roger Dowling, as Head of Programme Services and Engineering in Manchester, I was allowed to book valuable studio time together with some of the BBC's technical facilities in order that James could further his researches into Binaural Sound with us, most ably assisted and advised by David Fleming-Williams and Chris Webb of the Audio Unit. It was David and Chris who spent three days on a sailing ship getting me the stereophonic background sounds and effects I've already mentioned for *Hornblower*. They were the key men in 'TTTT', as David named Trevor's Tireless Technical Team. These two valued colleagues did great work on *Sons and Lovers* which starred Peter McEnery, Rosemary Leach, Billie Whitelaw and Rosalind Shanks, and on another D.H. Lawrence serial, *Women in Love*, with Peter joined on this occasion by Sarah Badel, Eleanor Bron, Penelope Wilton and Clive Francis. With casts of that calibre who come to the studio having read the books and studied the parts in detail, and then give of their time and enthusiasm as well as their talents, then stereo drama has a lot to offer in terms of creativeness. It also has the bonus of being heard by a *pair* of human ears. To date, the television and the film camera posses only one eye – the lens.

Dorothea Brooking was to produce a delightful version of *The Secret Garden* from London for Children's Television and at my request agreed to audition both 'Bunkle' (Billie Whitelaw) for the role of 'Martha' and my talented *Children's Hour* colleague, Herbert Smith, for the role of 'Ben Weatherstaff' the old gardener. Both got these respective parts in her 1952 production. Just to put the record straight I *did* receive a letter from a young person who, if memory serves, came from Huddersfield. What *is* fact is that I got Herbert to read out that letter during *Out Of School*, our North Regional teenage magazine, on Saturday 24th June 1952:

> 'Whilst I am enjoying *The Secret Garden*, I like even more the plays on radio because the scenery is better.'

That letter was picked up by John Stratten who used it the following week in the *Manchester Evening News*.

I can always trust Gillian Reynolds. She got it right in her *Daily Telegraph* column in recent times – unlike some others. One lens, perhaps, two ears, definitely, but even TV in stereo isn't capable of reproducing quite the same 'scenery'.

By the late 1970s, we were working towards the very first radio programme ever to be broadcast in Binaural Sound, which appears the more natural since it seems to come from all directions. It was to be transmitted on Radio 3 as part of a Northern Weekend. Listeners would be advised to listen to the broadcast on a pair of good quality headphones, 'in order to enhance the experience'! But, I was warned, *no* advance publicity. The BBC had often been an Aunt Sally; decried for what a large part of the British press love to be able to label as 'a disgraceful waste of licence payers' money'! Fears were of headlines such as 'Just how much public money did the BBC waste on bringing us Binaural Sound with *The Sound of The City*? MP demands an investigation'.

The idea of this first feature programme had sprung from a scripted talk written by the artist Harold Riley. It traced the change from his pre-war boyhood to the present-day sounds of the city as he heard them. Those 1930s sounds of trams, mill hooters, clogs, the street lamp-lighter, we recorded in 'narrow' stereo, and all the post-war sounds – Manchester Airport concourse, video games in an amusement arcade, a modern swimming bath, et cetera – we captured by using binaural microphones no thicker than a pencil and placed for greatest effect, or so we discovered, just inside the recordist's own ears.

I was on my way with David Fleming-Williams in his estate car loaded with gear to record a 1930s mill loom which was to be run especially for the occasion, when we heard it. The sound of a fast-approaching fire engine which then roared past. Giving chase, David caught up with it on a housing estate in Wythenshawe. Only a chip-pan fire as it turned out but, yes, the fire crew would be very pleased to assist us. David quickly set up the Nagra stereo recorder and the binaural microphones. We recorded that fire engine passing and re-passing at various speeds, siren sounding; that wonderful sudden 'tone drop' in sound, when things like sirens and bells pass the human ear at speed. Ah yes! I and the members of 'TTTT' felt very smug when it was brought to our attention that the celebrated Angus McKenzie had written about *Sound Of The City* in the technical press and of 'the remarkable sense of realism and the impression that sounds were projected in front, at the sides and, in many cases, behind me, in a quite extraordinary way which I found enthralling!'

I think it was really thanks to Mr McKenzie that I was invited to take our tapes to Berlin and then on to Copenhagen in order that German and Danish listeners could hear radio's first binaural feature, with a commentary in their own language of course.

Looking back, I cannot say I felt that 'enthralled' when we'd bid thanks and farewell to that fire brigade crew at the time we made our very first Binaural recording for *Sound Of The City*. They were already well out of sight and sound when Mr Fleming-Williams made a discovery. He hadn't put any tape into the recording machine – or so he *told* me!

'Come on, Granddad, I'm not serious. Time for a coffee?'

* * *

When another splendid David, now Sir David Hatch was appointed by the BBC in its wisdom as Network Editor, North, I as second-in-command took him on a tour of the old BBC buildings and studios and then, on to New Broadcasting House and to the complex of radio studios in the course of construction there. I knew quite a bit about these as I had been chairman of the Radio Planning Committee in Manchester right from the start, thanks to my former boss, Grahame Miller, who would be retiring before our new headquarters were finished.

What soon became evident to this bright young Mr Hatch was that, in spite of all I've written about myself so far in this book, I *did* have certain shortcomings.

New Broadcasting House, Oxford Road, Manchester

The first radio production from Manchester's new headquarters in September 1975 was a reunion for Geoffrey Banks, Herbert Smith, Peter Wheeler, Billie Whitelaw, Brian Trueman, Philip Jenkinson and producer Trevor Hill

'Now be honest! You know every man-jack of the staff but less than half their names. How many more, "This is er ..." am I going to get? And another thing. You don't really know your way to the new Music studio. I swear we've been down this same corridor three times already!'

Charming chap. He remains one of my most favourite men who was in the BBC, and was, rightly, to become Radio's Director of Programmes. David is a very generous man in his help and praise. He insisted that as I had done quite a lot of the spade work, he should hand the Prime Minister on to me when it came to the tour of the BBC's latest stereo drama studio and complex at the official opening of New Broadcasting House, Manchester, in June 1976.

Knowing our senior drama producer, Alfred Bradley, only too well, I not only suggested that he might break the habit of a lifetime and wear something like a suit for this occasion, but also that it might be a good idea if *I* were to select which part of the play the PM would hear in rehearsal. *And* I had on David's advice remembered to carefully write down the full names of the studio production team and those of the cast on my copy of the play script.

'And this, sir, is Alfred Bradley's production assistant sitting just beyond him, Kay Jamieson!'

The PM replied that if Mr Bradley would kindly pull in his voluminous pullover a bit, perhaps he'd be able to *see* Miss Jamieson. I then invited our distinguished visitor to hear a little of the play. He thanked me, then to my alarm asked if he might borrow my copy of the script in order to follow what he was about to hear. The short play extract went perfectly. It was a fictional piece all about Local Government. Knowing full well that the Prime Minister's official party would include not only the Lord Mayor but also Manchester's Town Clerk, I had chosen with extreme care.

Next moment Alfred declared, 'Of course, Prime Minister, this is the bit we really wanted you to hear!' He turned several pages then handed him his script. Peering over his glasses, the Rt. Hon. James Callaghan roared with laughter.

'If this is the sort of thing you are allowed to do on Radio 3, then I must surely listen a little more often!'

On that particular page of the script, the Town Clerk is referred to as being 'a devious little fart'!

* * *

Several months later I invited author, Ken Whitmore, to lunch with me. He wrote excellent and amusing radio plays, like *Jump* which he turned into a book. In a much more serious vein perhaps, would he now be prepared to adapt for me Howard Spring's political novel, *Fame Is The Spur* as a Radio 4 Sunday night serial? As I came down in the lift Ken was standing at the reception desk. I shook him by the hand. 'Hello, nice of you to come and meet me. I'm Trevor Hill.'

I thought he looked a little bemused. 'Yes, I know who you are. You introduced me to the Prime Minister!'

* * *

As I've already noted, Norway was to feature large in the lives of Margaret and Trevor Hill – as had Germany where we first met. The Norwegian experience was really thanks to Richard Dimbleby with whom I'd worked whilst I was 'engineering' on *Radio Newsreel* and he was with the BBC's War Report Unit. And what a broadcaster and commentator *he* was. I doubt Richard would have said what one of his sons said during HM's Golden Jubilee celebration in telling viewers that 'the Royal coach is drawn by six gays'!

But going back to the 1960s, at home in Pott Shrigley one evening we were to see a film which Richard's own company had made on holiday in Norway, only days after Jan and Vlasta Dalibor had again been staying at 'The Croft' in order to discuss a possible second series of *Pinky and Perky* – the first having completed initial transmission of *Pop Parade* for adult viewers, to be followed by a revised version for Children's Television.

The reader will of course believe me when I state that, while tucking up the trotters of my young friends Pinky and Perky in our 'Guest Room 2', it was Pinky who whispered to me that they now had a splendid London Agent, Norman Murray, and *he* had got them both an engagement to appear in cabaret in, wait for it, Las Vegas. All I asked of them was that they would be sure to take both Jan and dear Vlasta with them, since they too had been working very hard. As indeed had Margaret and I. Richard, whom I'd assisted in the early 1950s when some *Down Your Way* editions came from the North, gave me more helpful information. Within ten days I'd put in for BBC leave then made our booking to stay three weeks in Stavanger which had been featured in Richard's film.

When the news of our holiday reached Edward Wilkinson who was in programme charge of the BBC's Newcastle studios – and he'd always been such a helpful and cheerful colleague – he told me that he'd often been asked if the BBC would consider doing a programme about the links between the ports of Newcastle and Bergen, since this sea crossing had been in existence for many a century. I'd already paid for our return fare and accommodation costs but OK, OK, yes I *would* take a mobile tape recorder on holiday with us. Meanwhile Ted would contact the Bergen Line in Trafalgar Square. And, begorrah, when I'd made that part of the journey wasn't it John O'Dell himself who said three weeks in Stavangar would be far too long; that we should do the 'Discovery Route' dating from Victorian times and again, begorrah, wouldn't he himself make all the necessary alterations and travel arrangements for us. 'Meantime, 'tis an idea to meet Captain Christiansen aforehand' – or words to that effect.

Next, a trip to Newcastle and there, indeed, was the Bergen Line's chief captain, not above five foot five, but what he lacked in height he more than made up for in both seamanship and stature. I'd be recording a crossing on the outward trip then visiting the Norwegian Nautical Museum in Bergen in order to get all the necessary information to enable me to write and make a studio sound reconstruction of a trip precisely one hundred years earlier. That museum visit came after a week of complete relaxation at the Solar Strand Hotel and the Bergen Line had then seen us both, and in comfort, all the way along that 'Discovery Route'. Little did we know it, but there was to be one astonishing 'discovery' within hours of our arrival at the port of Stravangar.

It all started the moment we were checking in at the hotel's reception desk. I was showing our passports when I felt a nudge. 'Darling, just look at that display cabinet!' It contained some lovely examples of pottery.

'You are vishing to see around de vorks?' the receptionist enquired. Indeed we *were* wishing. We saw her next just as we sat at our dining table 'It vill be at eight of the clocks tomorrow, sir.' Not a lot of time for sleep as it turned out, for our visit was to be at 8 a.m.

The factory, Stavangarflint, stood in sight of a lovely bay. To meet us was an extremely kind and courteous gentleman who was to introduce himself as a Mr Brekke and then take us firstly to design, then to all other areas including the kilns, decorating department and finally into the sales office. To our surprise all the range of the 'Mesterkokken' could be placed directly on top of a gas or an electric ring or into an oven. To us the designs were stunning – as was the revelation which Mr Brekke was to make having then invited us to take morning coffee with him in his own office. To my astonishment I was to note the sign on the door 'Direktor

Brekke'. Surely he did not take every foreign visitor around his factory himself?

A broad smile crossed his face as he looked down at his shoes. 'Not at all but the Hotel Solar Strand gives us your names yesterday afternoon. You are Mr and Mrs Tre-vor Hill, yes? And I think you call Mrs Hill "Margaret", yes?' By now we were both 'yours sincerely puzzled' as he continued, 'My first name is Trygvve. In Norwegian that is "Trevor". My surname, Brekke means "Hill". My wife is also called Margaret!'

We were to meet Norway's Margaret and Trevor Hill again in their own home before the week was out, also their children and again and again over the following years either holidaying at their lovely Norwegian chalet, in our own home in Cheshire, or aboard MV *Cleo* on Lake Windermere.

It was also as a result of being up that Norwegian mountain, when the 'Discovery Route' took us to Voss in central Norway, that we'd come across a young man who was fishing the clear waters of a fast-flowing stream – or rather putting down his rod to wander along the bank in search of something. As it turned out he was looking for a packet of sandwiches he'd brought with him – his lunch. And that, as I've already recounted, is how we came to bring a BBC North Regional film crew to Norway the following year in order to make *Focus On Fine China* and then *Bread And Cheese* using no actors for this one but only the residents, young and old, from Voss. The chap who played the brother to 'Nils' was, in fact, the very man who had mislaid his lunch on our initial meeting. That was the trigger for the story we wrote. Without the assistance of the Managing Director of the Bergen Line and the equally splendid co-operation of the Norwegian Tourist Board, we'd never have shot two films within a period of three and a half weeks. But before that, I had to complete the radio feature regarding those historic links between the ports of Newcastle, Stavangar and Bergen. Any skipper worth his salt would steer *Course Forty Five*.

* * *

But time for some refreshment. In the early days of *Round Britain Quiz* team members were given dinner in 'Hospitality', served by a Greek lady, Aphrodite Wall (of whom more later). There was the one participant who, once his glass was drained – which it so often was, would hold it aloft whilst still talking to others, having bellowed 'Aphro ... diiteee!' Oh God, not another. What'll he be like when we come to record?

Those were the thoughts which ran through my head. The teams would return to Hospitality once the recordings had been completed. On one occasion my understanding colleague Aphrodite took me aside.

'Please, Mr Hill. I show you.' I was led across the room to a side table on which stood the Hospitality drinks – and just one cup. 'In there you see the cork. Is soaking in gin. So for him I wipe the cork round and round the rims of the glass inside *and* out, fill just with tonic water and no more. It may *smell* like another large gin and tonic, so you must not have this worry any more!'

The time came for Aphrodite's retirement. Yes, she would be serving us for the very last time. A call to one of her children would ensure she came dressed up that evening rather than in the usual staff uniform – for on this occasion, Anthony Quinton would present our guest at that dinner with a French crystal vase engraved with the signatures of those of us whom she'd taken such splendid care of during several years of BBC Hospitality.

Now, I am the one who serves the food and drinks when Aphrodite's son kindly brings my Greek friend to lunch with me here in Cheltenham once or twice a year.

19

The Fortnum and Mason of Quiz Programmes

I was more than a little surprised to find Winnie the Pooh in a Warsaw flat: and not only the stories but also a cook book by him. Hastening back to England I passed this intelligence to the President of Trinity College Oxford over a plate of sticky cream-filled buns in a London restaurant. Both went down rather well. The information was then used to great effect by that clever, urbane, witty and gentlest of men, Anthony Quinton, later Baron Quinton of Holywell. On a July evening in 1979, Tony asked the two members of my Polish team in *Round Europe Quiz* the following:

> A blue one was preferred to a green one, as a means of deceiving some bees.
> A broken red one was given to a donkey as a birthday present. (He also got a container.)
> What are these things and who was involved?

This question was directed at Janusz Stefanowicz, journalist and editor of the principal Polish Catholic newspaper. I'd noticed some of his reading matter as I waited to meet him for the first time in his Warsaw apartment, and to see if I might persuade him to take part in this unashamedly highbrow, elegant and often, I trust, very amusing form of Radio Quiz. He not only accepted but now he rose to the occasion. Or, how about 'ascended'? You must excuse such clues, but as the producer of *Round Britain Quiz*, *Transatlantic Quiz* and *Round Europe Quiz* for several years, those sort of things remain in my blood. Janusz was quick to unwrap Tony's question. He hesitated but a moment or two before saying:

Janusz Stefanowicz:	The er, … something in both cases is balloons. In the first case, Winnie the Pooh was at pains to get to the honey which was collected by bees up in the trees. He does not know how to deceive them himself, so he asks Christopher Robin for a balloon and hesitated between the blue one, which would look like the sky under which Pooh would act as a cloud, or the green one which would make a part of a tree.
Anthony Quinton:	You are doing extremely well!
Janusz Stefanowicz:	Pooh picked the blue one, but it didn't save him from being bitten by the bees, I think!

Our newly discovered expert on the subject then went on to explain about another balloon associated with Eeyore who had a birthday which everyone forgot; how Piglet decided to give him one, but fell and burst it, so Winnie the Pooh made the legendary donkey a present of a jar of honey, only by the time he got there, it was an empty jar as he had licked out all the honey on the way over.

There then followed a question for the resident London team from my other regular quizmaster, Gordon Clough. Gordon could also be relied upon to set good questions and to wrap them up very nicely too – especially for Irene Thomas and for her partner, John Julius Norwich.

Gordon Clough:	Why might *prunus incisa*, a noble dwelling place, a tail-less member of the *Apterygidae*, or even the common or garden bluebell, put you in mind of our visitors?
John Julius Norwich:	*Apter … Apterygidae*! A word, I'm bound to say, which is not constantly on my lips but which I conceive must mean having no wings.
Irene Thomas:	A tail-less member of the family, you said, Gordon!
John Julius Norwich:	Something which has no tail or wings; … the only one I can immediately think of is a kiwi.
Irene Thomas:	Which only comes out at night, I believe!

John Julius Norwich:	Oh, I don't know. What about Kiwi polish – in the days when people often used to polish shoes.
Irene Thomas:	And *prunus incisa* ... that would be the cherry tree? Ah, 'Cherry Blossom' is another sort of polish. A noble dwelling? That would be a 'Mansion'. Did you ever use a button-stick in the services, J.J.'
John Julius Norwich:	Certainly I did. Yes, I can smell it now. 'Bluebell'. And, oh the joy when one was promoted to 'Duraglit'!

It was at this point in the quiz between London and the visiting team that Karol Malcuzynski, a member of the Polish Central Committee, said:

> You know, when I used to be the Press Councillor at our embassy in London, I subscribed to the English Press cuttings service, and under the general heading of 'Poland' I received hundreds and hundreds of adverts for shoe Polish!

* * *

There are a number of people I have to thank for the fun and joy of having done these quiz programmes during almost ten years of my time with the BBC. First and foremost there was the one and only Irene Thomas, 'Brain Of Brains', 'Brain Of Britain' – and as delightfully down-to-earth and amusing as they come. If you haven't already read her autobiography, *The Bandsman's Daughter*, then I heartily recommend it.

If Irene had not written nice but persistent letters to Anthony Whitby, whom I was privileged to work to when he was Controller of Radio 4, then as he said himself, he would not have decided to see if *Round Britain Quiz* could be revived after a break of several years. Many of us still mourn Tony Whitby's untimely death. I thank him for asking me to try out a number of likely contestants from around the British Isles, and to become the series producer. I had invaluable help in selecting team members from Michael Green, then head of Network Radio for the North of England and before he was to succeed David Hatch as the BBC's MD Radio. At the time, Michael was working within my group of radio producers and it was he who suggested I should try Anthony Quinton – an excellent choice – and, later, also our Polish Winnie the Pooh fan. There was also Professor Henry Appia who became a member of the French team, and Dr Hilde Spiel who was in the Austrian team during the run of *Round Europe Quiz*. And *that* series came about through Ian McIntyre. Amongst those I tried out for *Round Britain Quiz* were a former Director General of the BBC, Hugh Greene, who thought I was wrong not to let Sooty have that girlfriend, and Ian, then a freelancer – and both at the suggestion of Anthony Whitby. Please note. I selected neither man for the *Round Britain Quiz* teams!

Not many years after his 'exclusion', Ian McIntyre was himself appointed as the Controller of Radio 4. Shortly after he had taken up his staff appointment so I received a memorandum from the new Head. It was marked,'Radio 4 Quizzes'. No, it didn't inform me that I had been fired. On the contrary, Ian stated that whilst he felt there was still a lot of good mileage left in *Round Britain Quiz* shouldn't we think in terms of widening our horizons? Big men think big. At Ian's instigation I went round quite a bit of Europe armed with more names given to me by George Fischer, the then Head of Radio Talks and Documentaries who was another I list in the 'very helpful colleague' category. Needless to say each European I saw had to have, in the first instance, a very good knowledge of the English language plus the ability, when I tested them, to take part in and enjoy that essentially English pastime of doing crossword puzzles. For that is what I had already turned these radio quiz questions into: a sort of 'verbal crossword', usually consisting of three or more parts and with liberal 'clues' where required from my quizmaster-question-setter. These clues were as much for the benefit of the listeners as for the team members in peeling away the layers of wrapping and arriving at various parts of the complete answers.

I discovered quite early on, when *Round Britain Quiz* restarted under my guidance, that it was no use for one person to set the questions, however inventive and amusing they might be, and then for another person to pose them. When contestants are seeking clues and guidance the quizmaster has to know all he can about the background in order to 'feed' the teams and often to get their minds working on another tack so that they see the common link between one part of the answer and the other parts.

For *Round Europe Quiz*, I found out as much as I could in the time I spent with European contestants about their work, hobbies and other activities and then listed these for Anthony Quinton as a basis for one or more of the questions he would so skilfully devise. The European teams were, after all, having to think and to broadcast completely off the cuff and in another language.

When I had accidentally discovered that Janusz Stefanowicz happened to be a 'Pooh' buff, I also found out that the Marquesa de Casa Valdes was not only a specialist in gardens and their history, and with a British degree in botany, but that she could recite page after page of Lewis Carroll learned at the knee of her Scottish nanny. That discovery came about when the Marquesa invited me to meet and to stay with her at her summer residence in northern Spain. I arrived by air, the plane disgorging lots of Spaniards who'd flown, like me, from Madrid. I had only a small case. They had mountains of luggage including a lot of livestock and were met by a flood of friends and relations. There was no tannoy system at this small airfield to announce arrivals and passenger names. Amid the press of persons, I noticed a lad jump up on to a crate of livestock. He held a length of cardboard aloft. I read 'Trevor Hill'. It was the butler's son who had been sent to collect me, the chauffeur and his housekeeper wife being on holiday. He drove me through the countryside to Valdes and to a house which fronted the village square.

Being the direct descendant of a Spanish Duke accounted for the fact that the Marquesa's lace-frilled sheets and pillows on the guest bed bore the family crest and a crown. The library in this house, one of her four residences, consisted of beautifully bound and well preserved books – none later than the year 1710! Some of the paintings were pretty ancient too. Flakes from the large canvas fluttered down into my fresh orange juice when the Marquesa's butler allowed the bedroom door to blow shut with a bang. I particularly enjoyed the moment I stood with my hostess in the long drawing room overlooking the square and the town which she and her husband owned, and we gazed at a family portrait – not one of the Marquesa's side.

'A lady of quality,' remarked Teresa gripping the ornate walking cane given to her by Salvador Dali, 'A lady of quality does *not* allow herself to be painted holding a silk handerchief – however precious silk may have been in those days!'

Having long been familiar with the various scales of BBC expense allowances for staff and for contributors, I was a little alarmed when my new-found friend and Quiz competitor phoned to say she was looking forward to coming to London for the programme and if I wanted to contact her, she would be staying, as usual, at Claridges. Her BBC overnight allowance will hardly stretch even to breakfast there, I thought.

I was then quite unexpectedly to be introduced to the Marquesa's equally charming and delightful daughter who had decided to accompany her mother to England and to visit her English dentist at the same time. An additional table setting and one additional dinner were hurriedly ordered.

At my request we always met in the Hospitality Room in the basement of Broadcasting House, London. Here, the visiting teams for *Round Europe* and *Round Britain* could then meet the resident London team members and the Questionmasters, and then settle down and relax over a meal before we all went along to the studios, recording Round 1 and then Round 2 of the quiz, with only a short break between the two programme recordings.

It became something of an unwritten rule that for *Round Britain Quiz* at least, we simply *had* to have Mrs Aphrodite Wall with us for the evening. This lovely Greek lady would set the table with style, see that the flowers were freshened up, since they'd probably attended a lunch the same day or even the day before, then she would serve drinks and then the dinner. She immediately knew when someone felt a little apprehen-

Anthony Quinton and Aphrodite Wall at the dinner in her honour for 'services rendered to our Quiz Teams'

sive or nervous. A quiet word with them and they'd soon be smiling and at ease again. In some instances she would top up a glass; in others, she would pass discreetly by, such was her understanding. Early on in the series, a celebrated broadcaster turned up for the quiz dinner only to discover that, on this occasion, Aphrodite was *not* part of our team. A letter of protest was received by the BBC's Catering Manager.

One evening at Broadcasting House, London, I was invited to attend a dinner in honour of a retiring colleague in senior management. As I entered, a very familiar voice called out to me from the far end of the Governors' dining room. 'Aaah!, Meester Hill! Will it be the usual?'

As Aphrodite came forward with my drink, so a voice just behind me said into my left ear, 'Oh! And do you come here often?' That was the moment I first met our new Managing Director, Radio, Aubrey Singer.

I had some delightful meetings, too, with those I went to talk to about *Round Europe Quiz*. I arrived at Charles de Gaulle airport, Paris, to be greeted by Professor Henry Appia and a big smile. I wasn't kissed on both cheeks or even asked if I'd had a good journey. In point of fact, his first words to me were, 'Mr Hill, I hope you realise that you have a quite excellent secretary!'

Yes, I did realise that. Audrey Robins was with me for almost the whole time I did the Radio 4 quiz series. She organised everything – including Gordon Clough in the hope that we got his questions *before* the day after the broadcast had taken place! Audrey typed them out and then had each most carefully checked by the Question Researchers. Bernice Coupe, the BBC Librarian in Manchester, could be relied upon not only for complete accuracy, but also for turning up quite delightful and fascinating 'Additional Notes' for use by the questionmasters if they so wished. There was always considerably more checking required on those questions sent in by our listeners and in discovering the source of their information.

Besides bringing back *Round Britain Quiz*, I was also invited to revive *Transatlantic Quiz*, the programme series I had worked on in wartime as a junior BBC engineer at 200 Oxford Street when this series first began. I'd be at Broadcasting House with Louis Allen, my questionmaster for *Transatlantic Quiz*, Irene and John Julius, whilst Anthony Quinton was at the BBC's studios on Fifth Avenue with the New York team. For two or three weeks prior to the start of recordings, Audrey and I were busy in our Manchester office getting together questions for the series of six programmes. That meant some 96 questions in all, half for the New York team, the rest for the London team. They would be duplicated and despatched to Heathrow airport where the BBC's own Shipping Department would put them on board a flight to New York.

At 8.30 a.m. on the day we were to record for the start of a new *Transatlantic* series, I was woken in my hotel bedroom. Audrey hadn't wished to disturb me before this hour, but at 11 p.m. the previous evening she had heard that our precious cargo had never arrived in New York. The airline had lost them! But I wasn't to worry, Audrey had got her husband, Bunny, to drive her from their home to the office and, together, they had sorted out and marked up another complete set of questions for the series and packaged them up. Audrey would be leaving Manchester in twenty minutes and bringing them down with her. Meantime, could I arrange to have the questions and answers for the first two programmes teleprinted to our New York office? Oh yes, and as an added precaution Audrey had also arranged for a despatch rider to meet her off the Manchester train in order to take the package to Heathrow, and then for a courier to travel with them personally to the Rockefeller Building in New York City.

No one would say that the questions and answers for these programmes were short and simple, so I was very impressed when an Indian member of BBC staff in the teleprinter section at Broadcasting House, London handed me pages of copy at around 11 a.m. that morning and said, 'I managed to get quite a few of the answers as I was sending these off to New York!' Later, our teleprinter colleague devised a couple of questions himself for *Round Britain Quiz*.

Meanwhile, feeling quite weak at the knees, I made a bee-line for the trolley service outside one of the lifts at Broadcasting House. I'd missed breakfast in my anxiety to get to 'Traffic' and to the teleprinter office. Now, I'd just ordered a large black coffee and two doughnuts when a voice behind me said, in tones I knew only too well, '*I* used to enjoy "elevenses", you know, only now I *do* have to watch my figure!' I was about to turn round and slap Janet Brown on her bottom, when, fortunately, I paused. It wasn't Janet doing her celebrated impersonation, it was the real thing, as I realised when I caught sight of Ian Trethowan and our Chairman, George Howard! They were escorting the Rt. Hon. Margaret Thatcher to the studio for the *Jimmy Young Show*.

We were not to lose our *Transatlantic Quiz* questions again. From then on, I accompanied them myself to New York each year and remained there whilst we recorded a series. But Professor Appia was quite right about the true power behind the quiz throne. The programme would doubtless have petered out long before but for Audrey Robins and her

New York with Anthony Quinton, Brendon Gill and Shana Alexander

unfailing strength and enthusiasm. Henry Appia and the man we selected to partner him, Paul Gabriel Bouce, an expert on Tobias Smollett and on French naval matters, did very well together in *Round Europe Quiz*. It was clear that they thoroughly enjoyed themselves right from their first visit to London. The letter of thanks for the experience of taking part and for the pleasure of meeting Anthony Quinton, Gordon Clough, Irene and John Julius ended by sending a word of love to Audrey, and a PS for me. It read, '*You* may call us Frogs!'

The year France won *Round Europe Quiz*, back I went to Paris this time bearing two rather impressive illuminated scrolls on vellum which I was to present to the victorious 'Frogs'. The one for Professor Henry Appia bore the coat of arms of Paris, for Professor Bouce, those of Normandy. For as Paul had told me in the course of our first meeting, 'I am a Norman, my dear fellow, and proud of it. After all, we did lick the English!'

They *really* talk like that – these foreigners! And I had hoped that Paul and Henry would have sounded at least a *little* more like Charles Boyer. This complete lack of any accent is something which clearly distressed the always gentlemanly and diplomatic Anthony Quinton for I distinctly heard him say on his first meeting with Hilde Spiel at dinner, 'Doctor Spiel, I wonder if you might affect a slight Austrian accent when we get to the studio – or I fear you may make the rest of us sound like second-class Custom officials!'

Now I will not claim that *all* our European team members were without any trace of accent, but they all spoke and broadcast very much in the English idiom. When Karol Malcuzynski's Polish partner was in full flight about some further aspect on his favourite bear, his partner interrupted him in tones which would surely have delighted Professor Higgins had it been Eliza Doolittle. There was a loud sigh and then Karol exclaimed 'Oh *do* shut up!'

Whilst *Round Europe Quiz* was still being broadcast, I received a letter from the State of Israel. Could they enter a team one year? Had the series continued, and it would have done but for rising costs, then I would have done my best to put them with a team from the Arab world, for such programmes do at least a little in helping to break down barriers and, above all, prejudice.

I could be sure of receiving a number of abusive letters every time our erudite and amusing team from Dublin took part in *Round Britain Quiz*. There was one persistent writer in particular. Later letters sent reminded me of that morning when I got to the office earlier than usual and telephoned our BBC newsroom in Belfast to inform them that Dr Michael Dewar, the rector of St Helen's Bay, and his gentle and informative partner, Martin McBirney, QC, had won *Round Britain Quiz* that year. Would they let the Ulster papers know.

'But haven't you heard? Martin was murdered only an hour ago by the IRA. They shot him in front of his young daughter.'

It became even more of a tragedy when it transpired that the IRA had, in all probability, executed the wrong man.

Far more listeners accused the programme and the producer in particular, of being very prejudiced over the business of the marks awarded. We were always, so we were told, hard on the resident London Team. But then, surely *they* appeared in every programme in the series and, in my book, doing a weekly crossword enables you to get to know the mind of the question-setter and the manner of his working. The challengers had to record their two rounds at one sitting – except for my delightful New York team of Brendan Gill and Shana Alexander. They would spend three consecutive lunchtimes with Anthony Quinton, myself and our Girl Friday, Ursula Kenny, at the BBC's New York offices, record six programmes which made up a *Transatlantic* series, and go away swearing never to work with me again – until the following year, when Ursula would again do all the spade work for us.

It was Irene Thomas who referred to *Round Britain* as 'the Fortnum and Mason of quiz programmes'. Not for me the, 'What's the highest mountain/longest river' type of question. Nor, perhaps, the sort of question contained in a *Radio Times* cartoon which appeared above an irate letter and my reply, about a score bias:

> The Wigan team has correctly answered, 'The Charge of the Light Brigade'. Now, London – what were their names?

At its best, a *Round Britain Quiz*, *Round Europe Quiz*, or *Transatlantic Quiz* question had three or more answers since, as a rule, it was in three linking parts. The listener could therefore often be ahead of a team in relating one answer to another, or in picking up the quizmaster's clues quicker than the team members. What is more, my question format was for *team* answers, the two partners working together to arrive at the answers. Again, in my book, two heads are invariably better than one.

In going 'Round Europe' in my quest for teams, I took several test questions with me. This was one of them:

> How can the odd numbers between 91 and 99 be said to contribute to the manufacture of jams.
> What am I talking about?

Start with those numbers – 91, 93, 95, 97 and 99. If they don't mean anything at first sight then think about 'jams'; those which normally occur just after breakfast and, again, just *after* tea-time. Ah, *traffic* jams! And what causes those? And what goes into the majority of motor vehicles on the roads? And besides being sold in various grades, what about octanes? I was a little taken aback by Señor Pedro Schwartz who partnered the Marquesa as members of the Spanish team. He looked at that question for a moment, said nothing, then looked at another I had given him. 'I like your "petrol" question,' he said. 'But this one needs a little more thought!'

Of course, *the* expert at coming up with part of an answer quickly, was surely John Julius Norwich, before breaking off to tell an always true but highly coloured story which may or may not have the slightest thing to do with the question in hand. He would then 'invent' the rest of the answer in the hope that he might bamboozle the questionmaster. 'J.J.' sometimes got a bonus mark for being so inventive. I do not recall if such skill enabled him and Irene Thomas to be a mark or two ahead of all the other teams so that London won *Round Europe Quiz* one year. As the 2nd Viscount Norwich, John Julius possesses his own family coat of arms. Irene chose those of the London borough which was to be enhanced by her presence, Chiswick.

The Royal Calligrapher illuminated their respective scrolls most splendidly. I even had them both framed. The day they were to be presented by Sir Ian Trethowan I took them to his office for him to sign as Director General of the BBC. Unfortunately, in removing the scroll done for Irene from its frame, Ian cut his finger on the glass. That evening at the dinner I had arranged, he made the presentation. I have this lovely memento of the occasion. In the photo, Sir Ian is showing Irene just where his blood fell upon the virgin vellum – before we mopped it away!

Irene and John Julius with Sir Ian Trethowan. On the right, my guide and mentor, Audrey Robins

Sir Ian Trethowan, as DG, with Irene Thomas. He shows her where his blood soaked her vellum scroll!

'Oh dash it but that's unfair,' protested John Julius. 'There's not a mark to be seen on mine! I'd just *love* to have had the blood of a Director General of the BBC hanging on *my* wall.'

Ah, well. Even in the world of quiz programmes, you can't win 'em all! However, it was only fair that Poland should have won that match I mentioned at the beginning of this chapter. I'd purposely chosen a highly regarded Catholic, Janusz Stefanowicz, to partner Karol Malcuzynski who, at that time, was also a leading light; in his case highly regarded within the then Polish Communist Party.

It was after the 'Winnie The Pooh' question that Karol asked if he might interrupt to tell the Radio 4 listeners how during the German Occupation and the herding of so many into ghettos, the 'Pooh' stories became a source of comfort to many parents and Polish children – so much so that after the war the children held a referendum for the naming of a new street in the centre of the city of Warsaw. Complete with a reproduction of the original drawing of their hero the sign reads in Polish, 'The Street of Winnie The Pooh'.

'You see now how Polish Democracy works,' chipped in Janusz, to be followed by Gordon Clough's remark, 'And to show you how British Democracy works let me tell listeners that Poland is leading by six marks to five.'

How could I look upon such people as being any part of 'work'? As my beloved Margaret and I used to say, after either I or she had been away and were telling each other all about those we'd just met as a result of programme making, 'Aren't we lucky – *and* we're being paid!'

20

'Am I Still With You?'

By July 1980 I had been watching many a screen over the years. Now, lying in a comfortable bed in the Intensive Care Unit of the Macclesfield Infirmary, I was watching my own screen. The 'peaks' were beginning to fall – fast. I pressed the 'night' bell. In came a nurse without delay. By now there *were* no 'peaks'. 'Have I just died?' I enquired. Luckily for me it was a very elderly gentleman whose heart attack moments before had proved fatal – his screen had been placed in front of mine whilst the staff attended to him.

When Michael Green brought Margaret to see me when daylight came he simply said, 'We're not going to get rid of you that easily, are we?' Such a kind and understanding chap. He was now the Network Editor. But then, both Michael and Christine Green were the sort of understanding people who would even loan their own children to those who didn't possess any in order that they might go to see a Disney film without embarrassment.

I had to see the BBC's doctor in London as soon as I was deemed to be 'fit for duty' once again. Awaiting that 2 p.m. appointment I spent a short lunchtime at the BBC's Staff Club, then situated in the Langham Hotel. And who should I bump into but my old BBC Programme Engineering pal, Bobby Jaye, who at this time was Head of Light Entertainment, Radio. He asked what brought me to London.

'Ah! Did you see the fellow you're to meet on television last night?' enquired Bobby. I hadn't. The BBC doctor was a kind and gentle man possessed of a highly refined Edinburgh Morningside accent and one which I'd rarely heard whilst training in wartime at nearby Dreghorn camp with the Royal Scots. As a rule I'd been intrigued by those in my platoon who hailed from the one area of Glasgow. To me, some sounded as if they spoke only through either their left or their right nostril, particularly when we were out on manoeuvres. Ordered to crash through streams and with genuine live ammunition fired above our heads I'd be asked, 'Why don't you effing well swear. You're no a Minister of th' Kirk?'

After consulting notes and a *very* thorough examination I was buttoning up my shirt with feelings of some relief at being pronounced fit and well again when I happened to say, 'I hear you were on television last night, doctor?' The stethoscope dropped with a loud clang into the metal tray. 'And to whom have you been speaking, Mr Hill?' I told him. 'Ah yes, Mr Jaye. I might have known.' What I didn't know was that a new light entertainment series had taken to the airwaves the very night before. The doctor then handed me his card. It read 'Dr Eric Blackadder'. A certain Rowan Atkinson had been his patient at some time!

Biting my lip, I returned to duties but then about a year later it was back to the good doctor. As Michael's Assistant Network Editor I had a number of North Regional producers working to me and came to the conclusion I was no longer able to do nearly enough to sell their talents to BBC heads of departments during those 'Programme Offers' meetings held in London. Dr Eric, as it turned out at that second meeting, was also a keen sailor. 'You will keep as active as possible on Windermere – and above all, you *don't* treat yourself as an invalid.' I'm glad to report that Eric Blackadder was to do great work for BUPA having, like myself, then left the BBC. A short while later Margaret and I departed from Cheshire and came to reside in Cheltenham.

It was in 1985 that the first of some 1,000 manuscript pages of, proposed book entitled *BBC Children's Hour – A Celebration of Those Magical Years* were to come tumbling through the door of Crofton Lodge, a flow which was to continue in the many months ahead. There is only one person who *could* write such a book – Wallace Grevatt. This I had finally edited. Judith Chalmers' younger sister, Sandra, who'd started as a 13-year-old actress with us in the North was to become an editor of *Woman's Hour* and then in 1988 was Head of Publicity for BBC Radio, had the idea that Wallace's book should be launched that year at the Earls Court Radio and Television Show.

To that end I was invited out of retirement in order to devise and to produce such a celebration before and audience of some 3,000 people who were to be present that day. But first I had to go to a London firm in order to learn all about a 'video wall' – some fifty or sixty TV screens which would produce one enormous picture – then to select many excerpts in both sound and 'stills' besides recording on video some who could not be present on the day. I invited Judith Chalmers to introduce and interview a host of *Children's Hour* personalities. My own copy of Wallace's book bears the signatures, first and foremost, of David Davis, Billie Whitelaw, Judith, Patricia Hayes, Jo Plummer, Glyn Dearman, Bryan Martin, Barry McCulloch the widow of Derek, Ray and Sylvia Baxter, John Ogdon and Peter Maxwell Davies. There were also those special video contributions by the likes of Kathleen Garscadden and Robert Powell. On this occasion Peter Maxwell Davies was to entertain the audience with that very first composition of his, which he himself had played on radio. By way of introduction he informed his audience, 'The extraordinary thing was that I was *allowed* to play this on the BBC at all because I was a pretty rebellious schoolboy and I wrote, even then at the age of 14, pretty unconventional music. But there was one person there at the BBC (the name has now been censored) who had faith in what I did.'

Had that person really given encouragement to all that unconventional music which was to follow in the years ahead? It is therefore at Sir Peter's 60th birthday celebration that I felt bound to inform my fellow guests that amongst a veritable mountain of composition there *was* just the one item – and that composed at the age of 13 – which I have been able to whistle. It was Vi Carson who played it, appropriately enough, over the airwaves in 1950. It is entitled 'Clouds'. (For a little more information on this composer, there is an even better and longer read to be found in *'MAX' – The Life and Music of Peter Maxwell Davies* by Mike Seabrook, published by Victor Gollancz.)

Wallace Grevatt's knowledge of *Children's Hour* was, and remained, second to none. Back in the mid 1950s whilst still teaching he had formed a 'Listener's Forum' for me during the years I was responsible for *Children's Hour* from the North of England. The then Head of BBC Audience Research took a somewhat dim view of others stepping in, but here was a man who, in our opinion, could not appreciate that the views collected by his Research Panel were entirely those of adults. I needed those of children; some should be invited to the studio to give their views on what I had provisionally planned for the next quarter's schedule. Even Bryan Cave-Brown-Cave who was one of *the* very best Heads of Programmes I had the privilege of working to – who had also been largely responsible for the founding of Forces Radio in Delhi in 1943 –

MV *Cleo* on Lake Windermere

even Bryan would tell me what his own children enjoyed, 'And many of those are *your* programmes.' I wasn't impressed. On the way into our Dickenson Road Television studios of a Sunday, didn't I occasionally collect little Claire and her brother from their house in nearby Disley and then sit them both in the Control Gallery in order to watch the *Sooty* rehearsals and transmissions? What child in their right mind would then tell dad that my programmes were awful?

It was whilst aboard MV *Cleo* on lake Windermere in the autumn of 1989, having followed Dr Blackadder's advice, that I got another call from the BBC's Manchester office. As I'd spent almost 35 years in the North, Les Robinson who by now was the Head of Network Radio for the region asked if I would be willing to prepare and record *An Oral History Of North Regional Broadcasting*. He considered that as I'd known and worked with some of those who were there from the very start back in 1922, they might be more willing to be interviewed by me rather than by a stranger. Not so much time for boating now.

Luckily that fund of BBC Programme information, and owner of one of the largest private collections of the *Radio Times* from Edition 1, Wallace Grevatt, was now archivist for that magazine. After several meetings with Les Robinson I was given the go ahead.

It was a project which was to take me out of retirement, this time for two and a half years. Initially I prepared the wording for a form which could be sent to each prospective interviewee. By agreement, much of that information was then sent on to Wallace in order for him to undertake research, for this project was to be a history rather than concentrating on just the interviewee's own life and experience in broadcasting.

It was the very person who taught me the importance of remembering staff names, *and* which corridor to take in order to get to New Broadcasting House Manchester's music studio, David Hatch, who on hearing the edited version of his own interview observed, 'Um, you *do* do a lot of talking don't you?' Well my brief had been to fill in any gaps deemed to be a part of this *Oral History* – and those from Wallace Grevatt's tireless researches. Come to think of it, in all the 67 interviews I was to arrange and conduct, taking up some 110 hours in edited form, the only person to ask me to come back and record further *was* BBC Radio's then Managing Director. But bless him, on that occasion he took a keen interest in the portable digital recorder I used and then asked what I copied such recordings on to and did I then do all the editing myself? I did, for as far as I was concerned *no* interview was to be released to the BBC until such time as the interviewee had heard his or her contribution, now in the tidied-up version, and their Release Form was in my possession.

At the start of this project in 1990 I was taking my digital tapes down the road to BBC Radio Gloucestershire. Peter Gallimore's studio had just been completed but he found time for me to copy digital on to quarter-inch tape for editing purposes. It came to the point when I needed to have copying and editing facilities within my own home. BBC Manchester agreed and so I was to ring HHB Communications Ltd at Scrubs Lane, London, who already provided the BBC with such professional facilities.

'Er, good morning. My name is Trevor Hill. I am the former Assistant Head of Network Radio North …'

It was at this point that a voice cut me short. 'Hello, Trev. Long time no see. This is Brian, Brian Binding. Remember?' Of course I did. Brian had formerly been with the BBC's Planning and Installation Group with whom I'd worked closely whilst we were both engaged on New BH Manchester. Brian advised that the BBC now supply me with a Danish

'Lyrec' tape machine, which they did. I have used it to this day, all thanks to that former BBC Managing Director who remarked when I was invited back to London in order to record the additions to his interview, 'I won't ask what your financial arrangements have been but as far as I am concerned you will keep all equipment the BBC has paid for.'

My 'arrangement' had been that as a heart problem patient I would not wish to 'become unavailable' during the course of this welcome project, and therefore I would require only expenses for travelling from Cheltenham to Manchester, Leeds, and to Newcastle – and we would discuss fees once the project had been completed. However, I must admit that having interviewed some who had been involved with programmes like *Yesterdays Men* and a former Prime Minister, it *did* occur to me that if I were to give the *News Of The World* a recording or two, Margaret and I might be able to reside abroad – and in utter luxury!

21

Only a Little Lamb? *(Derek McCulloch)*

That's the title I gave a Radio 4 feature which, in 1990, I'd been invited to write and to introduce from London by a man whose work I'd always admired. At the time Simon Elmes was Chief Producer Features Arts and Education, Radio. He was about to launch a new series entitled *Radio Lives* – five portraits of the great names in radio commencing with Derek McCulloch, who'd died in 1967. I've written a little about Mac in an earlier chapter. It wasn't until taking up Simon's kind offer that I was to meet Derek's widow, Barry McCulloch – a splendid lady who had already been working for John Reith before Derek arrived on the scene – and also to hear first-hand from others.

Simon sent me some of the archive recordings: Mac's appearance on *This Is Your Life* in which his brother Douglas was to explain that at around the age of 4, Mac fell some 20 feet from circus seating and broke his collar-bone. I was to learn that at the age of 16 he got himself into the First World War. He was in the Battle of the Somme and was so badly wounded that a member of the German equivalent of the Red Cross took pity and shot the lad through the head, which took away a part of his ear. It was John Snagge who told Simon and myself, when we went to record at his home, that Derek was to join him and the team of BBC announcers in 1926 – having already undergone numerous operations and leaving him with one lung and one eye. I knew about the eye and the facial scars. His widow told me, 'I never saw those scars.' That's the sort of person Derek was to marry.

I also learned that Reith considered Derek to be 'uneducated'. By whose standards, I have to ask. Who was to start the first ever broadcast

Derek McCulloch

quiz programme, *Regional Round*; to put *The Man Born To Be King* on radio? He certainly became one of the most celebrated voices at the height of his fame pre-war. Who else could have narrated those *Toytown* stories so brilliantly *besides* being, 'Only a little l-a-a-mb?

Many of my age will recall that day in 1938 when we heard that Derek had been ready to alight from a Greenline bus at the Banstead stop when it had to suddenly brake, catapulting him right to the front. He spoke to us from his hospital bed on the 5th of May. 'Hello, children. Hello to you all wherever you may be. How to begin?' he asked. When preparing this feature some 52 years later I was to learn how the accident was to end –

with the removal of a foot. As my great friend David Davis was to tell me when speaking of Mac in his later years, 'He was often drifting off into sadness'. From the listening end, that was never apparent.

Toytown remained the best ever; Mac's jokes on *Regional Round* never portrayed his suffering, whilst from 1946 until 1966 there was also *Nature Parliament* which he so successfully and cheerfully chaired. I'd only had connections with Northern *Children's Hour* for about a year when, in September 1950, Derek left the BBC staff and, please note only *now* was he announced as 'Uncle Mac' when introducing *Children's Choice* on the BBC Light Programme. It was Derek himself who got rid of those 'Aunts and Uncles' titles way back in the early 1930s.

Roy Hattersley recalls *Children's Hour* as 'A nightly devotion with Mac as the High Priest'. I recall the last time we met. With Gwen Pain now in charge of *Children's Hour* North for a short period, we'd taken Derek to the American Airforces Base at Burtonwood. I was to make good contacts that day in 1950 with some of the Americans. Later two of their sons, William Crocker and Brian O'Neill, were to make their acting

William Crocker and Brian O'Neill

debut for me in a serialisation of Reginald Taylor's book *Wings Over Tewksley* which dealt with an American airbase and its relationship with the locals. The then Commanding Officer announced after we'd had lunch, 'Say, Mac ...' (there's a name which rolls off the American tongue even when half the mouth is filled with a see-gar) 'Come take a look at our latest babe!' We couldn't wait. Mac was assisted into a Jeep. The vehicle whizzed us away in the direction of giant hangars. A huge tractor had already roared into life as massive steel doors rolled back to reveal a truly gleaming monster. Soon it began to edge forward, the noise growing even louder as we covered our ears. It was then I felt Derek's elbow in my ribs. His one hand quickly pointed upwards as our mouths dropped open. We were the ones to notice that some form of protruding radar hadn't been lowered whilst the aircraft still stood within its massive hangar. We weren't to hear the ground controller's roar, 'Hold it, hold it!' nor his frantic 'Forchrissake' as a part of the bomber collided with the door mechanism. With a siren now giving a series of short, searing blasts, silence eventually fell after just one final 'tinkle' of metal. The cigar had already dropped from the CO's mouth. It was then we were to hear a distinctive voice say, 'And what do you do for the encore?'

I collected Derek McCulloch from Manchester's Grand Hotel the next morning, seeing him safely on to the London train together with a bottle of Malt. The label simply read, 'Only for a little l-a-a-amb'!

To me, to this day, the word 'radio' still conjures up his unique voice.

22

The Winds Of Good Fortune

Standing on the bridge overlooking Platform 1 of Cheltenham Spa railway station that May morning in 1998, the winds were nothing if not fair as the 11.08 train drew to a halt and passengers began to alight. Thanks initially to Carol Wyatt, the BBC's Radio and TV Correspondent in Bonn, I was now to meet a member of Krefeld University's staff, a Dr Gregor Prumbs of the Department of Media Studies. He'd written in March to tell me of his interest in pre-war and wartime broadcasting, and I was particularly impressed by his technical knowledge which must surely have been gleaned over many years. Now we were to come face to face – or so I hoped. I went down the steps towards the one solitary figure left on the platform but he looked to be in his early 30s and was holding the handle of a large case on wheels.

Catching my glance he came towards me saying, 'You are Tree-vor Hills?'

'Oh my God,' I retorted, 'You've come to tell me that your grand-father is dead!'

Not at all. This young man *is* Herr Prumbs – and to prove it, when I get him back to my home and we trundle that heavy case into the guest room, it is full to the brim with documents, some pre-war recordings and photos of German Broadcasting during wartime. As we take a glass of Niersteiner Gutes Domtal I ask if we might first drink a toast to my late beloved Margaret, WAAF 473788 Potter M., from our Hamburg days together. And what a number *she* turned out to be, for it is entirely thanks to her that within the 1910 addition of a Conservatory at Crofton Lodge, I now have the facilities for us to record a series of programmes.

Gregor edits in my studio at Crofton Lodge

As I said to Herr Prumbs, and I think he believed me, now and again I do stop talking and listen, just as I did that day on Lake Windermere when the BBC had phoned and asked if I would undertake the oral history project. Initially I had thanked Les Robinson for the kind offer but declined. Once you are *out* you should stay out.

'But why?' Margaret had asked as I hung up, 'At least give it *some* consideration. What a marvellous opportunity for many others besides yourself. Think of them and the contributions they've made to broadcasting.'

I did. 'Of course, dear, how right you are, dear.' And as usual she was. I phoned Les back later that same day and asked if, upon more 'mature' consideration, I might now come up to Manchester in order to discuss his project.

'Ah, and so without doing this oral history you would not now have all these facilities for the recordings and editings,' observed a bright young radio historian – or words to that effect. How right *he* was too.

Since our joint project would include the introduction of Forces Broadcasting during and after the war, Alan Grace had already been in contact with Gregor Prumbs. Now they were to meet. Alan had initially worked with BFN, then based in Cologne in 1957, as a sports reporter. He was to hold several posts within the British Forces Broadcasting Service in various countries, and during the 1991 Gulf War he'd worked on their satellite link. Alan and I had first met when I gave him a little assistance with his book *Forces Broadcasting in Germany*. Thanks to Alan I had also got to know an ex-BBC man who possessed a wealth of technical knowledge as well as a unique collection of historical recordings, besides his own facilities for digital editing, et cetera. He was Antony Askew, a former orchestral player and BBC balance and control engineer before he became a music producer of some renown. Antony was such an asset to us in the preparation and recording of what was to be the first of two four-part series of radio features concerning the 1939–45 war and, initially, the role broadcasting was to play in both England and in Germany. Two days after Gregor's arrival I introduced him to Antony. Later he was to stay at his home. We three were soon to embark upon what I had titled *Songs and Sounds of War*, four 'tapestries' of song, sound and music which came about directly as a result of conflict.

In the first programme, for example, a very 'snooty' voice from an HMV commercial recording (which incidentally was quickly withdrawn from sale since the Government felt it might well panic the public) informs us that 'This record demonstrates to you the system of signals which will be employed during war. Listen carefully!' Then, in one of the very few 'links' required by way of explanation, Gregor tells the listener that as the sirens begin to sound in London in 1939, air raids in his country were yet to come. There follows part of the soothing ballad '*Gute Nacht, Mutter*' and beautifully performed by Wilhelm Strienz. As he soothes a German mother to sleep, so his young comrades noisily celebrate in song the fact that '*Wir Fahren gegen Engelland*', followed by '*Bomben auf Engelland*'. There were many of those. From 7th September 1940 the Luftwaffe was to bomb London on sixty-five consecutive nights. As a then 14-year-old cockney lad tells about the whole house shaking all around him, so we hear the song's realistic sound effects of whistling bombs and loud explosions, after which the boy declares on a BBC recording from that year, 'I think it's a rotten shame to do it in th' night!'

There then follows one of several very clever parodies from Germany of well-known American songs. The 'St Louis Blues' lyric adapted well to the London Blitzkrieg. As vocalist Karl Schwedler announces by way of introduction, 'A negro from the London docks sings "The Blackout Blues".'

I hate to see the evenin' sun go down
Coz the German, he done bombed this town,
Wasn't for Churchill an' his bloody war,
I wouldn't feel – yeah – so doggone sore.

A clip from a government broadcast on 'Employment in Munitions' triggers off vocalist Marion Hutton with the Glenn Miller orchestra and 'The Five O'clock Whistle' (which, as some will recall, never blew). Now it is the turn of Arthur Askey to explain in song that:

It's the girl that makes the thing that holds the oil
That oils the spring that works the thingamy-bob
That's going to win the war!

After 'Mr HMV' has warned his audience what to do in the event of Gas, so George Formby picks up his ukelele and informs our listeners that 'Mr Wu's An Air Raid Warden Now' and later, after a Columbia Broadcasting System report on Hitler visiting the Maginot Line so George tells us:

At night myself to sleep I sing, to my old tin hat I cling,
I have to use it now for everything, down on the Maginot Line.

Vocalist Alan Breeze writes home to ma and pa in song saying he's sending them the Siegfried Line to hang their washing on and adds:

Tell my sister Mary that I've found a German sausage
That can sing like her canary!

The precise military march rhythm of that song is taken up by genuine members of the then German Reichsmusik Labour Service who ended Part 1 of our series with '*Parodie auf die Siegfriedlinie*' – and which they recorded in English.

Our ideas caught on – not with the BBC but certainly with the Head of the British Forces Broadcasting Service, Rory Higgins, whom I took Gregor to meet at Chalfont St Giles. The series was later to be broadcast worldwide by BFBS. We then assembled excerpts from our four programmes with material as supplied by Elmer Bantz from the German Radio Archives and by Antony Askew for a CD which, by contract, we allowed an English magazine to clear for 'Performing Rights' and then to issue the CD on a limited sale. Sadly two of our special friends, Antony and Wallace Grevatt, were both to die in 2003.

Now I was to return to Germany with a former BFN Hamburg colleague from the mid 1940s, Douglas Brown, and to attend a reception with Gregor at Krefeld's Town Hall. It was given for the three of us by the Bürgermeister of Krefeld, Bernd Scheelen, and by the German Minister of Culture, Herr Roland Schneider. For my services to broadcasting in Germany they kindly presented me with a plaque made by the students from the Design Department of their university. It was an added pleasure when Gregor then took us to meet some of those young people.

On later visits back to Germany I was to see just what he also did for other younger people: Turkish children there as a result of the influx of cheap foreign labour to former Western sectors of his country. Now I saw the reason why Gregor had asked myself and several of my friends he'd met whilst he was on his various visits if we'd make a collection. No, not money. Believe it or not, he wanted the inner cardboard tubes from toilet rolls; even more desirable were the longer inner rolls from our Christmas wrapping paper. Dr Prumbs spent many hours showing these children how to carefully wind wire round and round each cardboard cylinder as the basis for an electrical circuit. I was to be further impressed when later he was to put a new mechanism into the ship's clock aboard MV *Cleo*. On another visit he brought a disc recording of the NWDR Children's Choir conducted by Erich Bender. A lovely souvenir of past days. By the time I'd taken to my bed on that occasion, Gregor had begun to burn the midnight oil in order to fix another electric clock mechanism, this time with a spindle through the record's central hole. That was for the hands of a 'record clock' which now hangs at the foot of the stairs leading up to my studio area within the upper conservatory.

After our first series had been broadcast we were then to concentrate on the preparation of another, this time dealing with *The War of the Airwaves*: the wartime propaganda services in England, America and Germany. I knew *that* war had been cleverly won by German Broadcasting. On first meeting Gregor, who was already friends with many German artists of my age group, I'd hoped he might now be able to put me in touch with the one and only Karl Schwedler – or 'Charlie' as we youngsters came to know him when tuning in to Germany during the early part of the war. Unlike 'Auntie BBC' of a Sunday, he and the Lutz Templin propaganda orchestra were *never* boring. I'd tried to trace Karl when arriving in Hamburg at the end of 1945. We got the original 'Lilli Marlene', Lale Anderson, to broadcast for us from the Musikhalle – but I'd drawn a complete blank with 'Charlie'. It was Gregor who told me that Karl Schwedler had been so fearful for his own safety at the start of the Occupation by the British Army of the Rhine that he had hidden himself well away as a night porter in a Dusseldorf hotel.

Thanks to Gregor I was, however, able to make contact with Germany's 'Forces Sweetheart', the one and only Ilse Werner of both song and film fame. She'd married an American Major – and was taken off to the safety of the States having, like 'Charlie', played such an important role in wartime broadcasting to her fellow countrymen. Now she was back in Germany again. It is Ilse, in a song entitled, '*Wir Machen Musik'*, who not only does all the singing but all the skilful whistling too!

Thanks again to Gregor, I was also able to be introduced to German broadcasting's equivalent of Stuart Hibberd in the person of Elmer Bantz who sent me a pre-war photo. As the Russian Army had occupied '*Das Haus des Rundfunks*' so they imprisoned all members of staff. Elmer and others were condemned to serve 15 years as 'war criminals'. Fortunately a general amnesty of the German Democratic Republic in 1952 was to set free those who survived, including Gregor's friend. I was also to learn through the resourceful Gregor that back in 1930 on a visit to Berlin a certain John Reith had been so impressed by the number of Germans who listened in to the then BBC National Programme that he sent Berlin Radio photos of all the then current BBC announcers. These were duly assembled and displayed to the public.

Before embarking upon *The War of the Airwaves* which would consist of four 45-minute features, I returned to Hamburg. What changes from 51 years ago! The Musikhalle was still there – together with BFN's former teenage office boy from 1947 in the person of Gunnar Oldag. It gave me a very strange feeling to enter what had been a cloakroom but had become the office which Sgts Potter and Hill had shared for almost three years; to gaze up at the figure of Brahms once again.

Gunnar, bless him, was to take us to Nordwestdeutsch Rundfunk which also held many memories for me. Studio 1 remained as it had been originally designed pre-war, with walls which could move in or out together with a moving ceiling, thus enabling changes for the required acoustics. At the original organ console I could still see the figure of another Gregor, Gerhard Gregor – but took a photo of someone else instead. And I recalled in my mind some of the songs the Kinderchor had performed for me from this Studio 1, just as in the early 50s the Darwen Girls Choir had sung from our BBC Studio 1 in Manchester when we did our exchange programmes. That visit Gunnar was also to take me to Hamburg docks, bringing back memories of a very different kind: the

Die englischen Ansager

National-Programm • London • Mittel-, Nord- und Westengland
Nordirland • Schottland

BBC announcer sheet

Gregor sits in for Gerhard Gregor at the NWDR Studios, Hamburg

feature I'd done when a Norwegian vessel *Venus* was raised from where she'd recently been scuttled. Sailing in this very ship with Margaret on our trips to Norway in the late 1960s was an added experience, also going back to those U-boat pens from which I'd flown into Berlin with Leon Griffiths in a Sunderland flying boat in order to do the 1948 feature for the BBC on the start of the Berlin Airlift.

It was on this Hamburg visit that I was to be re-united once again with the talented Axel Alexander who had taken such trouble with our own piano scores, turning them into beautifully orchestrated 'Tyrolean Sketches', and who was later to compose the incidental music for the final play Margaret and I had written whilst with BFN, *Journey Into Darkness*. It was Martyn C. Webster who was to use Axel's evocative incidental music when doing his production of our play for the BBC. Axel was later to work for Walt Disney.

But now it was back to work, to find and select excerpts from programmes which had been skilfully crafted in England, Germany and in America in order to keep up the morale of both civilian and services personnel between 1939 and 1949. As early as 1928, programmes in both the Italian and German languages were to originate from London in order to counter propaganda from these countries. By 1935 the BBC had begun a draft report on its technical operations in the event of war. A new transmission distribution scheme for low-power relay stations was now evolved, since powerful radio transmitters in various locations could become a useful aid to navigation for enemy aircraft. The Munich Crisis of September 1938 became a 'dress rehearsal' whilst a small section of BBC monitoring staff had been set up in Broadcasting House, London. Their duties were to include listening to, reporting on and transcribing foreign-language broadcasts. As one of the female monitors was to declare, 'We were like members of the Foreign Legion, but men *and* women of all nationalities.'

Another described hearing and immediately reporting on the German announcement concerning the invasion of Poland, by which time larger premises had been found well away from London with emergency studios and a new home for the now expanding Monitoring Service. That was situated in wooden huts in the grounds of Wood Norton Hall, Worcestershire where, by 1943, some of us were to undergo our technical training. As from that September day in 1939, however, BBC programmes in England had been reduced to just the one channel, the Home Service. The Forces Programme came on air in February 1940. Television transmitter signals were like glowing beacons in a night sky. That service in Britain ceased altogether on the morning of September 9th 1939.

For *Let's Listen In*, as we were to re-title our series, Gregor introduced us to the 'New British Broadcasting Station' which claimed to be run by dissident Britons. On 5th March 1940 it was to report on the evacuation of British children whose parents were warned, 'It may have a profound effect on your boys and girls in the years to come'. That station was to continue to operate from the continent until the end of the war.

In order to make those of us listening on this side of the Channel believe it *was* British, the 'Station' would commence transmissions with such tunes as 'Loch Lomond' or 'Comin' Through the Rye'. But it was the voice of William Brooke Joyce ('Lord Haw-Haw') together with Kenneth Lander, educated at Pembroke College, Oxford, and Norman Baillie-Stewart who had the tones of authenticity.

As for cheerful 'Charlie', we English Ovaltineys remembered that 1938 version of 'All The King's Horses' which had been recorded in Abbey Road, London for Radio Luxembourg. Now we were to invite our audience to *Let's Listen In* as Charlie gave us *his* version which he recorded in 1940, informing us that those 'King's Horses' had unwisely ridden all the way over to France and now had to ride all the way back again because of Dunkirk!

With expert help and assistance from Rory Higgins, who did all the required digital editing for us at the HQ of Forces Broadcasting, we assembled our series, which also dealt with the setting up of the Allied Expeditionary Programme on D-Day Plus 1 and the start of the British Forces Network with excerpts from the opening concert. Our friend Douglas Brown described that event, since he was one of the technical team at the Musikhalle that memorable July day in 1945.

In the course of preparation for the broadcast series I'd been invited by the director of the Allied Museum in Berlin to prepare an exhibition of a selection of photos and articles from the post-war BFN Bulletins and also a 75-minute CD which Gregor issued through the BOS Records in Germany. It went on sale from Saturday September 29th 2001, when the exhibition was declared open. Former BFN Sgt Bob Boyle did the announcements for the CD, whilst BFBS arranged that our *Let's Listen In* transmissions would have completed their German run in that same month. For the Exhibition itself Gregor and Walter Voigt were to loan the Allied Museum some of their priceless collection from the Radio Museum which they had been instrumental in setting up in Duisburg. On this occasion one of the Wartime ENSA girls who broadcast for us from BFN Hamburg and acted for me in later times was to fly out to Berlin – Daphne Oxenford.

I found the concert the following day a particularly moving experience, for standing there on the stage was a musician who'd been a member of the renowned Helmut Zacharias Band whom I'd used on many occasions. When first we'd met in 1946, bass player Coco Schumann was still a skeletal 24 or 25 year old, having somehow survived life in a concentration camp. Now, happily, I could just about embrace Coco with two arms around a far healthier-looking figure.

Later that week Rory Higgins, Gregor and myself received an invitation from the German Bundestag in the person of someone who had become a very good friend, Bernd Scheelen. A busy but caring person, Bernd spent three hours of his valuable time in taking us around what I'd first seen back in 1946 as the burnt-out ruins of a Reischstag building and then again, hemmed in by the Berlin Wall, when I did the Airlift feature. What a truly incredible transformation due to the architectural talents of Sir Norman Foster and craftsmen from the Federal Republic of Germany. Yes, some original features have been reinstated but the ruins of a huge

'Are you sitting comfortably?' Then Daphne Oxenford will begin a dinner in Berlin 2001

original dome have now been replaced by shimmering steel and glass with an inside circular walkway from the base to the very top of the dome, whilst taking light down into the parlimentary chamber itself far below is a giant cornet-shaped funnel of metal and mirrored glass. The strength of sunlight controls the angles at which thousands of mirrors reflect such light.

'And of course you appreciate that up this funnel can escape much of the hot air which some of us generate – just as in *your* parliament in London!' explained the ever-courteous Bernd.

He was also to show us what had been carefully preserved below ground – including some of the Russian post-war graffiti – and to take us into areas not open to the general public. And finally, we three were given a splendid lunch within the Bundestag. A memorable visit indeed thanks to these winds of good fortune and even better company.

A year beforehand, I had introduced Gregor to what is now the University of Gloucestershire having at that time been a member of one of the committees. He was fascinated by the work of their design students and those who did media studies. As a result Gregor was invited to deliver a lecture. It would be on 'The History Of Recording', a subject he excelled in and could now amply illustrate with the additional recorded examples from Antony Askew's unique collection. I know from

Viscount Norwich how much he appreciated the translations which Gregor did and sent to him concerning what a certain Dr Goebbels wrote and published in wartime concerning John Julius's father, Duff Cooper. If I could speak German even half as well as Gregor speaks English then I would have given those members of the BFN Light Orchestra little cause to laugh at my knowledge of the German language all those years ago. As it was, Gregor was now to give what is a *technical* lecture in a foreign language. He sent me all his notes which I typed out and then went through with him once we'd decided on the precise wording he would use.

The students faced us in rising tiers of seats – and with excellent 'wraparound' sound facilities, required not so much for mono but for stereo, quadrophonic and for my own 'binaural' sound. Gregor began by thanking William Caxton who was the first English printer, having learned the art in Cologne in 1471–72. Next Gregor spoke about Thomas Edison who initially printed a newspaper aboard a moving train. By 1871 Edison had invented the Printing Telegraph before presenting his model of 'The Phonograph'. His Edison cylinder recording of August 2nd 1890 was well received – as was Clement Ader's first demonstration of stereophonic sound held in the autumn of 1881 during the International Electrical Exhibition. For this he'd used two separate telephone lines connected to two carbon microphones. Now I'd worked with Dr Ludwig Koch during my time with the BBC in Bristol, but only from Gregor was I to learn that Koch had been a Doctor of Music and a member of the Berlin Record Company, 'Electrola', in 1928 and had a father who could, around 1890, have afforded to own a cylinder recorder. The students were next to hear Johannes Brahms himself playing a piano. Within some 50 extracts his large student gathering was to hear examples of what, in my own experience, had been the greatest stride in the annals of recording: the German invention of magnetic tape. The very first recording was made on November 9th 1936 when the London Philharmonic Orchestra was in Ludswigshafen for a concert conducted by Sir Thomas Beecham, and recorded on the AEG K-2 recorder with DC bias. Gregor was also to let us hear an extract from a repeat of that concert done precisely 50 years later and on digital audio tape from the Barbican Hall – now with the London Philharmonic conducted by Vernon Handley.

What *did* make those students really sit up was when Gregor had been explaining to them the various stages of the Electrola and biased with HMV Tonschreiber 'C' as a portable tape recorder and the advent of 'Magnetophonband'. He'd already told them all about 'Series 5', then he declared to the assembled throng, ‘And now we come to Zex.’ At this point I felt bound to spring to my feet.

‘No, no, Herr Prumbs. I’m sure these young people already know *all* about sex. Might we please stick to your “History of Recording”?’

It was during the refreshment break that I distinctly heard an unidentified voice declare, ‘That Tree-vors Hill. He really *is* a swinney!’

23

Final Reflections

Of one thing I can be absolutely certain. Reflecting now in this year 2004 on the waters of my life, I have been extremely fortunate. A letter received literally out of the blue from Lewisham in London in January of last year, and after a period of some 39 years, states, 'This is just a short note to tell you so long after the event how much your work in *Children's Hour* gave joy and happiness to my family …'

I and countless others, besides John Symons who was to kindly send me that letter, are only too aware of just what this particular BBC programme gave to us in our own formative days of childhood and what a truly marvellous opportunity we were given to 'listen in and to learn' through a daily *Children's Hour*. As a listener I am indebted to Derek McCulloch, and, when I was myself to be associated with the programme, in particular to David Davis. David, like Derek Burrell-Davies in the North when *he* became my boss, was to open so many doors for those of us who worked for them.

The then long-running life of *Children's Hour*, as far as I, the late Wallace Grevatt and countless others were concerned, was only to be cut short by the guillotine imposed by Frank Gillard in order that, as Managing Director of Radio, he would have the necessary financial resources in order to start BBC Local Radio. Sir Hugh Carleton Greene was to admit that the storms of protest against such a closure were far stronger than any others to which he'd agreed during his time as DG. It was David Davis himself who decided that, as the very last programme would be broadcast on Good Friday, 1964, a day of national mourning, he would read Oscar Wilde's story *The Selfish Giant*. As he later wrote in Wallace's book, 'It seemed to me there was something unjustly symbolic about that.'

Gillard's own attitude to *Children's Hour* – and in particular his attitude to his then West of England Organiser, Mollie Austin, who did superb work on *Clara Chuff*, such serials as *Lorna Doone* and the introduction of Jane Austen in *Children's Hour* through *Sense and Sensibility* – had already persuaded me that I should not remain in the BBC's West Region but should apply for that vacancy in North Region as the then Controller in Bristol, Gerald Beadle, had kindly advised.

However, I most certainly wish to pay tribute to the Frank Gillard with whom I was to be associated during the wartime as a junior Programme Engineer, when he and Richard Dimbleby provided our War Report unit with newsworthy accounts from the battlefields which were to bring into the listener's own home, yes the real horrors of war, yet so often mixed with their own observations and in truly memorable and poetic language. I still cherish some of those recordings.

It is again in 2004 that I can reflect on another pleasurable meeting, arranged through the good offices of my friend Peter Worsley, who is a sub-editor with *This England* magazine which issued our 'Songs And Sounds Of War' CD. Peter was to invite me to a lunch at his home in order to meet up with Kenneth Wilkins, who happens to be a talented cartoonist. It was back in 1949 that as a young boy he'd heard the very first of my radio *Cameo Cartoons* and immediately wrote to the then organiser of *Children's Hour*, North, Nan Macdonald. It was Nan herself who'd encouraged me to both write and to produce *Floppy's Tail*. And what was 'Master Wilkins' to give me at that lunch but Nan's own reply, addressing him in that manner. Her letter is dated 3rd November 1949. Kenneth was also to give me one of his own illustrated cartoons concerning the BBC and which he has drawn in recent times.

Again peering into the waters of life, the greatest reflection for me was to come about on 17th June 1994 when I heard in a letter from Janet Johnstone, who at that time was secretary to the Principal of the Cheltenham Ladies' College, that a part of Margaret's script *Willingly To School*, which she had researched on Dorothea Beale, the founder of the College, could now be broadcast by the BBC Open University who were to feature two great pioneers in education, Miss Buss, founder of North London Collegiate College, and Miss Beale in *Ahead Of Their Time*. Scenes Margaret wrote concerning Miss Beale were to be used in this July, 1994 London production. It was entirely thanks to Janet and to the then Principal, Enid Castle, that my wife had much of the college archive

THE BRITISH BROADCASTING CORPORATION

Head Office: Broadcasting House, London, W.1

Broadcasting House, Piccadilly, Manchester 1

TELEPHONE AND TELEGRAMS: CENTRAL 2931

3rd November, 1949.

Master Kenneth Wilkins,
55, Kennan Avenue,
Leamington Spa,
WARWICKSHIRE.

Dear Kenneth,

Thank you for your letter.

The signature tune we used for the cameo cartoon, "Floppy's Tail" was "Willie the Whistler" by Robert Farnon. The recording we used was made by the Queens Hall Light Orchestra, directed by Charles Williams, on Chappell C.259.

The other music you enquired about was written by the person who wrote and produced this cartoon, Trevor Hill. He called it "Burrow with Your Paws", and it has never been published.

It is nice to know that you enjoyed this programme, and we hope that you will always find lots of things to interest you in Northern Children's Hour.

Yours sincerely,

N. Macdonald

(Nan Macdonald)
Organiser of Northern Children's Hour.

BAH.

Letter from Nan Macdonald to Kenneth Wilkins

delivered to our home. She'd noted that back in 1864 another of England's great reformers, John Ruskin, had stated to the city of Manchester, 'Let girls education be as serious as that for a boy. You bring up girls as if they were meant for sideboard ornaments …' Thanks

Cartoon by Kenneth Wilkins

again to the Ladies' College, we were to see some of the original letters which Ruskin exchanged with Miss Beale, whilst I was privileged to be put in touch with and to record two former college pupils reminiscing about their times when Miss Beale reigned supreme until her death in 1906.

For forty years Margaret was either to submit to the BBC, or to be commissioned by them to write countless scripts comprising many serials, single plays, features and many a series, before her death. This had been the one and only occasion on which her work was rejected, as she was informed in a letter from the then Head of BBC Features Arts and Education in December 1991. Margaret had already received a letter from the ever-helpful Features Editor, Simon Elmes, who had written to tell her, 'I really have lost hope for "traditional" Radio 4 ideas …'

Janet Johnstone's letter to me concerning Margaret's final contribution to broadcasting, received almost a year after her death in 1993, was to inform me that her feature on Dorothea Beale could now be heard via the BBC's Open University. Janet goes on to state, 'I do think it would be a marvellous tribute to her if it was broadcast after all'. I heartily agreed – providing the BBC paid the script royalties to the College.

Margaret Potter and I had every reason for thanking both 'Auntie' BBC and the British Forces Network in Germany for the enrichment of our own lives through Broadcasting, which was to give us both added pleasure when working for many fruitful years together as an author and a producer team on radio and television 'Over The Airwaves'.

INDEX